MW01062013

CONTROLLED RECKLESSNESS

CONTROLLED RECKLESSNESS

ED LEMMON AND THE OPEN RANGE

NATHAN SANDERSON

To Matt,

I hope you enjoy this look into Ed Lemmon's
life & his role in the development of our unique
West River country! Take care, sir!

Nathan B. Sanderson
12-09. 2015

South Dakota
Historical Society Press
Pierre

This publication is funded, in part, by the Great Plains Education Foundation, Inc.,
Aberdeen, S.Dak.

Library of Congress Cataloging-in-Publication Data
Sanderson, Nathan, 1980-
Controlled recklessness : Ed Lemmon and the open range / Nathan Sanderson.
   pages cm
Includes bibliographical references and index.
ISBN 978-1-941813-03-4 (alk. paper)
1. Lemmon, Ed, 1857-1945. 2. Cowboys—West (U.S.)—Biography. 3. Frontier and
pioneer life—West (U.S.) 4. Cattle trade—West (U.S.) 5. Lemmon (S.D.)—Biography.
6. West (U.S.)—Biography. I. Title.
F595.L48S26 2015
636.2'13092—DC23
[B]
         2015026217

The paper in this book meets the guidelines for permanence
and durability of the Committee on Production Guidelines for
Book Longevity of the Council on Library Resources.

Cover image: George Edward Lemmon. *Virginia Grabow collection*
Frontispiece: George Edward Lemmon. *City of Lemmon, S.Dak.*

Text and cover design by Rich Hendel

Please visit our website at sdhspress.com.

Printed in the United States of America

19 18 17 16 15   1 2 3 4 5

CONTENTS

List of Maps, vi

Acknowledgments, vii

Introduction, xi

1 Youth, 1

2 Cowboying, 25

3 Trespassers, 46

4 Roundups, 68

5 Cattlemen, 94

6 The Largest Fenced Pasture in the World, 121

7 Town Building, 150

8 Legacy, 175

Notes, 191

Bibliography, 227

Index, 241

LIST OF MAPS

West River South Dakota, 47

Lemmon and Environs, ca. 1915, 153

ACKNOWLEDGMENTS

If not for my father-in-law, Chuck Anderson, I would not have written about Ed Lemmon. Chuck and his wife Koreen ranch seven miles south of Lemmon, South Dakota, and their families have lived in the northwest part of the state since just after the turn of the twentieth century. During his travels on sheep-shearing crews and as a rancher and carpenter, Chuck has developed an uncanny knowledge of the countryside. He also has a keen interest in western history. In the summer of 2000, he started telling me about all the things "Dad" Lemmon had done as a cowboy and cattleman and how important he was to the region. At the time, I did not even consider writing about Lemmon, but a few years later I began looking for a dissertation topic. Another University of Nebraska-trained historian, Chuck Vollan, had used Lemmon's writings in his dissertation on the early years of Cheyenne, Wyoming, and suggested him. As I began researching the man, it became obvious that Lemmon not only had a great story, but he clearly altered the development of the Northern Great Plains. Many thanks.

A number of exceptional faculty members in the History Department at the University of Nebraska-Lincoln were helpful and encouraging. My advisor Andy Graybill, who has since become co-director of the William P. Clements Center for Southwest Studies at Southern Methodist University, provided a wealth of insight and advice. Will Thomas was a thoughtful mentor and introduced me to the exciting and growing world of digital history. John Wunder provided wise counsel, as only a man of his experience could. And David Wishart of the University of Nebraska Geography Department offered several unique insights that greatly improved this work. At the University of Indianapolis, James Fuller started the process of teaching this Great Plains aggie how to be an historian. And special thanks to Linda Iverson, one of the best teachers I've ever had.

Virginia Grabow of Tigard, Oregon, a great-granddaughter of Ed Lemmon's older brother Hervey, has been a tremendous supporter, sharing her family's genealogical research, reading portions of the manuscript, and providing several photographs of the Lemmon family. Janet Graham and Bill Sheidley helped put me in touch with Betsey Sheidley Fletcher of Mission Hills, Kansas, who generously welcomed me into her home to view records and papers from the Sheidley Cattle Company.

A number of librarians, archivists, public servants, and institutions helped with research for this project. Mary-Jo Miller, Matt Piersol, and the rest of the staff at the Nebraska State Historical Society were always helpful and patient. Thanks also to Robin Everett with the Wyoming State Archives; the American Heritage Center in Laramie, Wyoming; John Sieracki and Gayle Ecklund of the Milwaukee Public Library; Greg Wysk of the State Historical Society of North Dakota; the Chester Fritz Library at the University of North Dakota; the Wisconsin Historical Society; Nancy Tystad Koupal and Jennifer McIntyre of the South Dakota State Historical Society; the South Dakota State Library; and the staffs at the Adams County, North Dakota, and Perkins County, South Dakota, courthouses.

The citizens of Lemmon, South Dakota, have provided invaluable assistance and shown remarkable enthusiasm for my work. Nora Anderson spent hours in the Lemmon Public Library reviewing its collection of local newspapers. She saved me several days of research, but I think I did her the bigger favor, providing a good excuse to leave Jim at home while she delved into the town's history. Thanks also to former librarian Carol Rafferty. Phyllis Schmidt of the Grand River Museum in Lemmon authored *The West as I Lived It*, a compilation of the columns Ed Lemmon wrote for the *Belle Fourche Bee* during the 1930s. Her book, as well the loan of her digital files, made my job of organizing Ed's stories much, much easier. Carolyn Penfield opened the Petrified Wood Park Museum during the off-season so I could review its excellent collection of documents and artifacts, including Ed's intricately carved diamond-willow cane. Many others have expressed support and provided valuable insight that has made this book far better.

Ed Texley of Hettinger, North Dakota, generously allowed me to borrow and copy his collection of Lemmon's original typed stories. He discovered them in about 1958 while playing in the Lemmon office of the Production Credit Association where his dad Shorty worked with Ed Lemmon's eldest son, James. The office was on the first floor of the old First National Bank building on Main Street. James had an apartment upstairs, where Ed Lemmon lived on and off during his final years. While playing in the building's nooks and crannies, Texley climbed to the top of the bank vault, where he saw an old filing cabinet. Inside he found a stack of dusty papers, which he took to James, who recognized them as his father's stories and put them away in a safe place. Texley did not see them again until forty-five years later. Not long after Shorty passed away, Texley came across a packet of documents in his father's papers and instantly recognized them as the stories he had found on top of the bank vault decades earlier. Ed, thanks for sharing.

And of course, thanks to my family. My wife Tiffany and son Carter have been enthusiastic about this project from start to finish. Carter never complained when I spent countless weekends locked in my office rather than playing outside. Tiffany, thanks for being my best friend and strongest supporter. I could not have done this without you.

NATHAN SANDERSON
Pierre, South Dakota
June 2015

ix

INTRODUCTION

George Edward Lemmon (1857–1945) lived a life full of significant achievements and played an integral role in the growth and development of the Northern Great Plains. From the 1880s to the early 1900s, he was one of *the* central figures in the region, and his life demonstrates the triumphs and challenges that came with the settlement of the American West. A renowned cowboy and cattleman, Lemmon operated an 865,000-acre lease on the Standing Rock Indian Reservation, bossed one of the nation's largest roundups, probably saddle-handled more cattle than any man who ever lived, and became an early member of the National Cowboy Hall of Fame. Lemmon's unparalleled cattle-handling skills and reputation as one of the region's most important stockmen emerged as a result of his systematic, rational nature as well as his penchant for fast, fearless, decisive action. This dichotomy earned him success in business but also resulted in several severe injuries that crippled him for life. Later Lemmon became a town builder, guiding the Chicago, Milwaukee & St. Paul Railroad west across the Missouri River and helping to establish several communities. Throughout his life, Lemmon fought to manage the two competing sides of his personality: the controlled, methodical cattleman who employed a calculated, logical approach to getting the job done well and the reckless, fun-loving cowboy who took tremendous, often unnecessary, risks in the name of getting the job done quickly.[1]

The process of developing the Northern Great Plains exhibited a similar contradiction, juxtaposing the systematic nature of government-organized settlement with the chaos of building hundreds of communities and dispersing tens of thousands of pioneers within a few short years. Federal officials who sought to control Plains Indians by establishing reservations and teaching them to farm or raise cattle watched as tribal members allowed non-Indian ranchers to graze cattle on their land while they left the reservations to hunt game. The cattlemen who trespassed on the reservations actively worked to restrict settlement by the homesteaders—who would eventually end their method of grazing the public domain—and imposed their own sets of range laws, maintaining them by force. Would-be homesteaders visited federal offices to sign up for parcels of land, the size and location of which were determined by the government, then supplemented this careful planning with huge measures of personal and financial risk. Ed Lemmon's personal struggle with these competing experiences provides new insight into the growth and development of the region stretching from southern Nebraska north to the Canadian prairie provinces and from the Missouri River west into Wyoming and Montana.

Despite being one of the most widely recognized cattlemen on the Northern Great Plains at the turn of the twentieth century and entering the National Cowboy & Western Heritage Museum's Hall of Fame as a member of its second class—in 1958, along with renowned westerners Oliver Loving, Stephen F. Austin, John Chisum, and William F. ("Buffalo Bill") Cody—in the twenty-first century Ed Lemmon is virtually unknown outside the small, rural community of Lemmon, South Dakota. Those who recognize his name tend to associate it with the town and its school (whose athletic teams are named, appropriately, the Cowboys), tucked in the middle of nowhere in the far northwest corner of the state, almost one hundred miles from the nearest stoplight. In spite of Ed Lemmon's relative obscurity, many of the common themes that define the plains—among them, cattle ranching, buffalo, American Indians, cowboys, railroads, and boomtowns—are reflected in his life and experiences.

Lemmon's years as a cowboy and cattleman taught him many things, including the value of using Indian lands for personal gain. In the 1880s, he and his fellow cattlemen were among the few local non-Indians who opposed, rather than supported, opening "excess" land on Indian reservations to white settlement. Lemmon and others grazed thousands of cattle illegally on the Great Sioux Reservation in the western half of what is now South Dakota—an area known colloquially as West River—because the grass was free and they could avoid paying taxes on cattle that were not grazing within an organized county. Even though Lemmon had thousands of cattle trespassing on the reservation, he enjoyed an amicable relationship with the Oglala Lakotas in the southern part of the

Great Sioux Reservation and earned the respect of the Hunkpapa and Sihasapa Lakotas when he won his lease on the Standing Rock Indian Reservation in the northern portion of the old Great Sioux Reservation.

His contacts extended into the railroad industry as well. Lemmon's intimate knowledge of the landscape made finding an appropriate route for a railroad line west of the Missouri River an easy task; in exchange for his assistance, Lemmon received a choice town site and gleaned knowledge of the railroad's proposed route that facilitated his expansion into other business ventures, including banking and real estate. Lemmon's intelligence, hard work, and charisma earned him a substantial personal fortune as he altered the development of the Northern Great Plains. But in the end, his personal success was fleeting. Like many old cowboys—including Buffalo Bill Cody—Lemmon died penniless, though the effects of his role in building the region can be seen to this day.[2]

Throughout his life, Lemmon was known by a number of nicknames. As a child, his friends called him "Buckskin Ed" for the fringed buckskin suit he wore.[3] During his time on the Great Sioux Reservation, Red Cloud dubbed him Huste, meaning "lame" in Lakota or "Crooked Ass" as Lemmon translated it, because of his severely crippled right leg, which he had broken several times. Some of his cowboys corrupted the name Huste into "Usta," while most of his friends and peers simply called him Ed.[4] Sioux Indians on the Standing Rock reservation referred to Lemmon as Taspaze, meaning "yellow apple," since the Lakota language had no word for "lemon."[5] His children and the citizens of the town he founded called him "Dad," because just as he was a father to his three sons, he was the father of the town as well. In fact, many residents of Lemmon, South Dakota, still refer to "Dad" Lemmon. Later he earned the title "Dean of the Range" for his renowned cattle-handling skills and because he was "easily the most widely known cattleman on the western range."[6] Following the 1969 publication of Nellie Snyder Yost's collection of Ed's stories, *Boss Cowman*, some refer to Lemmon by that appellation, even though he never used it while alive.[7]

The variety of monikers bestowed upon Ed Lemmon speaks volumes about his life and legacy. He was a cowboy, cattleman, reservation trespasser, guide, town builder, land speculator, banker, sheep rancher, and eventually a pauper. Yet above all, Lemmon was a juncture between two eras, one rooted in the nineteenth century, the other in the twentieth. He represents the meeting point between Indians and whites, between humans and the land, between cowboys and cattlemen, and between the dusty days on a western cattle trail and the development of settlements and "civilization." He is the convergence of organized self-discipline and chaotic rashness. Lemmon personified the traits and lessons that came to be identified with life on the Northern Great Plains: overcoming adversity, rootedness in a place, violent conflict, the triumph that comes with hard work, and the devastating failures that accompany bad decisions. As one of the most important individuals guiding its progress, Ed Lemmon and his controlled recklessness altered the growth and development of the entire region.

A Note on the Sources

In his twilight, Lemmon began recording his adventures, thoughts, and insights on a wide range of topics, including Indian-white relations, the nuances of proper cattle handling, banking and business, town founding, statehood, county-seat battles, the shift from open-range cattle ranching to fenced pastures, and many others. Like famed showman Buffalo Bill Cody, Lemmon used storytelling to create an image of himself for public consumption.

Lemmon wrote more than eight hundred articles about his life, many of which appeared in the *Belle Fourche Bee* during the 1930s and 1940s as a column titled "Developing the West." As Lemmon was a poor typist—he never used a typewriter until he was in his sixties—and often wrote multiple copies of the same story for various purposes, the readable versions published in the *Bee* are cited in this work. Lemmon's *Bee* articles published between 1932 and 1936 are collected in Phyllis Schmidt's edited volume, *The West as I Lived It: Stories by Ed Lemmon* (Pierre, S.Dak.: State Publishing Co., 2007).

Lemmon's papers, which include hundreds of pages of typed stories, submission (and rejection) letters, and, in some cases, editorial comments about his work, are located in repositories throughout the Northern Great Plains. The Chester Fritz Library at the University of North Dakota houses hundreds of Lemmon's original typed manuscripts as part of North Dakota Congressman Usher L. Burdick's papers. These manuscripts include Ed's submissions to the *Belle Fourche Bee*, which were heavily edited to prepare them for publication. Lemmon appears to have typed his stories as he recalled them, in a stream-of-consciousness method that transferred his memories directly to paper with little self-editing. As he recalled additional details, he penciled them in above the typed lines or in the margins. Most of his submissions contained numerous typographical errors and required no small amount of editing for style and form. He also repeated many of the same anecdotes in different published articles, providing the researcher an interesting opportunity to compare and contrast multiple versions of the same stories, sometimes told over the course of several years.

The American Heritage Center at the University of Wyoming houses Burdick's unpublished compilation of Lemmon's stories, titled "History of the Range Cattle Trade of the Dakotas." This manuscript collection includes pages of handwritten notes, some apparently penned by Nellie Snyder Yost as she prepared her collection of Lemmon's writings in *Boss Cowman: The Recollections of Ed Lemmon, 1857–1946* (Lincoln: University of Nebraska Press, 1969). The Wyoming State Historical Society has an interesting collection of Ed's stories, gathered during the 1930s as part of a Work Projects Administration project to document histories from plains residents. In addition to the stories themselves, the collection contains signed statements in which the author swears to the accuracy of the accounts. The Nebraska State Historical Society has a few of Lemmon's papers, as he tried on several occasions to persuade the society to publish his stories. Included in the collection is a typewritten comment on Lemmon's writing by famed plains author Mari Sandoz, who worked for the society at the time. A smaller number of Ed's stories are housed at the Kansas Historical Society and in the private collection of Ed Texley of Hettinger, North Dakota. Together, Lemmon's rich, compelling stories offer a comprehensive look at his personality and character while demonstrating the various ways in which he altered the course of development of the Northern Great Plains.

The process of organizing, categorizing, and cross-referencing Ed's many stories was difficult and time-consuming. After cataloging his writings and arranging them into a rough chronology whenever possible, I compared Lemmon's claims with historical records and secondary sources to verify their authenticity. For many of the major events he recounted, including the aftermath of the Wounded Knee Massacre and his acquisition of the lease on the Standing Rock Indian Reservation, his accounts help to clarify what is already known. On other occasions, it was impossible to verify Ed's claims. In these instances, I relied upon a thorough examination of the available sources to establish a clear picture of the man.

Because he sought to build a legacy of his achievements, Lemmon exaggerated or fabricated some of his accomplishments, particularly in relation to the famous figures he claimed to have met and interacted with, such as Wild Bill Hickok and Charles Goodnight. Lemmon wanted a place in history. Because it is often possible to identify those instances in which he took liberties with the facts, readers can be confident that in the majority of cases, Lemmon's recollections of his experiences are largely factual.

CONTROLLED RECKLESSNESS

1 YOUTH

As Ed Lemmon guided his horse-drawn buggy toward the top of a tall butte in south-central North Dakota in early May 1902, he basked in the glory of his wealth and power. A few weeks earlier, the seasoned cattleman had secured a private meeting with President Theodore Roosevelt to request a cattle-grazing lease on the Standing Rock Indian Reservation, which straddled the North Dakota-South Dakota state line. Early on that May morning, Lemmon harnessed a team and headed out for Leaf-on-the-Hill Creek to survey his new empire: 865,000 acres of prime grassland, to which he had acquired grazing rights for the next five years. As he drove to the top of the butte, Lemmon took in the grandeur of his hard-earned kingdom, which extended in every direction as far as the eye could see. Rolling grasslands, steep draws, wooded river bottoms, broken badlands, and majestic buttes caught his eye as he slowly made his way to the summit. Once on top, he later recalled, "I . . . stopped my team, stood up in my buggy, drew a long breath of fresh air and shouted to the universe that I was Lord of all."[1]

Lemmon had good reason to celebrate his achievements. His lease, which covered an area larger than the state of Rhode Island, was the culmination of a thirty-year rise from poor cowboy to respected cattleman. Lemmon's success was a product of his unlimited ambition, steadfast determination, strenuous effort, and natural talent. He had a sixth sense about cattle—Lemmon always seemed to know how they would act in a particular situation—and he was a hard worker. He started in the cattle business at the age of thirteen and by twenty had earned a position as a trail boss for a large cattle outfit. In this capacity, he demonstrated another talent: leading men.

Throughout his twenties, Lemmon regularly led and directed teams of cowboys several years older than himself. Standing only five feet, five inches and weighing no more than 150 pounds, Lemmon did not have the physical size to garner immediate respect from his men, but he displayed a determined intensity that quickly compensated for his small stature. In addition to his modest size and slight build, Lemmon had a baby face, which made him appear much younger than his years. His thinning hair may have hinted at his real age, but because few people saw him without the hat he wore for more than eighteen hours on most days, few thought him much older than a teenager even as he approached the age of thirty. Despite these physical limitations, Lemmon proved an effective leader who demonstrated a powerful work ethic and a natural, likable attitude. His even temper and cattle-handling skill earned him widespread recognition as a capable leader and cattleman. He was intelligent, thoughtful, and fun-loving. As one of his cowboys noted, "His horses were fast, and so was he, and those of us young fellows who were a little on the 'wild cowboy' order enjoyed working with Ed Lemmon's outfit. Everyone liked him."[2]

This likeability was more than a product of his engaging personality; his achievements in the cattle industry were almost unequalled among cowboys. In 1897, Lemmon "bossed" one of the largest roundups ever staged. This huge undertaking held on the Peno Flats near the Bad River in west-central South Dakota included twenty roundup wagons, five hundred men, and fifty thousand cattle. On another occasion he "cut" (separated from the main herd) nine hundred cattle in a single day, "riding 8 horses to near exhaustion in so doing."[3] At the 1905 National Live Stock Association annual meeting in Denver, association secretary Charles Martin recognized Lemmon for having saddle-handled more cattle than any other man who ever lived—over one million head. By the early 1900s, Lemmon owned a 15-percent interest in fifty-three thousand cattle, grazing them on what was then the world's largest fenced pasture.[4]

Lemmon's accomplishments were especially remarkable in light of his physical condition, which, in addition to his small size and youthful appearance, included a severely crippled right leg. The result of three separate breaks over thirty years in the saddle, Lemmon's shrunken, contorted appendage prevented him from achieving anything faster than an unsightly hobble. Although slow on his feet, when in the saddle he rode with a controlled recklessness that impressed other horsemen. One cowboy said later, "Lemmon rode

James
Hervey
Lemmon,
Sr.
*Virginia
Grabow
collection*

horses that were high-headed and thrashed around in a roundup more than most cowmen liked." But they kept a roundup moving quickly, and he "got the job done to [a] cowboy's satisfaction . . . and he was an easy man to work with."[5]

Lemmon proved himself by working harder and longer than other men. As a trail or roundup boss, he often put in twenty hours per day during the peak of the cattle-handling season. As Ed noted years later, he regularly rose at 2:45 A.M., worked until 9:00 P.M., and sliced out a two-hour night-guard shift as well. Lemmon was known for his uncommon physical energy, but his capacity for work was not a product of energy alone. He also had the motivation he needed to rise above his apparent limitations in the eyes of others—and the work ethic that he learned from his family.[6]

Lemmon's father, James Hervey Lemmon, was born in New York state on 26 August 1820 and moved to Lower Sandusky (later Fremont), Ohio, at the age of seven. As a young man, James moved to Indiana and later to northern Illinois, where he worked at odd jobs, including clearing farmland. In 1847, he sought new opportunities in the West, leaving Illinois for St. Joseph, Missouri, where he joined an emigrant wagon train headed to Oregon Territory. While on the trail, James passed through southern Nebraska, traveling a route that would later become a critical part of his life and livelihood.[7]

Upon arriving in Oregon Territory, James established a small store and worked as a freighter. He also appears to have participated in a regional war. As white settlers spread throughout the region, they encroached on lands belonging to the Cayuse nation and brought new, lethal illnesses, including an 1847 measles epidemic that spread to the local Indians. Angered by the outbreak and unleashing years of pent-up frustration, Cayuse warriors killed two missionaries on 29 November and touched off a conflict known as the Cayuse War.[8]

In later years, Ed would proudly recount his father's exploits in the war in several engaging, though likely embellished, stories. According to Lemmon, on one occasion James faced off against an entire Indian village with nothing but an octagon-barrel Sharps rifle and a pepperbox pistol. An Indian had stolen a few hundred dollars' worth of clothing and supplies, and James and a friend tracked the thief to a nearby village. Several armed Indians confronted the duo as they attempted to reclaim their property, and James and his associate had to make a rapid escape when they saw "Indians by dozens swarming from the lodges in hot pursuit with every conceivable kind of weapon they could hurriedly grab up."[9] After killing several of the attackers, James managed to escape unhurt. Ed also noted that throughout the course of the conflict his father had several horses shot out from under him but came out unharmed every time. Ed wrote these stories in the 1930s, more than eighty years after James first arrived in Oregon Territory, so although these accounts may have some truth in them, they are most likely apocryphal.[10]

Such stories clearly played a key role in the development of Ed Lemmon's character. As a young boy, he listened with awe to his father's exciting exploits. He looked up to James as a role model and sought out similar adventures for himself. According to Ed, James was the best boxer, wrestler, and fighter of anyone he knew; he was an excellent athlete who could make a standing jump as high as he was tall. His father's rugged persona inspired Ed to mirror these qualities in himself. James acted decisively, with intelligence, forethought, and courage, and Ed aspired to live up to James's (real or fabricated) model.[11]

Above all, James's vivid accounts of his life in Oregon inspired Ed with the power of a well-told story. While in cow camp, Ed entertained his men with tales of Indian battles, horse races, fistfights, gunfights, uncommon examples of courage, and other manly exploits. Late in his life, Ed published many of the stories he heard from his father and others, along with tales of his own adventures. At times, his recollections do not match the historical record, but Ed did not see a significant difference between the stories he told in cow camp and the memoirs he wrote for publication. For Ed, stories were an integral part of life—an enjoyable pastime that earned the attention and respect of his men and, later, the praise and recognition of an interested public.[12]

When word of the California gold strike spread in 1849, James left Oregon Territory and started a lucrative business freighting supplies for miners in the gold fields near Sacramento. Two years later, he quit his freighting activities and traveled to San Francisco, where he secured passage to Central America. After crossing the Isthmus of Panama, he traveled by steamship to New York City and returned home to northern Illinois.[13]

In October 1852, James married twenty-six-year-old Lucy Elizabeth Whittemore in Marengo, Illinois, a small town west of Chicago. The newlyweds decided to settle in California, and in early 1853 James gathered a group of emigrants to accompany them. Their small wagon train included three of Lucy's siblings and several other families. They had traveled only as far as what they called Skunk Creek, a small tributary of the North Platte River somewhere in western Nebraska, when Lucy gave birth to the couple's first child on 20 June 1853. Born in a tent pitched near the creek bank, James Hervey Lemmon, Jr.—called Hervey by his family—arrived eight months after his parents' marriage and likely slowed the train's progress even further. The pregnancy had been difficult, and when they reached Bountiful, Utah, in the fall of 1853, the Lemmons decided that Lucy and Hervey would be better off remaining there for the winter. James purchased a small farm, entrusted his shorthorn cattle herd to the care of his brothers-in-law Benjamin and Nathaniel, and left his wife and infant son behind as he guided the wagon train on to California.[14]

As James came and went on various freighting trips, Lucy and their expanding family remained on the Lemmon farm near Bountiful, about ten miles north of Salt Lake City. Lucy gave birth to her second son, Moroni Stowell, on 19 July 1855, and to a third, George Edward ("Ed"), on 23 May 1857. The family had frequent contact with Mormon settlers, making a number of Mormon friends for whom James often freighted goods. Some non-Mormons refused to trade with the Latter-day Saints, but the Lemmons evidently had no such qualms; indeed, their second son was named for the angel who appeared to Joseph Smith in 1823.[15]

According to Ed, the Lemmon family managed to earn the respect and admiration of Brigham Young himself. On the return leg of one of his California freighting trips, James happened to travel through a valley where local farmers had harvested a bountiful early wheat crop. Since the Salt Lake City area was in the midst of a serious drought, he loaded several wagons with flour, which he sold to needy citizens at a minimal profit. In the course of another trip, James met a group of starving Mormons pulling handcarts and helped to bring them to Salt Lake City without compensation. Years later, Ed related a statement by his friend Joe Lee, who claimed "that Brigham Young just swore by [James], although he was no Mormon, and [Lee] had seen Brigham point [James] out saying he was a better Mormon than any of them, and to just pattern after him and he would be suited."[16]

The Lemmons' association with Mormons clearly engendered mutual respect and left a lasting impression on the family. Ed recorded a barroom confrontation in which James kicked an eastern traveler into the street for claiming that "every plural wife of a Mormon was a prostitute."[17] Ed's lifelong abstinence from alcohol and tobacco may also have stemmed from Mormon influence. However, there is no hard evidence to suggest that the Lemmons themselves practiced Mormonism or were members of the Church of Jesus Christ of Latter-day Saints. As a freighter, James often left

Lucy and the children at home while he traveled, and it seems possible that they named their second son for a Mormon angel out of respect for those who watched over the family during his absences. In his reminiscences, Ed described his family as "not being Mormons," and in later life, he did not openly embrace any religion.[18] Lemmon's religion was cattle, and his church was the open range. He probably believed in God, but the prairie was his passion, his livelihood, and his home.

On 25 June 1859, Lucy gave birth to her only daughter, Alpharetta Elizabeth, whom James and his wife named after a character in an American folk song, "The Blue Juniata." Just a few weeks later, the Lemmons headed east to see family. While visiting Lucy's parents in Marengo, Illinois, the conversation turned to recent events in Utah. Two years earlier, in June 1857, an armed dispute known as the Utah, or Mormon, War had broken out. President James Buchanan sent the United States Army into Utah to quell what he perceived as a Mormon rebellion. The Latter-day Saints viewed this action as federal repression and blocked the military from entering the Salt Lake Valley. For more than a year, Mormon militiamen engaged in skirmishes and minor confrontations with soldiers. The Utah War peaked on 11 September 1857, when a Mormon militia and its Paiute allies attacked and executed more than one hundred members of an emigrant wagon train in what historian Will Bagley has called "a ritual of blood and vengeance" known as the Mountain Meadows Massacre.[19] The Utah War ended in April 1858, when Brigham Young finally bowed to federal pressure and surrendered the territorial governorship.[20]

Even though the Lemmon family had faced no immediate threat during the war, Lucy's parents urged their daughter and son-in-law to move their young family to a safer location. With the army maintaining a presence in Utah and the potential for additional confrontations, James probably considered his routine freighting expeditions to be risky endeavors. On the return trip to Utah early in the fall of 1859, the Lemmon family passed through Nebraska, where James purchased the Liberty Farm stage station, a 160-acre farm with a small assortment of wooden buildings.[21]

James was eager to relocate before winter, so he quickly sold the farm near Bountiful and put his affairs in order. Reluctant to spend extra time trailing cattle with winter fast approaching, he left his herd of shorthorns in the care of a Mormon friend named Rideout. The Lemmon family packed their belongings in James's freight wagons and within a few weeks of purchasing Liberty Farm arrived at their new Nebraska home.[22]

Liberty Farm was a collection of several small log structures located on the north bank of the Little Blue River in south-central Nebraska, a half-mile north of the present-day town of Deweese, near the point where Liberty Creek enters the Little Blue. The riverbanks were fairly gradual at that location, offering several easy crossing points. Liberty Creek's banks were quite steep, however, making a crossing (or an attack) impossible on horseback and difficult on foot. The buildings, like many others at stations along the Oregon Trail, featured sturdy split-log walls with mud packed between the cracks to keep out the elements. They were constructed from the trees lining the river and provided ample protection against attack. The surrounding tallgrass prairie was broken by small, intermittent creeks lined with cottonwood trees and the occasional ash or oak. Adequate moisture and fertile soil supported abundant grass for buffalo, cattle, and horses. The land north of the river had been cleared of vegetation to accommodate the station, while the south bank featured a thick cover of trees and brush.[23]

Liberty Farm rested on the Oregon Trail, a well-established route. As James later noted, "In the year 1860 there were never less than three hundred and sometimes over five hundred wagons passing over the road every day for over five months, not counting any teams coming from the West."[24] The road was up to one hundred yards wide and occasionally carried three wagon trains traveling abreast. "Just imagine five hundred wagons strung out on the same road," he reflected, "each team taking up at least one hundred feet, making a distance of over nine miles."[25] As an accomplished freighter, James may have selected the location for this very reason. He had passed over the route on his initial trip west in 1847, an experience that likely influenced his decision to relocate his family to a ranch on the trail. Sixty years after that initial passage, James called the Oregon Trail "the greatest thoroughfare that was ever traveled in any country."[26]

One of the opportunities James realized in this location was selling teams of wagon-broke oxen (cattle trained to pull a wagon) to fellow freighters and emigrants heading west. He had a systematic method for breaking the animals, which consisted of yoking two young, "green" oxen and tying their tails together to keep them from turning around. James would harness several pairs in this fashion and then, using two to four horseback riders, would teach the oxen how to work together and follow commands. He would eventually hitch several pairs together and train them to drag chains or heavy cottonwood logs, placing a well-broke team of older oxen in front to help educate the younger ones. Later the oxen would pull the front wheels of a cart until they were deemed ready to be hitched to a full wagon. Using this method, James trained a large number of oxen, which he sold or kept for his own freighting enterprise.[27]

This main travel route would also host one of the most storied endeavors in American history, the Pony Express. Beginning in April 1860, the Pony Express carried mail overland between California and Missouri in an attempt to reduce delivery times and earn organizers William Russell, Alexander Majors, and William Waddell an exclusive government contract. The competing Overland Mail Company held the contract, using stagecoaches to carry the mail along a 2,795-mile southern route that required a month or more to traverse. The Pony Express instead used a series of mounted carriers to travel a 1,966-mile route, reducing delivery times to around ten days. The riders passed mailbags called *mochilas* (Spanish for "pouch") in relay fashion and rode between stations located roughly every twelve miles. Liberty Farm was one of these stations.[28]

Although just shy of three years old in April 1860, Ed would later recall the Pony Express with fondness. His youth limited his firsthand knowledge of the endeavor, but he vividly remembered the character of some of the young men the Pony Express employed. When Majors hired riders, he gave each a Bible and required them to sign a document pledging not to drink alcohol, fight with other employees, or curse. Ed later wrote, "I have read how the riders were allowed to use no profanity, however, I am convinced some did not strictly observe the rule, for Bill Trotter, and Jim Moore, especially would have made poor Sunday School teachers."[29] Trotter and Moore worked as freighters for James throughout the 1860s, and their linguistic tendencies left an indelible mark on the impressionable boy.

In the summer of 1861, Lemmon may have encountered a legendary western character who would appear in his stories for the rest of his life. According to Lemmon, James Butler ("Wild Bill") Hickok stopped overnight at Liberty Farm only days after the lethal shootout at the Rock Creek Pony Express station that laid the groundwork for his reputation as a gunfighter. During Hickok's stay, Ed, Moroni—whom the family called Rone (pronounced ROAN-ee)—and Hervey, "three boys, aged four, six, and eight, followed him around all evening admiring him as a great hero."[30] Ed later claimed to have been well acquainted with Wild Bill, having met him several times, but his recollection of these meetings seems false. While Hickok may have stayed at Liberty Farm in 1861, Ed's description of the other encounters is noticeably vague. Lemmon may have realized he had stretched the truth on this occasion, once tempering the story of his relationship with Hickok by noting that Hervey "was a very intimate friend of Bill's while I was always rather an observant admirer."[31] In virtually every area in which he had some experience, Ed had strong convictions. In this case, he was certain that Hickok had adhered to the Code of the West and acted reasonably in the Rock Creek shooting. In fact, Lemmon claimed, the state of Nebraska should build a monument to Hickok's "heroic and appreciated act."[32]

The excitement of 1860 and 1861 evaporated after the federal government completed the first transcontinental telegraph line on 24 October 1861 and the Pony Express came to an end. Russell, Majors, and Waddell lost several hundred thousand dollars in their failed endeavor and turned over their assets, including all the stations, to Ben Holladay, the wealthy "Stagecoach King" who had financed much of their operation.[33]

When Holladay took over these assets in 1862, he enjoyed a solid reputation as a competent businessman. He had owned and operated a number of successful stage, freighting, and express endeavors and seemed determined to do the same with the route he had just inherited. The Lemmons appreciated Holladay's commitment to the old Oregon Trail route, and family members would always refer to Liberty Farm as a station on the Ben Holladay Stage Line. This change in operations also brought Ed into contact with a large number of freighters; these whip-cracking, gun-toting, foul-mouthed men gave him a memorable exposure to the wider world.[34]

Holladay's various freighting enterprises came with a great deal of overhead, not the least of which was his bill to feed the freighting animals. Holladay owned more than 150 stage stations, and each used between forty and eighty tons of hay per year. All told, he had to feed more than two thousand head of animals each day, which required a total of about twenty thousand tons of hay per year at a cost of more than five hundred thousand dollars. Some of the stations used hayfields nearby to supply their needs, while others had to haul hay up to one hundred miles. In addition to managing the Liberty Farm station, James had a contract for putting up hay for the stage company. At prices ranging between fifteen and fifty dollars per ton, hay was a valuable source of additional income for his young family. This venture also demonstrated James's ability to recognize and capitalize on business opportunities, a tendency that his young son Ed would inherit and use later in life as he sought out new investments.[35]

Liberty Farm's wild and beautiful surroundings, highlighted by abundant game, vast prairies, wooded creeks, and a winding river, became a special place for Ed Lemmon. Many of his first and most memorable experiences took place near the banks of the Little Blue. At age five or six, he embarked on his first "courtship," involving a neighbor girl named Sadie. During this time, he also had his first experience with alcohol. While attending a wedding party at Liberty Farm, Ed discovered eggnog. He "tipped the Jug" several times and within a few minutes was "full to overflowing."[36] This occasion marked the only time he ever tasted whiskey. Years later, Ed would drink beer and champagne while on his honeymoon in Mexico, but those instances aside, he abstained from alcohol completely. It is possible that Ed modeled his behavior on his first employer, cattleman John Wesley Iliff, who "was noted for his friendliness toward the Indians, for his abstinence from drink, and his aversion to [guns]."[37] The ill effects of Lemmon's first drinking experience and his family's association with the Latter-day Saints were presumably factors as well.[38]

James
Hervey
Lemmon,
Jr.
Virginia
Grabow
collection

Ed's primary focus in the early 1860s was an ever-present desire to impress his older brother Hervey. Ed referred to him as his "chum and hero" and spent much of his young life trying to live up to Hervey's example. This goal was difficult to achieve, however, because in Ed's eyes Hervey could do no wrong. He was an "expert trailer of man and beast," was adept at handling all sorts of weapons, knew "practically all the tactics of both Indians and miscreant whites," was fearless in the face of danger, and owned "the very fastest and longest winded pony in the country." As an eight-year-old, Ed aspired to become a "man" just like his incomparable twelve-year-old brother, a figure only "a trifle inferior" in Ed's eyes to accomplished mountain men Kit Carson and Jim Bridger.[39] Ed's youthful view of Hervey's accomplishments, though embellished, demonstrates a deep respect for his older brother and a genuine admiration for his talents. Ed put these sentiments on paper decades after his childhood on the Little Blue and his older brother's premature death in 1886 at age thirty-three. Clearly, he regretted that Hervey had not had the chance to equal or exceed his own achievements. Ed could be sentimental about certain things, and his boyhood at Liberty Farm was among his happiest memories.[40]

During his years at Liberty Farm, Ed also began learning to read and write. James placed a high value on education, often moving the family closer to towns with schools while he traveled on his freighting trips. The closest school to Liberty Farm sat near Cub Creek, a small stream about twelve miles west of Beatrice, Nebraska, and eighty miles east of Liberty Farm. The Lemmons occasionally stayed at the Samuel Kilpatrick farm nearby so the boys could attend classes. James once moved the entire family to Nebraska City for several weeks while he hauled freight to Salt Lake City. Hervey, Moroni, and Ed later attended school in Beatrice as well, again staying with a family in the vicinity.[41]

In the summer of 1864, James embarked upon what he hoped would be a lucrative freighting venture hauling heavy quartz-mining equipment to the Pike's Peak area in Colorado. Miners had discovered gold near Pike's Peak in 1858; the subsequent Colorado gold rush lasted for several years and brought more than one hundred thousand fortune seekers to the area. After the gold ran out, miners began searching for other valuable minerals, including silver, copper, and quartz, and James's heavy mining equipment was intended to help with their extraction. While James started his freight train for the mines, the rest of the family moved to Marysville, Kansas, so that the children could attend school.[42]

The move was fortuitous, for southern Nebraska suddenly became a conflict zone. For four years, the Lemmons had lived and worked along the Little Blue River without any confrontations with American Indians. As James noted, "We did not mind them any more than we did the birds that were flying about us."[43] Now, however, the Cheyennes, Arapahos, and Sioux began a series of violent raids along the old Oregon Trail.

The attacks had their origin in the United States-Dakota War that began in southern Minnesota in August 1862, when several bands of Dakota Sioux resorted to violence in the face of famine, treaty violations, Indian-agency corruption, the loss of traditional hunting grounds, and increasing encroachment by white settlers. The conflict spilled into neighboring regions, fueled by additional pressures on Indian lands and resources, including white hunters' slaughter of buffalo for the hide trade as well as the arrival of thousands of new settlers on the Nebraska plains in response to passage of the Homestead Act of 1862. Gold strikes in Montana and Idaho provided further incentive for military campaigns to drive the Sioux from the region; these developments sparked a series of retaliatory attacks in Nebraska and elsewhere.[44]

In the mid-summer of 1864, bands of Sioux, Cheyennes, and Arapahos began raiding white settlements throughout central and southern Nebraska. On 7 August, well-coordinated groups of Indian warriors launched an assault on outposts along the old Oregon Trail. More than thirty freighting stations and 150 ranches were hit. The raiders burned scores of buildings, killed or ran off livestock, and left a path of destruction in their wake. Dozens of individuals died; dozens more were taken captive. Liberty Farm escaped the first strike, but two days later, on 9 August, Indians attacked the Lemmon family's station as well. Two Denver-bound wagon trains—one loaded with crockery and hardware and valued at twenty-two thousand dollars, the other filled with liquor—were destroyed. Nine men died in the Liberty Farm attacks, more than twenty wagons were burned, 150 oxen were scattered, and many of the goods were taken.[45]

On 10 August, refugees from the various raids reached Marysville, Kansas, one of the closest large settlements and the Lemmon family's temporary home. As an early historian noted, "Teams with wagons filled with settlers, station-keepers and ranchmen, with their families, flowed into the town, each bringing stories of the outrageous murders and torture of men, women and children, and beseeching aid in recovering their captured friends."[46] The local militia mustered in response, and several men borrowed horses from Lucy Lemmon, who had a number of mounts the family had brought to Kansas from Liberty Farm. The hostilities continued for the next several months, exacerbated by the November 1864 Sand Creek Massacre, in which Colonel John M. Chivington and his two

Colorado cavalry regiments killed more than one hundred women and children belonging to Black Kettle's band of Southern Cheyenne Indians. Enraged, several tribes responded with a series of attacks from Montana to Texas, including a raid on Julesburg, Colorado, that burned the city to the ground. The United States-Dakota War finally ended in the fall of 1865 after three years of fighting. Both sides signed treaties pledging to end the violence, though the result was only "a makeshift and very provisional peace."[47] Had the Lemmons not been in Marysville in 1864, they might have been victims of the attacks as well.[48]

This providence had to serve as consolation for James, who realized a near-total loss on his Colorado freighting enterprise. During the raids, several of his hired freighters abandoned their loads in fear of the Indians. As a result, much of the freight, including the expensive mining equipment, had to be abandoned near Julesburg. Although James later returned to claim the heavy pieces, they had been stolen. He was not alone in his misfortune, as dozens of families lost buildings and equipment; others lost their lives. Stagecoach king Ben Holladay suffered extraordinary financial losses along his stage line, including thirty-seven horses, fifty-five sets of harnesses, 331 tons of hay, 3,143 sacks of corn, and many barns, corrals, and warehouses. All told, he claimed almost $250,000 in damages during the raids.[49]

The following spring, the Lemmons returned to what was left of Liberty Farm. The attackers had burned the Liberty Farm station and all the other buildings, except for a string of log corncribs that were too rough and ramshackle to ignite easily. Without useable structures, Liberty Farm could not serve as a regular stop on the Holladay stage line, so James set out to rebuild the farm, hiring men to plant a corn crop and reconstruct the buildings. During the growing season, guards kept watch for Indians while others tended the fields. Sometimes even the young Lemmon boys would stand watch with rifles.[50]

By early 1866, nearly all the old ranchmen had returned to the Little Blue River, and the Lemmon family continued to raise corn successfully. Again, however, an alarm was raised warning of further Indian attacks, including one less than twenty miles from the Lemmon home. Many families prepared to leave the country again for the larger settlements farther east, but James determined to stay and defend Liberty Farm with three hired men. He wanted Lucy and the children to go to Beatrice, Nebraska, but she refused to leave. For several days, the men had sporadic encounters with Indians, driving potential attackers away whenever they appeared. On one occasion, according to Ed, he and his two brothers took up pistols as well, but the incident ended before they needed to use them. As the summer drew to a close, the Lemmon family escaped unharmed once again.[51]

Ed was just nine years old during these raids and later claimed to have found the danger exhilarating. Over the next several decades, these experiences would serve as fodder for the many stories he told in cow camp and in writing. He boasted that he "never even went out for the Milk-Cows, one mile distant from [the] Ranch without a Six-Shooter belted around me" and claimed that he always carried pistols when working in the fields or traveling along the Little Blue—tales that kept his cowboys entertained and boosted his reputation as a man skilled in the ways of Indians and weapons.[52]

On 20 August 1866, just six weeks after the Indian raids on Liberty Farm, the Union Pacific Railroad reached Kearney, Nebraska Territory, on its way to completing the nation's first transcontinental railroad. Construction had begun in earnest at Omaha on 10 July 1865. After a slow first season, the line grew rapidly in 1866, with 191 total miles of track completed when the railroad reached Kearney. The arrival of the Union Pacific brought a sudden end to the Ben Holladay stage line's lucrative freighting enterprise in eastern Nebraska. Just as the completion of the telegraph line in 1861 had rendered the Pony Express obsolete, the arrival of the railroad signaled the end of overland freighting. With his profits falling, Holladay sold his holdings to Wells, Fargo & Company on 1 November 1866 and retired from the stage business. Facing the lack of future overland traffic, the devastation of the 1864 Indian attacks, and the potential for good wages from the railroad, the Lemmons decided to leave Liberty Farm. They were not alone. According to Ed, practically all of the station managers "from the Hackney ranch at the west foot of the eighteen mile ridge, near the present city of Hebron, Nebr., to Kearney joined U. P. construction."[53]

James owned several heavy wagons and had a number of good

ox teams, and he soon found work freighting for the Union Pacific. The family gathered a few belongings and traveled 110 miles northwest to Kearney, where they joined the construction crews. Before he left Liberty Farm, James collected all of the family's nonperishable goods, including furniture and tools that could not be taken along, and placed them in an underground cellar. He padlocked the wooden door and sealed the structure with well-packed dirt, anticipating returning to his property later.[54]

As the Lemmon family prepared to leave after five years on the Little Blue, James hired two men to stay and tend the corn crop. Harvest was just a few weeks away, and sometime later James sold the crop, together with several thousand bushels of corn bought from farmers near DeWitt, Nebraska, to the railroad to feed its construction crews. This sale—another example of James's ability to capitalize on a business opportunity—supplemented his regular freighting income, which included contracts to cut and haul wooden ties for the construction crews. As Charles Edgar Ames noted in *Pioneering the Union Pacific*, high-quality "lumber for the crossties, bridges, and other purposes, including fuel, was very scarce and costly, and was to remain one of the UP's chief difficulties."[55] Construction required about twenty-five hundred ties per mile, and although local cottonwood was considered inferior to hardwoods, it remained the cheapest, most abundant option. With ample money to be made cutting and hauling timber, James spent much of the next three years supplying the Union Pacific with ties.[56]

The Lemmon family followed the construction crews westward, camping at junctions and moving forward as the building advanced. James and his son Hervey, now a teenager, worked to cut and deliver ties ahead of the tracks, traveling with the construction crews each day while the rest of the family remained in camp. Hervey regularly worked alongside his father and from a young age shouldered important responsibilities in the family's business ventures. For his part, Ed loathed life in camp, which he considered "quite tame" compared to his adventures at Liberty Farm.[57] The Union Pacific reached North Platte, a townsite 305 miles west of Omaha, on 3 December 1866. When construction shut down for the winter, the Lemmons spent several months in the town, a rough amalgamation of cloth tents and crude wooden structures that one Irish resident called "a place where people suffer for a time before going to hell."[58] Like many of the larger towns established during the railroad's construction, North Platte was a wild place, featuring multiple saloons where drinking, gambling, and prostitution were the primary forms of entertainment. It was the Lemmon children's first exposure to such an atmosphere, but not their last.

Construction resumed in the spring of 1867, and the Lemmon family followed the railroad, which reached the city of Cheyenne, in what is now Wyoming, on 13 November 1867. General Grenville M. Dodge, the Union Pacific's chief engineer, had staked out the town that summer and named it for the Cheyenne Indians inhabiting the area. Cheyenne became the railroad's winter headquarters, housing thousands of construction workers, freighters, and their families. As in North Platte and Julesburg before it, "stores, saloons, and haunts of vice" abounded, and Cheyenne emerged as the "third burgeoning 'Hell-on-Wheels.'"[59] In December, James settled the family in Cheyenne, where they would remain for several years.

Although only fourteen, Hervey Lemmon was already a well-respected young man. He regularly collected payments and distributed wages for his father's teamsters, sent important messages, and acted as James's representative in business dealings. His independence and level of responsibility became a model for Ed, who continued to idolize his brother. In actuality, Hervey may not have lived up to Ed's admiring, larger-than-life portrayals, but James obviously deemed him competent and trustworthy, even in a dangerous town.[60]

Whereas the city of North Platte had quickly established a rigid system for enforcing law and order, Cheyenne remained a rough place for several years. Between 1867 and 1869, the *Cheyenne Leader* documented more than a dozen murders and shootings, so when Hervey traveled into its less desirable areas he armed himself with two .36-caliber Colt revolvers. Although Cheyenne passed an ordinance on 30 September 1867 banning the carrying of firearms and dangerous weapons, few citizens observed the rule. The lack of respect for this law was so blatant that the *Leader* pleaded for authorities to "Enforce the Laws, or Repeal Them."[61]

Members of the Lemmon family saw Cheyenne's violence first-hand on 21 March 1868. They awoke that morning to see the remains of accused murderer Charles Martin dangling at the west end of Cheyenne Street in plain sight of the Lemmon home. Martin had recently been acquitted by a local jury and celebrated his freedom by cavorting at the Keystone Dance Hall. Around one o'clock that morning, someone lured Martin outside, where members of the local Vigilance Committee struck him on the head with a pistol, hauled him away, fashioned a noose from a clothesline, and strung him up on a tripod made of three clothesline poles fastened together. As Ed recalled, "the Vigilantes were then cleaning up Cheyenne . . . and they made quite a thorough job of it."[62]

Throughout 1868 and 1869, the Vigilance Committee dispensed similar frontier-style justice to suspected murderers, thieves, and other ruffians. Rather than being appalled or scared by these events, Ed reveled in the town's danger—or so he claimed. In his view, the good guys had lynched the bad guys, who deserved what they got. Cheyenne was a welcome change from the boredom of the railroad camp and regularly offered some new or unusual event to satisfy his inherent need for adventure. Others approved of the violence for what they believed to be practical reasons. A Cheyenne business directory published in 1868 defended the vigilantes, stating: "People living in old settled communities may at first think that the Vigilance Committees of the Rocky Mountain region are a source of evil, but on a moment's consideration they will recognize the necessity of having either an extraordinary powerful city government, or in lieu thereof, a power that will make crime hide its head and give a feeling of security to law abiding citizens. Such a power is the Vigilantes. They restrain desperadoes from practicing their lawless work, and give an assurance of safety to the honest man who desires to make this region his home."[63] The directory listed several instances of vigilante justice, designed to offer potential businessmen and travelers a measure of comfort. Indeed, some members of the Cheyenne business community appear to have participated in the Vigilance Committee's activities, although public support for the organization varied.[64]

In the spring of 1868, James Lemmon partnered with a Nebraska acquaintance named Ute Metcalf to subcontract for tie-cutting with the Coe and Carter Company, which had a large contract to provide ties for the Union Pacific and Denver Pacific railroads. James had known Metcalf for some time and considered him resourceful, if a little untrustworthy. They established a camp near present-day Rawlins, Wyoming, where they worked for several months in the Medicine Bow Mountains cutting and hauling lodgepole pines with several hired men, including Hervey. After a few months in the mountains, James returned to Cheyenne to visit Lucy and his other children, leaving Hervey at the camp. During James's absence, Metcalf collected payment from Coe and Carter and abandoned the camp, taking several thousand dollars of James's hard-earned money. When Hervey discovered Metcalf's theft, he wired James in Cheyenne, who immediately boarded a train in pursuit. An evening stop at a road ranch and saloon cost James the use of his left index finger when he carelessly handed his handgun, a unique pepperbox pistol with four rotating barrels, to the bartender, who allowed another patron to examine the weapon. As James took the gun back, it went off, shooting him through the finger. This painful wound did not slow James down, however, and the next morning he resumed the chase, which ended fruitlessly a few days later when he learned that Metcalf had murdered a rich mine prospector and had already been hanged for the crime.[65]

When James returned to the Medicine Bow Mountains to gather his wagons and equipment, he learned that Metcalf had failed to pay wages for any of their employees and had left a large bill for groceries, feed, and other supplies. James had to sell a number of his wagons and teams to pay these debts, leaving him with just three freight wagons, a fraction of his earlier fleet. In typical Lemmon style, he moved on from his losses and acquired another tie-cutting contract, but with considerably less equipment, he was unable to secure large, lucrative contracts as before. Twenty years later, Ed learned that Ute Metcalf had not been hanged but had fabricated the story of his death to throw James off his trail.[66]

While James and Hervey worked cutting and hauling railroad ties, Moroni, Ed, and Alpharetta attended school in Cheyenne. Aside from attending class and working a few odd jobs, including capturing prairie dogs to sell to eastern tourists, the Lemmon brothers had a great deal of spare time and occupied themselves with various boyhood pursuits, including honing their skills with bullwhips and taking notice of the city's beautiful young women.

Finally, on 10 May 1869, the Union Pacific's tracks reached the terminus of the Central Pacific Railroad at Promontory Summit, Utah, completing the nation's first transcontinental railroad. James Lemmon watched as Leland Stanford, president of the Central Pacific and later founder of Stanford University, used a silver maul to drive a symbolic golden spike, finishing the line. James probably felt a sense of pride for having participated in the historic endeavor, but he also lost the tie-hauling job that had been his primary source of income for the previous three years.[67]

The meeting point was about seventy-five miles northwest of James's old farm near Bountiful, and on the return trip to Cheyenne he stopped to inquire about the seventy head of shorthorn cattle he had left in Rideout's care when the family moved to Nebraska almost ten years earlier. James discovered that Brigham Young had sent Rideout on a foreign evangelical mission, leaving the herd neglected. Unable to restore James's cattle herd, Young compensated him with fifty-two horses from the church's large Antelope Island herd. The horses on Antelope Island in the Great Salt Lake—also known as Church Island because the Latter-day Saints used it to graze their herds of cattle, sheep, and horses—were well-known for their quality, serving as mounts during the Utah War and for the Pony Express. These fine "Church Island horses," as the Lemmon family called them, more than made up for the loss of the seventy shorthorn cattle and provided James with a new source of income. James, Hervey, and a Mormon boy named Ruben ("Rube") Taylor trailed the horses back home to Cheyenne, along with about twenty head of work stock used during the Union Pacific's construction.[68]

A short time after returning from Utah, Hervey went to work for John Wesley Iliff, a wealthy cattleman with a huge ranch in northeastern Colorado. Iliff was one of the region's first cattle ranchers; he owned or controlled thousands of acres of grassland on ranges stretching from Julesburg to Greeley, Colorado, a distance of more than 150 miles. To look after his more than twenty thousand head of cattle, he employed between twelve and thirty-five men, depending on the time of the year (many cowboys were let go before winter, as the cattle required far less tending during those cold months). While Hervey started "punching cows" under Iliff's Bar F brand, Ed—now twelve—joined Iliff's crew as a part-time courier. Iliff owned a retail meat market in Cheyenne and also had beef contracts with several area forts, including Laramie, Fetterman, and D. A. Russell. Ed regularly traveled between the ranch headquarters located south of Sidney, Wyoming, near the present-day town of Iliff, and these places to deliver messages.[69]

When not working for Iliff, Ed looked after his father's fifty-two Church Island horses at the Chalk Bluffs, a unique geological formation about thirteen miles south of Cheyenne in the present-day Pawnee National Grassland.[70] Ed stayed in a cramped cabin with a crew of wood-choppers, many of whom had worked as freighters for James Lemmon. Rube Taylor assisted Ed in retrieving strays, a chore repeated often, as the ponies had strong homing instincts and sought to return to Utah. One day, Ed and Rube tracked several stray horses to an area more than twenty miles from the wood-choppers' camp. By the time they gathered the horses, it was too dark to make the return trip, so they cached their saddles, hobbled the animals by tying their front legs together so they could graze but not travel far, and prepared to spend the night in a deserted trapper's cabin not far from a known Indian winter camp. Ed later recalled:

> The cabin was only 12 by 14 and had a wall bunk in the southeast corner. There was in the west side a small three paned slide window, covered with white oiled paper. The wide wall bunk took up the greater portion of the part east of the south door, leaving scant room to set our carbines at the head of the bed, so we had placed them at the foot but had our six-shooters under our heads.
>
> It was a moonlight night and we had scarcely gotten in bed when we heard a slight commotion to the west and looked and espied three Indian faces crushed against the window, apparently trying to pierce the interior darkness, for they had likely seen our horse sign around the house and were wondering if the owners were in the cabin. I slipped my six-shooter from under my head but the Mormon boy seemed to prefer his carbine and reached for it at the foot of the bed and in so doing evidently made a slight noise from which the Indians

sprinted away in a flash. So I lost my best opportunity to have killed an Indian.[71]

Neither boy slept that night, and they thoroughly scanned the surrounding country before cautiously setting out from the cabin the next morning.

In later life, Lemmon would have countless dealings with American Indians. While working as a cowboy, he trailed cattle to Indian agencies on numerous occasions, including trips to the Standing Rock and Pine Ridge agencies. Ed regularly ate, talked, and traded with Indians; he would come to know Red Cloud, Young Man Afraid of His Horses, and other notable leaders. In the early twentieth century, he would acquire a huge lease on the Standing Rock Indian Reservation and would hire nearly three hundred Indians to help fence the pasture. He looked upon several Indians as friends and tried to maintain an amicable relationship with the local tribes. Given his apparent respect for Indians, his recollection of what he later called "My Lost Opportunity to Kill an Indian" seems out of character.[72]

The story's title suggests that Lemmon would have liked to have shot at the silhouette in the window. He did not kill anyone during his lifetime, and the apparent regret expressed in his story is probably the result of a desire to impress the public. When Ed first published a version of this story in 1932, he had been preparing articles and reminiscences for publication for several years. He wrote his stories for a white audience and colored them with details and insights he hoped would rival the tales produced by popular western authors like Zane Grey. In his correspondence with Lewis F. Crawford, a North Dakota historian whom he contacted about editing his writings into a single collected volume, Ed apologized for the tameness of his accounts, which, as he regretfully admitted, could not rival the "blood and thunder" exploits the novelists produced. As he noted in a 1926 letter, "I realize you are going to have trouble living my stories up as to tales so, Bear in mind I have at least 10 more good Indian stories . . . I can vouch [for them], as they are truth and not fiction. One can't expect such Blood-Curdling Stories."[73] He sought to produce a factual representation of his life, but he also wrote with entertainment in mind. Just as he did in his cow-camp stories, Ed made a point to highlight the action of his encounters, taking great pains to flesh out these events in minute detail, just as popular western novelists and memoirists did. He admired tales of danger and armed exploits, including his father's, and he did not want his own life to seem untouched by that kind of adventure. In the end, this story must be read in the context of both values.

Far more important than cool nerves and skill at arms were the values of respect, honesty, conviction, and hard work that Ed Lemmon learned from his father and older brother. James and Hervey's example helped to instill in Ed an entrepreneurial spirit that he would carry for his entire life. Thirty-two years after his "lost opportunity to kill an Indian," Ed reflected on his experiences during the long buggy ride to Leaf-on-the-Hill Creek in North Dakota to inspect his newly acquired cattle empire. As he stood surveying the 865,000-acre lease, shifting his weight to his left to accommodate his badly crippled right leg, he was a confident, content cattleman reveling in the product of a life's work. Lemmon was at the pinnacle of his career; he was successful, well-to-do, and had a satisfying sense of his place in the world. Perhaps he reflected on the carefree days with his family on the Little Blue. And perhaps he thought back to the origins of his career in the cattle business, when he followed in Hervey's footsteps to become a cowboy.

2 COWBOYING

Ed Lemmon's introduction to the open-range cattle industry began in an ordinary fashion, with no fanfare and little indication that he would become one of the world's greatest cowboys. When his older brother Hervey began working as a cowhand for J. W. Iliff's Colorado and Wyoming ranches in 1869, Ed managed to secure a part-time job carrying messages for the wealthy cattleman. Although he had worked around livestock as a child, Ed's first significant exposure to cowboys came in 1870, when at age thirteen he began spending a great deal of time with Iliff's outfit. Lemmon was short, wiry, and looked even younger than his years, but he was also tough, determined, and showed a keen interest in cattle handling. A short time later, he managed to secure a job tending beeves for Iliff on the open range. Ed's early experiences in Wyoming and Colorado marked the beginning of a fifty-year career in the saddle, during which he worked more than one million head of cattle on horseback and earned recognition for his talents as a cowboy and cattleman.

In the fall of 1870, after three years in Cheyenne, the Lemmon family packed its belongings and returned to Liberty Farm, their road ranch on the Little Blue River in eastern Nebraska. After the Union Pacific Railroad had been completed and Ute Metcalf had absconded with the earnings from their Coe and Carter tie-hauling contract, James Lemmon had little reason to remain in Cheyenne. He still owned the 160-acre property in Nebraska and planned to take up farming and freighting once again. James, Lucy, and their four children traveled with seven of Iliff's cowhands who helped drive their herd of fifty-two Church Island horses. Before starting work with Iliff, the cowboys had been members of James's freighting outfit; now they were heading back to their homes and families in Nebraska, since Iliff would soon be cutting his hired help down to a skeleton crew for the winter.[1]

When the Lemmons arrived at Liberty Farm, they discovered a former soldier named Benjamin Royce living on their property.

Royce had been stationed near Liberty Farm during the previous year, and in the Lemmon family's absence he contested their homestead and filed his own claim of ownership, contending that they had abandoned the farm. "He had jumped father's homestead by moving right into father's house scarcely making a new improvement," Ed recalled. In addition, "Royce had broken open a large cellar that father, upon leaving, had filled with furniture, fixtures, windows, doors, farm implements and lumber removed from the houses."[2] Royce and three other area homesteaders had found the cache and divided it among themselves, leaving the Lemmon family with none of their former possessions.

Although the cowboys wanted to remove Royce forcibly, James decided to leave Liberty Farm to him. As a former soldier who had fought for the Union in the Civil War, Royce might garner some sympathy for his case, and he had officially filed paperwork on the property. For James, the time and expense of contesting the claim in court were probably not worth the effort, given that more land was available in the area. The Lemmons took up residence on a section of land about twenty-four miles east of Liberty Farm, near the town of Kiowa in Thayer County, Nebraska.[3]

James may have been willing to give up Liberty Farm without a fight, but the loss deeply affected Ed. He had spent his formative years there and felt a strong attachment to the place. Liberty Farm was the site of many boyhood adventures, where his family had fended off Indian attacks and hosted Wild Bill Hickok. It was a stop on the Pony Express, part of the Ben Holladay stage line, and the spot where two of Ed's infant brothers were buried beneath a stand of cottonwood trees. To the end of his life, Ed cherished the memories he made there. As he later wrote, "With all my roamings, successes, failures, devotions, and annoyances, the old place will always seem my real home. Even with a good thrifty town named for me in South Dakota, I will never have the attachment for it I have for Old Liberty Farm."[4]

With few job prospects available during the Nebraska winter, seventeen-year-old Hervey left for Texas to continue his career as a cowboy. He would remain there more than five years, depriving Ed of his longtime friend and hero. Hervey's absence, combined with the clean break from his childhood endeavors at Liberty Farm, would prompt thirteen-year-old Ed to begin his cowboy career as well. He attended a local school during the winter of 1870–1871, but when spring arrived, he stopped going to class and started working full time.[5]

Two Texas cattlemen, whom Lemmon identified as Lawhorn and Hardigan, drove several large herds into southern Nebraska that spring, fattening them on the open-range grasses and selling them to area residents for beef. The cattle grazed for several months near the town of Oak, just a few miles from the Lemmon home at Kiowa. At that time, homesteaders capitalizing on the 1862 Homestead Act were arriving in southern Nebraska, seeking free title to up to 160 acres of land. The Lawhorn and Hardigan herds had a penchant for stampeding at night and began to cause significant damage to crops, so the cattlemen hired Ed to gather up the strays and compensate homesteaders for any damages. Lew Slover, the brother of Hervey's future wife, also worked with this outfit. "One night," Ed recalled, "I was with a herd of three year old steers and they met in a head-on collision, in quite a deep gulch, with a herd of all steers, [four-year-olds] and upwards. As the herds neared one another the bosses hollered for all hands to quit the leads and drop out of their path. The results were that about one hundred steers were killed and many more crippled; but not a single man or horse [was] killed, owing to the knowledge of the bosses and their hollering for all hands to quit the leads."[6]

This incident was illuminating for Ed; indeed, it was one of his closest calls during a stampede. Even as a teenager, he was acquiring the necessary skills for success as a roundup and trail boss.[7]

From 1871 to 1874, Ed worked at various jobs, including carrying mail, herding mules, tending horses, and trailing cattle. He probably felt similar to cowboy W. H. Hamilton, who was "young and tough and did not mind [the hard work], tho no one had to rock me to sleep when I did get to bed."[8] In the summer of 1871, Ed contracted to carry mail from Kiowa southwest to the Guide Rock outpost on the Republican River, then west to Red Cloud, Riverton, and back. Guide Rock and Red Cloud were also called the Lower and Upper stockades, because local homesteaders had built wooden stockades there to protect themselves from the Indians who still inhabited the area. One morning while making the return run from

Riverton, Ed came upon a group of homesteaders gathered on the north bank of the Republican and inadvertently put himself in an awkward situation.[9]

Earlier in the day, a small party of Indians had launched a surprise attack on these homesteaders while they were digging a well. The settlers managed to wound one member of the war party, but the wounded man had escaped across the river and hidden in a plum thicket. Unsure whether he was dead or alive, the homesteaders stood at the edge of the river, too cautious to go across but too curious to leave. When Ed asked why they "didn't swim over and see if they had a dead or badly wounded Indian," they claimed not to know whether their horses would swim the river.[10] When Ed offered the loan of his horse, which he knew would swim, the settlers were suddenly "troubled with rheumatism or something" and suggested to the young mail carrier that since he was well acquainted with his own horse, he would be the best candidate to do the swimming.[11] Though only fourteen years old, Ed had been bragging for some time about his skill as a frontiersman. He could hardly "falter and show a yellow streak" now, so he asked for a pair of field glasses and a rifle and began to swim his horse across to the other side.[12]

Ed headed downstream for a place with no vegetation that could conceal an ambush, and when he reached the bank, he began searching for the wounded man with the field glasses. He soon saw a horse, and "upon more careful scrutiny located the Indian close under the horse's nose, with flies buzzing over his face. But for fear of a ruse I rode up with cocked rifle, but found the Indian stone dead."[13] Ed swam back across the river, reported his findings, and resumed the trip to Kiowa. He later learned that the homesteaders traveled several miles to get a boat and retrieved the Indian's remains the following morning. In retrospect, Ed wished he had pumped "a few shots into the carcass" so he could "claim the honor of finishing him off."[14]

Like the incident in the tie-cutting camp two years earlier, this episode was another lost chance to kill an Indian. The young Ed was likely relieved to find the warrior already dead, but his disappointment in not being able to *claim* that he had done the deed may have been genuine, for he was not one to miss an opportunity to take credit for a heroic act or a dangerous feat. On the other hand, his conscience was clear, and Ed also surely realized that the story's anticlimactic outcome did not diminish the daring of his actions: as a fourteen-year-old boy, he swam alone across the river to confront an armed opponent while a group of adults stood idly by. Foreshadowing the man he would become, he had demonstrated a willingness to take risks, both to quench his own thirst for excitement and to prove his bravery.

Lemmon's stories can be unreliable, however, sometimes having more in common with the informal atmosphere of the cow camp than with careful attention to accuracy. His account of an event that supposedly happened while he was working on Kansas cattle drives in the early 1870s provides an apt example. As Ed told it, in about 1872 he and several other cowboys were trailing a herd when they came across a group of Comanche Indians hunting buffalo. Neither party showed any hostile intent, and each let the other go about their business unmolested. As the cowboys rode by, Ed saw a Comanche shoot a buffalo and dismount to skin it. The hunter had straddled the animal's neck to cut its throat when the still-alive buffalo rose to its feet with the man on its shoulders. One of the buffalo's horns slipped through his leather belt, and the animal dragged him along as it pounded across the prairie. The disoriented man still held his skinning knife and attempted to cut the belt, but as he did so the knife slipped and he stabbed himself. According to Ed, the man "cut his own bowels out and the buffalo literally tramped them off before anyone could shoot the buffalo and rescue him." One of the cowboys galloped over and killed the buffalo, but the man had already died. Lemmon recalled that "even [though] we were not much in love with the Comanches, the sight stirred us to a high pitch and we expressed to one another the horror of the thing, and it cast a pall over the entire outfit for several days, even as used as we were to horrible sights."[15]

While Ed's first-person perspective lends considerable drama to the story, he almost certainly did not witness this event, if it occurred. In another of his articles, chronicling "a couple of the Hashknife outfit [adventures] in the early eighties," he included a substantially identical story.[16] Ed never worked for the Hashknife outfit, however, and it seems clear that he heard this story from one of the outfit's cowboys and repurposed the tale to make it more interesting and enhance his own standing as an expert on Indians and trail drives. This approach was consistent with Ed's penchant for telling exciting stories around the campfire, but it complicates his later assertion that "it is a shame for persons to express their views on hearsay, and not from real experience and use."[17]

Ed had ample reason to contemplate life and death in 1873, when his mother Lucy died on 26 December at the age of forty-seven. The cause of her death is unclear, but she had experienced several difficult pregnancies, which may have been a factor. Lucy's family buried her next to the Little Blue River, though subsequent flooding caused them to move her remains to a hilltop cemetery above the site of the old Oak Grove Pony Express station.[18]

The effect of Lucy's death on her youngest son is difficult to determine. In his writings, Ed rarely mentioned his mother and said next to nothing about her death. Her role in his stories was limited; Ed did not brag about his mother in the same way he did the rest of his family. Perhaps her death was too painful to write about, but more likely Ed and his mother simply were not close. He was a man who lived in the realm of men and appreciated their exploits. Women were pleasant to look at and a necessity for raising children, but their lives and labors held no interest for him except when they reflected manly qualities, as in the adventures of Calamity Jane, who appears in several of his reminiscences. Ed was not prone to displays of emotion, at one point writing, "It seems I am not built that way," and he probably did not dwell for long on his mother's death.[19]

A few months later, the McCumpsey family, a widow and her four sons, moved into the Lemmon home near Kiowa. The widow's former husband, Richard, had mysteriously disappeared some time earlier, and after Lucy's death, James needed a woman to care for the home. The nature of their relationship is unclear, but the McCumpsey family would live with the Lemmons for the next three years. Ed quickly became friends with Tom McCumpsey, who was the same age, and they spent a great deal of time working with the Church Island horses.[20]

According to Ed, "These horses were hot blooded stock bred for cavalry horses on which to mount troopers."[21] Since the Mormons had isolated them on Church Island, they had become wild and somewhat inbred, which reduced them to a medium size. The animals were fast, however, and when Hervey and Ed worked for Iliff in 1870, the brothers had attempted to train them as roping or cutting horses.

Although roping and cutting were both done on horseback, they were different activities that required two different types of horses. When roping, a cowboy would throw the noose of his lariat around a calf's neck and then quickly wrap the slack end around his saddle horn, a maneuver called "dallying." With the rope secured, the cowboy would turn his horse and drag the calf to the branding fire. Cowboys often roped unbranded mavericks out on the range as well. Four-year-old beeves could weigh more than one thousand pounds, and a heavy roping horse with a broad chest and wide hips was needed to absorb the jolt when a running half-ton steer reached the end of a cowboy's thirty-foot line. "A horse that likes roping will do his utmost to carry his rider to where his loop will catch," observed cowboy Ike Blasingame, "and he doesn't mind the jerk that follows. But a horse that doesn't like roping can cause a loop to miss, even if he has been spurred to the right place and can do a good job of working the rope once the catch is made."[22]

In contrast, cutting horses were generally smaller, narrower-fronted animals built for speed and agility rather than strength and stability. A cutting horse's job was to remove, or cut out, an animal from a larger group of cattle without using a rope. Instead, the rider and his horse used proper positioning to drive the animal to a particular location. Cutting horses could therefore be lighter than roping horses and, consequently, quicker and more nimble. Cowboys used the cutting technique when they needed to move a number of animals rapidly, without having to "work" each individual animal. This was especially true during roundups, when large herds needed to be sorted by brand. When Ed selected his cutting mounts, he knew exactly the type of animal he wanted. "Most of our durable cutting horses were narrow breasted and flat limbed, especially the hind limbs," he wrote, "which took the jar off when they stopped on them."[23] He liked horses with front ends so narrow it seemed that "both front legs [were] coming out of one hole."[24]

Ed also preferred narrow-fronted horses because he thought they aged better than their broad-chested counterparts. Cutting horses had a propensity to stiffen up in the shoulders when they reached fifteen to twenty years old, and during the winter Ed employed a technique called roweling to keep them limber for the spring roundups. To rowel a horse, Ed used a knife to make parallel incisions in the horse's shoulders. He would then carefully insert the knife blade just beneath the hide between the two incisions, to separate it from the muscle underneath. Finally, he would thread a braid of rope or horsehair through the slits so the cuts would remain open throughout the winter, "thus leaching out all impurities."[25]

Not surprisingly, Ed also had strong opinions on how cutting horses should be trained. Some cowboys preferred to give them a loose rein, thereby allowing the horses the ability to select how they would move and react to an animal during pursuit. Ed emphatically dismissed this approach, arguing, "I think I can anticipate the next move of the cow better than any horse." He further contended that "a horse working on a loose rein . . . covers a wider swath than a stiff reined horse" and tends to "stir up" the cattle in a roundup, making them nervous and more difficult to handle.[26] A few years later, Ed would cut nine hundred head in a single day, a statistic that suggests that his stiff-reined approach served him well. For the average cowboy, whose ability to anticipate the movements of cattle was less acute, using a loose rein ("giving a horse its head") may have been more effective.

Unfortunately, the Church Island horses were not well suited for cutting or roping, and the Lemmons never used them for either purpose. They made fine courier horses, however, and Ed rode them while traveling his mail routes. With their speed and small size, they were "the cream of the region for go-getters," and Ed boasted that he could even run down antelope on them.[27] James knew an opportunity when he saw one and used some of the Church Island horses as racers. Throughout the mid-1870s, he traveled around the region with them, competing in match races and at local fairs. Tom McCumpsey often served as the jockey. James's horses were moderately successful, and they may have been the mounts that renowned female racer Minnie Pinneo used in the eastern United States and Europe.[28]

In the summer of 1874, Ed had the first of two accidents that would change his life forever. While trailing a wild Lawhorn and

Hardigan cow in south-central Nebraska, his horse fell, pinning him and crushing his right thigh, "the break cropping out in two places."[29] As a result of this severe compound fracture, Ed was bed-fast for four months and on crutches for a year and a half. He was only seventeen years old and might have made a complete recovery if not for a similar accident the following year, when he broke the same leg a second time. On this occasion, Ed and Tom were racing their horses behind a herd of cattle moving toward a night corral when their youthful exuberance got the better of them. Sixty years later, in an article titled "The Bitter with the Sweet," Ed described the mishap:

> Tom was riding a young mare half broken, and with my bridle[,] while I rode with rope around my 1200-pound mount's nose, and after running about 200 yards both flew the track, which was a wagon road, each bolting outward, [and] as we pulled them inward, they clashed together with terrific force, piling Tom's mount up in a heap and killing my mount on the spot, and crushing my partially healed leg in similar manner as the year before, and rendering me unconscious for an hour, from which I was rendered a cripple for life, for besides the breaks, rheumatism set in, drawing my defective leg all out of shape.[30]

Healing the injuries sustained in this second accident took several months and gave Ed ample time to reflect on his life and his new situation. He must have known the injury would be permanent, and coming to terms with this realization probably took some time. Nevertheless, the Lemmon family had a history of taking adversity in stride: James Lemmon rebuilt his business after his partner absconded with their earnings, and the family started over with a new homestead after the loss of Liberty Farm to a claim jumper. Ed did not wallow in misfortune; his youthful recklessness had cost him the normal use of one leg and forced a change in how he sat in the saddle, but the accident also made him more mature. He knew the challenges life could present and made a concerted effort to overcome them. Ed did not seek pity and would not accept charity. He understood that he had to adapt and work harder to match the physical capabilities of other cowboys and demonstrate skill in specialized areas in order to earn his place, and he embraced the challenge.[31]

As a cowboy, Ed found his niche in the tasks that best suited his condition. During roundups, for example, several cowboys worked at branding and castrating each calf. A mounted cowboy roped a calf around its neck and dragged it near the fire that heated the branding irons. There, one or two ground-based men wrestled the calf to the ground, removed the rope, and held the animal as still as possible while another man applied the red-hot iron to its ribs or hip, scorching the hair and leaving a permanent identification mark, or brand, on the hide. If the calf was male, another cowboy castrated it, cutting off the end of the young bull's scrotum with a knife, pulling the testicles from the sack and cutting them away, after which the cowboys turned the animal back into the herd. This dusty, tiring process—rope, drag, wrestle, hold, brand, castrate— was repeated hundreds of times each day. Lemmon's crippled leg and small size—he stood less than five and a half feet tall and weighed less than 150 pounds—made wrestling difficult, but he demonstrated great skill in castrating calves. Castration prevented unwanted reproduction, improved fattening, and made the castrated animals, or steers, more docile and easier to handle. Lemmon made certain that the procedure was done correctly to ensure the animal's health.[32]

Such physically taxing work proved strenuous for men with two good legs, so Lemmon had to work even harder to keep up. Cowboys were noted for avoiding ground jobs if they could, but Lemmon's infirmity made him even more eager to be on horseback than the average cowhand. He worked hard to distinguish himself as a roper or cutter, a mounted cowboy who removed individual animals from the larger herd. In time, he would become legendary for his skill in this role, and while on horseback he gleaned the information that would serve him well as he acquired greater responsibilities.

By 1876—the year Charles Goodnight settled in the Texas Panhandle and the centennial of the Declaration of Independence— the Lemmon brothers had begun to establish themselves in various trades. Hervey had been trailing cattle in Texas since 1870; Ed worked as a courier and cowboy in Nebraska; and Moroni sought freighting opportunities in the Black Hills of Dakota Territory. By

Moroni ("Rone")
Lemmon.
*Virginia Grabow
collection*

the time Jack McCall shot Wild Bill Hickok in Deadwood on 2 August, Moroni had already made a significant profit freighting goods and supplies for the miners in the area's various gold camps, as his father had done in California in 1849.[33]

The Black Hills Gold Rush began with an 1874 scouting expedition led by Lieutenant Colonel George Armstrong Custer. Although the 1868 Treaty of Fort Laramie had guaranteed the sacred Black Hills to the Lakotas as part of the Great Sioux Reservation, the discovery of gold by miners and scientists attached to the expedition triggered a massive influx of white prospectors. Attempts to stop them were halfhearted and politically unpopular, and when negotiations for federal purchase of the land failed, the Lakotas, Northern

Cheyennes, and others defended their lands with force. The Great Sioux War ended disastrously both for Custer, who was killed in the Battle of the Little Bighorn, and for the Indians, who saw a wide swath of present-day western South Dakota, including the Black Hills, removed from their reservation.[34]

While Moroni sought his fortune in the Black Hills, Ed remained in Thayer County for the rest of 1876. But when spring came, he and Tom McCumpsey—who had become too heavy to serve as James's racehorse jockey—left for the town of Ogallala, Nebraska, to find work as full-time cowboys. Ogallala was a major cattle-shipping point, sending more than 175,000 animals to market in both 1875 and 1876. Dozens of cattle companies had operations there, and the young men soon obtained positions with a large outfit, the Sheidley Cattle Company, managed by Dave Clark. During the 1870s, the Sheidley Company had driven more than thirty-two thousand cattle north from Texas and operated a large ranch near the forks of the Platte River in western Nebraska. Brothers Ben, George, and William Sheidley had been involved in the livestock business since the end of the Civil War and owned large herds of cattle, sheep, and horses. They owned or controlled land in both Texas and Nebraska, had built a large mansion in downtown Kansas City where they based their operation, and were involved in a number of other business and real estate ventures. Clark, just nineteen years old in 1877, was "a handsome man and good mixer, with a finished education and weighing about 240."[35] He hailed from the Sheidleys' hometown of Tiffin, Ohio, and showed tremendous skill as a cattleman and leader of men.[36]

Tom soon soured over punching cows and returned home, but Ed thrived as a cowboy. He participated in his first large-scale roundup during the spring of 1877 and quickly earned the respect of his superiors. In June, he bossed his first cattle drive. The Sheidley brothers loaned Ed's services to a friend and fellow cattleman, "Major" Seth Mabry, who had contracted to provide beef to soldiers stationed in the Black Hills. Lemmon was just a month over twenty years old and one of the youngest cowboys in the outfit when he was selected to lead a three-man crew on a 160-mile drive from the North Platte River to a soldiers' camp. Guided only by a crude map the troop commander had sent showing the location to be somewhere in the southwestern Black Hills, Lemmon managed to find the camp "without encountering a single Indian or other obstruction."[37] After the lieutenant in charge finished counting the cattle, he asked who was responsible for the herd. When the other cowboys pointed out the small, boyish, crippled Lemmon, the officer looked him up and down and remarked that "it was a damn shame to place a stripling of a boy in charge of such a precarious undertaking."[38] Lemmon's men seemed proud of their young leader and defended his abilities, saying, "If you would just follow him on a long difficult ride and try to lose him [on] a dark night, or fool him about the habits of these northern Indian[s], you would soon change your mind."[39]

Ed's successful trail drive established him as a competent and trustworthy employee, but he still remained a line-rider on the lower rungs of the Sheidley Company hierarchy. In western Nebraska during the 1870s, individual companies did not own land, but each cattle outfit nevertheless had clear and acknowledged boundaries to its range. As a line-rider, Ed followed the edges of the Sheidley Company range to keep its cattle from straying onto areas controlled by adjacent ranches and to keep other cattle off the Sheidley range. He also watched for rustlers, shot or ran off wolves and coyotes that would prey on weak cattle or calves, rounded up stray cattle, and trailed the herd to locations with ample grass for grazing. Line-riding was essential to maintaining order on the open range where the cattlemen, not law enforcement, set the rules.

According to Ed, this "code of the open range" was usually strictly observed, and cattle outfits rarely placed livestock on land they did not control or drove them onto another outfit's range to "steal" the grass.[40] On the established ranges of public land, this gentlemen's agreement extended only to white, large-scale cattle ranchers in good standing with other cattlemen. Ranchers with less than a few hundred head, Indians, newcomers, and sheepmen—whom cattlemen almost universally detested—were not covered by the terms of this unwritten code. Ed may have felt superior to sheepmen, but as a young, low-ranking cowboy, he followed orders and honed his skills. He worked hard and earned about a dollar per day for his labors. Although the pay was low, each day on the range brought a new adventure, and he thoroughly enjoyed the excitement and uncertainty of being a cowboy.[41]

A number of writers have described the boredom and loneliness of tending the same cattle over the same country on the same horse day after day; even renowned cattleman Charles Goodnight commented on "the monotony of the range."[42] Far from finding his work tedious, however, Ed thrived in it. His clear preference for life in cow camp rather than in town—or even in his own home—was a key factor in his successful career. A cowboy's work might change little from day to day, but the natural environment—weather, season of the year, terrain, and wild animals—made each day different from the previous one. While working on the open range far from shelter, lightning could be both dangerous and awe-inspiring. As cowboy Ike Blasingame recalled:

> Working livestock in natural lightning country, we had many close calls. Among ourselves, we had a theory that hot, sweaty cattle or horses "drawed" electricity; that they were a likely target when the fire-devils in the clouds got to splitting the sky apart. Most any old cowboy can tell of the way a horse's mane and tail almost sparks just before a storm. The hairs stand out separately as if a little hurricane is blowing in from underneath. On nights when a black storm hovers overhead, soft phosphorus lights glow on the tips of a horse's ears, like little candles, moving as he twitches and turns them while watching everything out in the dark. On many bad nights, I've seen these same little balls of light on the tips of the cattle's horns, and the glow is considerable when many cattle are bunched.[43]

Ed wrote dozens of stories about incidents on the range, including his occupation's hazards and opportunities. In one colorful account, Ed recalled a run-in with a badger:

> When I hired out to the Sheidley Brothers, near Ogallala, Nebr., on the Platte River in 1877, with Dave Clark, manager, they were furnishing saddles if desired. In addition to the saddles there were many harnesses to oil. Badger oil was excellent for the purpose, so Dave gave it out that he would pay us boys one dollar for each badger we would kill and render the oil from. Since we were then only getting thirty dollars per month, every added dollar was a temptation, especially as it

was gotten on company time, so we were all on the look-out for badgers.

My duties at the time of this happening was as line rider between the Sheidley cattle and the neighboring outfit, west, known as the 100 outfit as that was their brand. One day, as I was out on my line, I espied a very large badger some distance away and rode for him, but, before I could reach him, he was partially down a hole which he evidently had hurriedly sought. It was a tight squeeze for him and he was just about one-half down when I jumped from my horse and grabbed him by both hind legs and gave a great heave. Out he popped, and I whirled him in the air, turning him over completely once. As he left my hands, I pulled my six-shooter, and as he came up facing me, I let drive, hitting him as square in the brain as one could have stuck one's finger. He fell stone dead, on my toes, but he had made his grab and his dying teeth stripped the whole front top of patent leather from my boot and he still retained it in his teeth. The act from the time he plopped from the hole couldn't have been more than three seconds. This is what in "western gun vernacular" would be called in the "split second."[44]

Ed was proud of his accurate shot and no doubt appreciated the additional dollar for his pay, especially since the badger had ruined a boot in the process. At the time, he was among the lowest paid of the Sheidley employees, and he soon sought greater opportunities elsewhere.

Like most open-range cattle outfits, the Sheidley Company used a skeleton crew during the winter, and when it cut its payrolls for the winter of 1877–1878, Ed was among those left without a job. Employing line riders during the winter was an unnecessary expense, because another outfit's cattle could not injure a company's range grasses while the plants lay dormant. Likewise, most of a cowboy's other responsibilities—branding, castrating, driving cattle to railroad heads, and so on—occurred only during the warmer months. Most cattlemen avoided shipping their animals to slaughter in Chicago or elsewhere during the wintertime in part because the cattle were much lighter due to "shrinkage." Cattle expended additional energy to keep warm in the winter and had difficulty finding adequate forage to maintain their weight, so cattlemen who shipped their animals to market in the winter had fewer pounds of flesh to sell and, thus, lower profits.[45]

After collecting his wages, Ed returned to his father's home in Thayer County to spend the holidays. In the spring of 1878, Ed hired out to the 100 Cattle Company, whose range ran adjacent to the Sheidley Company's holdings. The manager of the 100 outfit, George Green, also hailed from the Sheidley brothers' hometown of Tiffin, Ohio, and based his operations about thirty-five miles northeast of Sidney, Nebraska, along Rush Creek, near the present-day town of Lisco. The 100 consisted of about four thousand head and was the first cattle ranch on Rush Creek. Ed worked for Green throughout 1878 and impressed him well enough to keep his job when the 100 cut employees for the winter. During those months, his duties ranged from tending horses to cooking meals. Despite the dangers of the open range in wintertime, domestic duties could prove just as hazardous. In fact, Ed narrowly escaped a gunfight over a dirty dish towel.[46]

One day a heavily scarred middle-aged man with "a keen piercing eye and nerve as steady as clock work" called Red River Red

> came to our ranch . . . on foot hunting a job. At the time the
> cattle were turned to the four winds to flutter until the coming
> spring roundups, and the ranch force was cut to the ranch
> owner (one Geo. Green) and myself, for he only had about 3800
> cattle, and as there was splendid sand stone building material in
> a bluff near our pole stable, over which a strong spring gushed
> forth, and building logs were scarce, George was desirous of
> building a stone stable, at which Red said he was an expert. So
> George took him on for the special job. As I positively refused
> to milk, George always did the milking while I [made] breakfast
> and supper, and dinner was [made] by whoever was on the
> ground first. As at that time cow-men lived almost exclusively
> on beef, it was unusual to use bacon, only for bean seasoning,
> but Red expressed his preference for bacon for breakfast,
> and as he had arrived at rather the peevish age we somewhat
> catered to his wants. I prided myself on keeping the kitchen and
> cooking paraphernalia in neatness, especially the drying cloths.

But one morning I forgot to fry his bacon and he rather peevishly jumped up, grabbing the slab of bacon and knife and slicing half a dozen slices of bacon, he had previously slammed the skillet on the stove rather far back and when he had the bacon ready, he grabbed the drying cloth, instead of the dish rag with which to handle the hot receptacle, when I drew his attention to the fact . . . he flared up, saying he would not be dictated to by me.[47]

The discussion between Ed and Red continued to escalate over breakfast until "finally our epithets became so heated we both started to draw our six-shooters, but soon we observed the muzzle of [a] Winchester [rifle] weaving back and forth between us, in the hands of Green, who said very convincingly that if there was any shooting to be done on the ranch he would do it."[48] The confrontation ended without incident.

Ed may have exasperated his boss with an armed defense of his organizational methods, but this systematic attention to detail was an inherent part of his personality and played an important role in his development as a cowboy and cattleman. Ed was neat, organized, and extremely particular about certain things, including the type and style of horses he preferred for roping and cutting. He adamantly refused to perform some chores, such as milking the cow, yet this stubborn streak did not negate his ability to reason in difficult situations. Although Ed often proved unwilling to back down from a confrontation, he would choose peace over violence when given the chance. He and Red parted on good terms, just as he would with most men with whom he disagreed. This ability to move beyond quarrels and petty arguments without holding a grudge had important ramifications for his success as a cattleman, because the men he employed always received a fresh slate after making mistakes. Ed did not forget their transgressions, but neither did he overreact to them. His innate ability to get along with a broad spectrum of personalities formed a lasting impression on his employers and made him popular with his employees when he became a boss himself.[49]

A few weeks later, Red left the 100 Cattle Company, and Green headed east with a shipment of cattle for market, leaving Ed in charge of the ranch. Green planned to spend the rest of the winter in his hometown in Ohio, giving Ed his first opportunity to manage a cattle outfit. His "management" responsibilities were limited, since the cattle were out on the range and his main occupation was tending to the horses. Life on the open range was unpredictable, however, and his tenure was not without incident. While trailing horses one day, he was caught in a blizzard almost ten miles from the ranch house. Before the blowing snow and strong winds cut all visibility, he managed to find shelter in a deep canyon filled with small trees suitable for firewood. Ed had plenty of matches, but only his chaps, a light overcoat, and a dirty saddle blanket for protection from the elements. For three days, he managed to keep a fire going, but he could not sleep, he reported, because "the cold was so intense the outer side of my person from the fire would freeze in short order" and he had to adjust his position continuously. He tried going to sleep between two fires, but "the canyon was sharp bottomed [and] the wind current would whip sparks and smoke over me."[50] When the fierce storm finally broke up, he made his way back to the house and treated himself to a well-deserved eighteen-hour nap.

Lemmon proved a capable manager of the 100 ranch. On one occasion, his caution and foresight saved the ranch's horses from theft, even though other area outfits lost dozens to Indian raids. A group of Northern Cheyennes led by Dull Knife and Little Wolf had fled their reservation in Indian Territory in present-day Oklahoma for their ancestral homes in Wyoming and Montana because they were homesick, starving, and dying of disease under the care of the federal government. By the time the group reached Nebraska—a trek of five hundred miles—they were cold, hungry, and ill-clothed for the cold winter weather on the Northern Great Plains. While Dull Knife took most of the women and children to surrender, Little Wolf pressed on with between thirty and forty men. In late 1878, he and his warriors raided white ranches throughout western Nebraska for fresh mounts to resume their flight. Ed knew they were in the area, for "it was an advertised fact that Little Wolf was almost nightly raiding the country for horses," and had wisely staked the 100 outfit's horses in deep draws close to the ranch where they were less likely to be seen or heard.[51] One night, a group of Indians stole twenty-three horses from several neighboring cowboys who had stopped at the 100 ranch for the night. The visitors had picketed their horses only seventy-five yards from the cabin, but Ed's skillful planning ensured that none of the 100's horses were missing.[52]

When Green returned to the ranch in the spring of 1879, he acknowledged Ed's reliability and aptitude by assigning him a task given only to the most trusted men in any cattle outfit—repping. A roundup representative, or "rep," was "sent to a neighboring cow outfit or round-up to gather the estray cattle of his respective outfit."[53] The rep made sure that cattle carrying certain brands were returned to their home ranges so that they did not blend into herds belonging to other cattlemen. The rep shouldered a great deal of responsibility because the annual spring roundups determined the number of cattle each outfit owned. Since the business of cattle ranching depended on an accurate count of beeves to be shipped to eastern markets, reps were among a cattle outfit's best-paid men.[54]

Spring cattle roundups were large, colorful affairs that included scores of cowboys and could last two months or more. During a typical roundup on the Northern Great Plains, cowboys gathered at a designated location and spread out in all directions, collecting every animal they came across, regardless of brand, and driving them to a central collection point. As the cattle were brought in, cowboys rode around the herd constantly, singing to keep them calm. When night came, each man took a two-to-four-hour shift as a night guard, while a skilled cowboy called a "nighthawk" cared for the horses. According to Ed, the first task when daybreak came was to cut the branded cows with their new calves from the main herd and into separate collection points for each cattle outfit. Keeping these pairs together was important, because the calves were to receive the same brand as their mothers. Next, cowboys began to sort the remaining animals according to brand, working efficiently by cutting out cattle from smaller outfits and leaving in place those from the brand with the greatest number, which typically belonged to the owner of the range where the roundup took place. These cattle would likely stay on the roundup range throughout the summer. Following each roundup, the crews would move on to the next one until all of the cattle in the area had been gathered and sorted and the calves castrated and branded.[55]

George
Edward
Lemmon.
*Virginia
Grabow
collection*

During his first experience as a rep in 1879, Ed was responsible for cattle from a number of other outfits in addition to the 100 Cattle Company. His obligations included gathering cattle for the 100, the Sheidley Cattle Company, Walworth Brothers, Paxton and Ware, the Bosler Brothers, and Keith and Barton. To make his job even more complicated, several of these outfits had more than one brand. As Ed later recalled, "I deemed it necessary to have all brands I was gathering, stamped on a wide leather hat band, that encircled my ten dollar Stetson, and if the brands had been in varigated colors, as I broke a rise, I would have presented the appearance of a rainbow, breaking over the horizon."[56] As he prepared for the roundup, Ed chose a string of four horses and packed the rest of his equipment, which included "two soldier blankets, and a strip of wagon sheet to wrap the blankets in, a war-bag [made] of a seamless sack, in which was enclosed one clean shirt, one pair of sox, one change of underwear, and four pair of rawhide hobbles, to be placed on my four horses [when] not picketed, to insure them staying put nights."[57] This equipment would be his standard outfitting for spring and summer work. When he moved to ranges farther north, he supplemented his "war-bag" with a thick blanket, extra socks, a heavy overcoat, and warmer underwear.

Ed excelled at repping, as he did at almost every other task involving cattle. Despite his inexperience and the large number of brands he had to recognize and cut accordingly, his "untiring mien," "ability of defining directions either day or night," and obvious cattle-handling skills drew the attention of several company mangers.[58] A few offered him work with their outfits, but he turned them all down. After finishing his repping responsibilities, Ed stayed on with the 100 ranch for the rest of 1879 but continued to entertain job offers. When winter arrived, the twenty-two-year-old quit the 100 and once again left for his father's home in Thayer County, where he mulled over employment opportunities with three different cattle companies. It took Ed two months to decide, but when he came back to work in early 1880 he took a position with a familiar outfit—the Sheidley Cattle Company. Ed's return marked the beginning of a twenty-seven-year association with the Sheidleys. This relationship proved lucrative for both parties, and their early success came largely as a result of trespassing on Indian lands.

3 TRESPASSERS

Over the course of his career with the Sheidley Cattle Company, Ed Lemmon benefitted from good wages and eventually an ownership stake, while the Sheidley brothers gained the services of an outstanding cattleman and natural leader. In addition to sound ownership and good on-the-ground management, their success depended on another ingredient—Indian lands. During the 1880s, the company grazed thousands of cattle in western Dakota Territory, many of them illegally on the Great Sioux Reservation.[1]

It is often assumed that ranchers sought to expel Indians from their lands as a matter of principle and profit. Yet while many whites saw Indians as just another obstacle to progress, not unlike the region's frigid winters or lack of rainfall, some large-scale ranchers, such as Lemmon and others at the Sheidley Company, looked on Indians (and their land) as an opportunity. These men supported the existence of Indian reservations because they believed that they could use those lands, legally or illegally, to make a profit. Most ranchers were not concerned about the Indians' prosperity, but on reservations they saw vestiges of the open range that was disappearing elsewhere, and they found common cause with others who wanted to keep Indian lands out of the hands of white homesteaders.[2]

On 28 February 1877, in the midst of the Great Sioux War, the United States government signed an agreement with the Sioux, Northern Arapahos, and Cheyennes that deeded the Black Hills to the United States and redrew the boundaries of the Great Sioux Reservation. The "new," reduced reservation extended from the Missouri River on the east to the Belle Fourche and Cheyenne rivers and the 103d meridian on the west, and from the Nebraska border on the south to the Cannonball River on the north.[3]

The opening of the Black Hills to non-Indian settlement brought hordes of gold miners, freighters, settlers, and soldiers into the area, but these groups were not the only new arrivals. The growing popu-

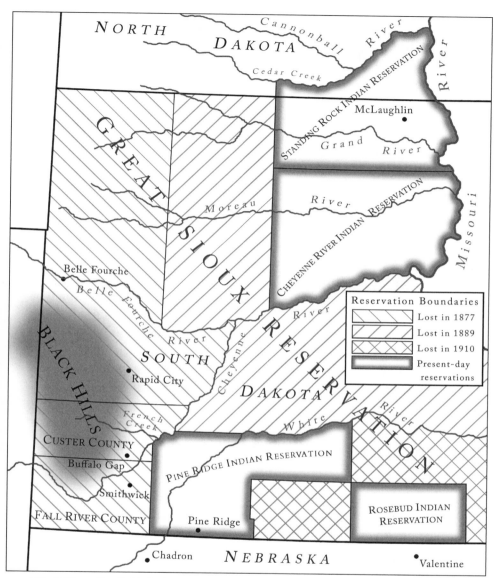

West River South Dakota

lation needed a ready supply of beef, and cattle ranchers quickly stepped in to provide it. Cattlemen capitalized on the excellent meadows of the Black Hills and established large-scale cattle operations in western Dakota Territory. Antoine and Nicholas Janis, brothers who had worked as traders in Wyoming Territory and served as interpreters during the 1868 Treaty of Fort Laramie negotiations, were among the first to bring cattle into the Black Hills. Dozens of other outfits followed, including the Matador, Diamond A, Turkey Track, BXB, VVV, Diamond M, and the Sheidley Cattle Company.[4]

Although they had enjoyed considerable financial success in Nebraska, in 1880 the Sheidley brothers sought even greater opportunities in Dakota Territory, which encompassed the present-day states of North Dakota and South Dakota. Early that year they created a new entity, D. H. Clark & Company, a cattle outfit not directly associated with the Sheidley Company's other interests. Managed by Dave Clark, this business would be the "silent" Dakota branch of the Sheidley empire. Clark & Company records would not be part of the Sheidley Company's official business, and an outside party would handle all transactions. This new entity would allow the Sheidley brothers to insulate themselves from the potential repercussions of grazing cattle illegally on the Great Sioux Reservation. Some stock remained in Nebraska and were identified with the Sheidley Company's traditional OSO brand, while most were sent north to graze the Dakota range under a new brand, the Flying V ($\mathbf{\curlyvee}$). Clark hired Lemmon as his range manager and prepared to move their cattle into Dakota Territory.[5]

In July 1880, Clark and Lemmon cut out twenty-eight hundred head of two- and three-year-old cattle from the Sheidleys' large Platte River herd and headed north to a new range near the southern Black Hills. They steered their herd to the Cheyenne River without incident and set up company headquarters north of the river near the mouth of French Creek. Clark had selected the trail route, while Ed, as his right-hand man, supervised the cowboys. Their responsibilities were not fixed, however, and the two men enjoyed a close working relationship. Clark, a large man at 240 pounds, and Lemmon, almost one hundred pounds lighter, were both in their early twenties but had years of experience working cattle and respected and trusted each other. In the coming years, Clark would often leave for weeks at a time in order to conduct business in Rapid City, Belle Fourche, and other towns. He served as president of the Black Hills Stock Growers Association, was a roundup foreman and a member of the Wyoming Stock Growers Association, managed a wholesale and retail meat market in Rapid City, and in 1888 was elected the city's mayor. During Clark's absences, Ed was in charge. He saw the Flying V as "his" outfit and managed it accordingly. Even though he did not become a full-fledged partner until 1891, Ed took ownership in the operation.[6]

Clark and Lemmon turned their cattle loose on the open range north of the Cheyenne River, which marked the boundary between United States government land and the Great Sioux Reservation. Within days, some of the cattle had recrossed the river, which was only a few feet deep, and had begun grazing on Sioux land. This development did not bother either man in the least; in fact, it was probably part of Clark's strategy from the start. While other cattle companies competed for grazing land on the Black Hills range, Flying V cattle roamed the "untouched" reservation. This land received little grazing pressure because most cattlemen chose to avoid the possible legal consequences of trespassing and ran their cattle on nonreservation government land west of the 103d meridian. Large-scale operators were the primary trespassers. Controlling large expanses of territory and thousands of cattle, they could readily claim that their animals grazed on the reservation by happenstance. Small operators did not have this luxury or the political connections to avoid prosecution for their crimes should they be caught. Those who could afford the risk of trespassing not only faced less competition from other cattlemen but also a minimum of natural competition for grass. Pronghorn antelope, deer, and the occasional mountain sheep remained, but most of the bison that had once grazed the area had moved to less occupied places or been slaughtered.[7]

The reservation land was far better than the Sheidley Company's Nebraska range. The needlegrass plains of southern Dakota Territory featured a different grassland ecosystem from the shortgrass prairies of western Nebraska, including a broader range of grasses that provided better forage for livestock. The presence of taller, more voluminous grasses such as little bluestem allowed cattlemen to stock the ranges with more animals per acre than farther south, while succulent plants like threadleaf sedge and needleleaf sedge proved more palatable to the cattle. In addition, the terrain south of the Cheyenne River featured a number of wide, deep draws that offered excellent protection during the bitter winter months. With the reservation's "virgin" grass, ample winter forage, and natural shelter in mind, Clark located his headquarters on the free government land available across the Cheyenne River from the western border of the Great Sioux Reservation. Ed later referred to Clark as "the very best picker of ranges of any man I ever knew," suggesting that his selection of reservation lands for grazing was hardly an accident.[8]

This strategy may also explain why the Sheidley brothers created D. H. Clark & Company in the first place. As respected members of the Kansas City business community, the Sheidleys had a vested interest in avoiding the legal issues that might arise from trespassing on the reservation, and by putting the operation in Clark's name, with substitute management and different cattle brands, they insulated themselves from that danger. In his numerous articles and reminiscences, Ed often stated that he was always a Sheidley employee, even when working for Clark & Company. Clark must have understood the arrangement, because he participated in every aspect of the venture. He probably accepted this personal risk as part of what he owed the Sheidley brothers for bankrolling the operation. At only twenty-five, Clark had no capital to begin a herd of his own and no collateral to back a traditional loan from the Sheidleys, so he made a simple decision: he traded the threat of potential legal problems for the opportunity to be a partner in a major cattle business.[9]

Years later, Lemmon described the operation in detail and explained how both the cattlemen and the reservation Sioux came to a living arrangement. Since the Indians were required to stay within the confines of the reservation, they kept the land "rather well skinned of game . . . excepting the wily mountain sheep that abounded in the bad lands," and since they regularly camped near the Cheyenne River, "it was very tempting [for them] to cross over to the north where both deer and antelope were in vast numbers. Upon such occasions as the Indians slipped off the reservation, say a mile or two, they did not care to be seen and reported to the agent for disobedience of rules," so they tried to avoid contact with the cowboys.[10] Meanwhile, Ed described the cowboys' perspective:

> My duties did not necessitate my coming in close proximity to [the Indians'] filched hunting grounds, for my job was line riding on a body of cattle that had been left on French Creek . . . while the other two riders, viz. Sam Bell and John McNabb, rode line on the balance of the cattle along the river, presumably to keep them from ranging on the reservation, only a very short distance. So one can readily see the Indians were not the only ones that were trespassing, for our boys had no right on the reservation, and neither had our cattle.
>
> Naturally, when the boys espied Indians, when throwing the cattle near the line or off the reservation, they shied clear of them as much as possible, often hiding until the Indians passed from view . . . and vice-versa.[11]

Ed believed that if the cowboys kept quiet about Indians hunting north of the Cheyenne, the Sioux would not complain about cattle south of the river. In 1875, the commissioner of Indian affairs had announced that any Indians hunting on lands outside of the reservation would be considered "hostiles" subject to military action, so the Lakotas were naturally eager to avoid being reported. In Lemmon's view, since each group looked the other way when they saw trespassers, there was no reason to stop.[12]

Within a short time, Clark & Company started trailing more cattle from Nebraska into Dakota. In August 1880, they brought up eighteen hundred yearling steers and later that fall trailed in more than one thousand cows with calves. Although the subsequent winter caused substantial losses—Lemmon held that "the winter of 1880–81 was the very hardest we, the Sheidley Cattle Co. . . . ever encountered," with an estimated 50 percent loss on yearlings and 20 percent on two-year-olds—their venture began to take off.[13] By placing cattle on the protected range of the Great Sioux Reservation, Clark managed to save most of his herd from the devastating winter weather. He also found excellent grazing lands that offered huge potential for stocking cattle. Flying V cattle remained on reservation lands for most of the decade.

Lemmon believed that the Oglala Sioux and the Indian agent at the Pine Ridge Agency, Dr. Valentine T. McGillycuddy, were willing to overlook this encroachment. He claimed that

> the doctor and I soon became fast friends, so much so that he, together with Chief Red Cloud, advised me to come and go on their reservation very much as I pleased, with the proviso from Old Red, as we called him, that I treat him and his sub-chiefs hospitably while rounding up their domain, which I of course did by saving all lump-jaws [cattle unsuitable for market] for them, besides feeding them sumptuously when they came to our camp and mess wagon, sometimes half a dozen, composed of Old Red and . . . leading sub-chiefs, even accompanying [us] through the whole round-up of a week or ten days. . . . [But] we were at all times grazing on their reservation and grasses nearly if not quite ten thousand cattle. I believe I was absolutely the only cow-man allowed to come and go over the reservation as I pleased.[14]

Lemmon estimated that throughout the 1880s "nearly, if not quite, two thirds of our cattle were at all times trespassing on the Pine Ridge Reservation," yet "during this period I never had any reason to believe [the Sioux] butchered a single beef animal . . . or in any manner pilfered even the smallest article."[15] He attributed this situation to his practice of treating the Indians with "liberality." In addition to Red Cloud, Young Man Afraid of His Horses, another respected chief of the Oglalas, would often set up camp near the Flying V headquarters. On such occasions, Huste—as many of the Oglalas called Lemmon—would "put on a big pot of beans and another of beef" and invite them to supper.[16] He and his cowboys would eat, talk, and trade with the Sioux, which helped ease relations between them. This amicable interaction convinced Ed that the Indians did not have strong objections to whites grazing their cattle on the reservation. In his estimation, they "never really figured I was sponging that grass" because it was being obtained in exchange for "good treatment of the border settler Indians."[17]

Lemmon's policy of liberality apparently worked; he noted that a single run-in with an Indian hunter in 1880 "was the last Indian scare we had until the great Sioux uprising, the fall and winter of 1890–91."[18] In 1879, McGillycuddy had instructed the Pine Ridge Indians to put the agency's FOF brand—which he registered with the Wyoming Stock Growers Association that year—on any stray cattle found on the reservation, but he did little about animals already wearing a brand. In his 1881 report to the commissioner of Indian affairs, McGillycuddy made light of illegal grazing, noting only that "many stray animals belonging to the stockmen have been picked up on the Indians' land and returned to the rightful owners by the Indian police and individual Indians."[19]

McGillycuddy's report for 1882 showed more concern for protecting white stockmen's animals than for preventing them from grazing illegally on the reservation. "No crimes have been committed on the reserve," he wrote, "and no depredations of any kind have been committed on neighboring settlers or stockmen off the reserve."[20] A year later he said nothing at all about illegal grazing but pointed out the Indians' ambivalence to stock-raising. "Under the nonsensical treaties at present in force," he wrote, "these people are guaranteed plenty of beef to eat, whether they work or not, so what earthly object has an Indian in going to the trouble and labor of raising beef? The consequence is that he either permits his cows and bulls to stray off or eats them."[21] McGillycuddy's apparent lack of concern over illegal grazing probably contributed to Ed's characterization of him as "the best Indian agent ever, excepting Col. J. H. McLaughlin, of the Standing Rock."[22] In 1902, McLaughlin would support Lemmon's bid for a lease of more than 865,000 acres on the Standing Rock Indian Reservation, accounting for Lemmon's bias.

The Indians' lack of opposition to Clark & Company's illegal grazing was not solely due to handouts of food. The same values that agents denounced as detrimental to the Indians' assimilation—a belief in community, shared property, and common-use practices—also created a tolerant perspective on the open range. As Janet McDonnell noted in *The Dispossession of the American Indian*, Indians "did not regard land as real estate to be bought, sold, and developed. Rather, they valued it for the things it produced that sustained life."[23] The Sioux were not using the grass for their own livestock;

consequently, most of them saw little reason to prevent others from doing so. Since the cattlemen faced no legal repercussions and the Indians themselves did not attempt to deter them, white ranchers in the pre-allotment era continued to run their cattle on the reservation. In this respect, the Sioux and the cattlemen alike treated the reservation land less like private property and more like the open range.[24]

Historian Peter Iverson has argued that white encroachment forced Indians to forge a new identity by creating a society based on cattle ranching, but this society had not yet emerged in the early 1880s. As Red Cloud told McGillycuddy, "The white man can work if he wants to, but the Great Spirit did not make us to work. The white man owes us a living for the lands he has taken from us."[25] Consequently, white cattlemen operated on the range with little competition from Indian stock raisers. They may have been "buoyed by their own needs and their own cultural assumptions" as Iverson contends, but his statement that "these intruders hardly ever seemed to recognize that they were, in fact, intruding" is inaccurate.[26] Cattlemen like Ed Lemmon may not have appreciated the full social and cultural implications of their actions, but they knew perfectly well that they were trespassing on Indian lands. Given all the circumstances, they simply did not think it mattered.[27]

Having used the grass of the Great Sioux Reservation to feed its cattle, Clark & Company then sold the animals to reservation agencies, which distributed the beef in fulfillment of the "nonsensical treaties" that McGillycuddy opposed. In August 1881, Lemmon bossed one of many trail drives to Indian agencies when he guided a herd of 738 cattle to a location on Oak Creek, near the present site of McLaughlin, South Dakota. This 180-mile cattle drive was "a hurry-up call for beef to supply the Sitting Bull Indians," who had recently surrendered after a five-year exile in Canada.[28] The herd included cattle from three outfits, the Sheidley Cattle Company (acting as Clark & Company), the W. B. Grimes Company, and Stearns & Patterson. Ed's use of three sources in gathering a herd of more than seven hundred head for the "hurry-up call" suggests that his outfit was not alone in tapping the reservation's readily-available resources.[29]

In 1882, after just two years of grazing the reservation, Clark shifted course and sought to legalize his company's activities by acquiring a lease on the Great Sioux Reservation. He and other Black Hills cattlemen proposed legally opening the reservation for cattle grazing because they believed it would encourage railroads to construct new lines into the region, furthering economic prosperity. The cattlemen also hoped that they could acquire long-term leases—perhaps up to a decade or more—that would guarantee their access to the land for years to come. The Sheidley brothers dissolved D. H. Clark & Company that year and reorganized all of their livestock holdings as one company; it is likely that after Clark's initial success (and a lack of government intervention in their illegal operation), they believed that the push for legal grazing leases would be better served by the backing of an influential, large-scale operator like the Sheidley Company.[30]

With the entire business again under the family name, the brothers looked to find a legal way to access the reservation and attract railroad companies, a development that could dramatically increase the marketing opportunities for their livestock. Clark, then president of the Black Hills Stock Growers Association, joined a number of other large operators in proposing to open the Great Sioux Reservation for grazing. Their plan called for grazing leases only, with no possibility that the land would be opened for settlement. Agent McGillycuddy and Agent Leonard Love of the Cheyenne River Agency favored the plan, which the Stock Growers Association presented to Richard F. Pettigrew, Dakota Territory's delegate to the United States House of Representatives. Although Pettigrew pledged support for the measure at first, opposition from businessmen, settlers, and small cattle ranchers forced him to reconsider.[31]

Most residents of the Black Hills opposed grazing leases because they wanted the Great Sioux Reservation to be opened for settlement instead. Many whites believed that the region's economic growth was "being restricted by the existence of the big reservation" and that a leasing system would only prolong its presence.[32] Although opinions on the issue varied, small cattle producers also tended to oppose the plan because they would not be able to bid competitively for the leases against operations with thousands of cattle. This opposition killed the proposal, so Clark and Lemmon continued to graze the reservation illegally as before.

The cattlemen's attempts to acquire legal grazing rights in 1882 probably did them more harm than good in the long run. As Bob Lee and Dick Williams noted in *Last Grass Frontier*, these efforts "hastened the eventual opening of the coveted country [for settlement]. It had alerted the people of the [Black] Hills to the possibilities of the surplus reservation lands and it had incited them to vigorous action that brought on extinguishment of the Indian title that the cattlemen wanted too."[33] Any attention to the grazing situation on the reservations included a risk that the convenient practice of illegal grazing would be challenged and ended, and the cattlemen who used the reservation took few chances. For example, while competition over choice ranges or mavericks often created disputes between cattle outfits, violent confrontations among white ranchers near the reservation were minimal. Even sheep ranchers, whom many cattlemen regarded with scorn, were not molested while grazing their animals on the reservation. "The Sheidley Cattle Co. . . . never openly placed a straw in the path of sheep," stated Lemmon, "for as we looked at it we were all trespassers, and one had as good [a] right as the other."[34] A disturbance on the reservation would have drawn attention to the ranchers' illegal activities, and both cattlemen and sheepmen understood this fact well enough to leave petty disputes to ranges on non-reservation land.

Grazing thousands of cattle on the reservation may have been illegal, but the flawed and often dishonest way in which white cattlemen and agency officials supplied beef rations to the Sioux was more immediately detrimental to the tribes. Several decades later, Lemmon described how the system was designed to work in the cattlemen's favor and illustrated the ways in which unscrupulous men manipulated it.

The Pine Ridge Agency—named for a nearby escarpment covered with evergreen trees in the southwest part of the Great Sioux Reservation—generally purchased about five thousand head of nine-hundred-pound steers each fall to distribute among the Indians. The cattle were issued throughout the year based on each animal's weight at the time of receiving. When the agents distributed the animals in winter, however, they did not account for "shrink," or the loss of weight during the cold months, which reduced each Indian's ration considerably. By the time the final steers were issued in the spring, most weighed 150 pounds less than when purchased.[35]

This practice denied the Indians their full ration during the time of year when they needed it most, but the cattlemen tried to gain an even greater advantage by working together to cheat the Indians when the cattle were weighed. As one of the conspirators later confessed, "Everyone made what he could and kept quiet about the other fellow."[36] Ed noted that "there was usually some method used at weighing pens . . . to bolster up the weights considerable. On one particular occasion it was found there had been, by night presumably, a trench dug under the plank runway by [the] side of the chute and scales, into which a man crawled before the weighing began."[37] Using an improvised lever, the man increased each animal's weight as it stood on the scale. He released the pressure as soon as the scale was empty, leaving it in balance. Each animal's actual weight was thus less than the scale indicated, cutting into each Indian's ration even more.[38]

This method was not the only one employed to cheat the system. In 1877, while Ed was working for Seth Mabry's outfit, the stock scales at the Red Cloud Agency mysteriously burned down. Instead of weighing every animal, the agency's receiver had to accept the herd based on its average weight per animal, which was usually between 850 and 1,000 pounds. To determine this average, the contract boss, Bill Campbell, selected the largest steer from his herd, while the receiver chose the smallest. The average weight of these two animals was used as the weight for every beef in the herd. On the surface this method seemed fair, but Mabry's outfit held a decided advantage: a massive twelve hundred-pound steer that somehow managed to be included in all of the company's deliveries that summer. Ed noted that "it is plain to see how he would bring the average up."[39] He also described the method used to disguise the animal and conceal the fraud. "First he was issued with a perfect set of horns, next he had quite a tip off one horn, which would change his appearance quite considerable, next he had a portion of both horns off, and next one horn entirely missing, and lastly a perfect muley. I, as merely a cow boy was not let into the secret of how this stag came to be gotten back and issued five times, but I had my suspicions."[40]

Writing years after these events, Lemmon demonstrated genuine sympathy for the Indians. He may have felt guilt at the time as well, but business trumped all other considerations, and one cowboy could not reform a system designed to exploit the Indians. The cattlemen who sold beef to the agencies stood together, even in their dishonesty, and did whatever was necessary to earn what they could. Ed saw a clear distinction between outright corruption—manipulating the livestock scales, reselling the same steer multiple times, or issuing cattle without accounting for shrinkage—and trespassing on the reservation. For him, the difference was stark: depriving the Indians of their full beef ration was morally wrong because they had been promised it and needed it; depriving the Indians of their grass was not immoral because they did not seem to want or need to use the land themselves at that time. Consequently, Ed had no qualms about using the reservation to graze his cattle, a practice that proved financially beneficial again in 1884 when county taxes came due.

The Sheidley Cattle Company had expanded considerably since first arriving in Dakota Territory in 1880. In 1883, it sold most of its Nebraska ranges to Alex Swan and moved the rest of its cattle into Dakota. The same year, Clark purchased 5,350 head from Texas ranchers for $147,000 and nine thousand more from the Grimes & Thornton Company for $160,000. With several thousand cattle already grazing on the Great Sioux Reservation, Clark needed additional acres for his growing herd. In 1884, the company moved ten thousand head north to a new range on non-reservation government land along the Moreau River near the boundary between present-day Harding and Butte counties in northwestern South Dakota, leaving the balance on their traditional ranges near the southern Black Hills. The cattle grazed on a vast swath of the range, including parts of present-day North Dakota. Cowboy Ike Blasingame, who would tend cattle on that range twenty years later, noted that "grass was good, and there was a heavy stand of timber—cottonwood, ash, elm, and many plum, chokecherry, and Juneberry thickets lined the river. The air was heavy with the fragrance of the fruit blossoms and millions of wild-rose blooms just bursting out."[41]

After just four years in Dakota, the Sheidley Cattle Company—with Dave Clark as general manager and Ed Lemmon as range manager—had one of the territory's largest herds. It also had a steep tax bill. The company had headquartered in Custer County since 1880, and in 1883, the year the railroads implemented standardized time zones across the United States and Canada, the county placed an assessed value of $100,000 on Sheidley Company holdings, primarily livestock. The following year, the county estimated the value of the company's holdings at $124,000, based largely on the increase in its herd size. However, most of the new cattle were 140 miles north on the Moreau River range, far beyond the boundaries of Custer County. Moreover, many more of the assessed animals were actually across the river on the Great Sioux Reservation. Clark filed an injunction to halt the collection of the company's 1884 taxes until he could meet with the county commissioners, arguing that Custer County could not tax his company for property outside its boundaries. The county commissioners agreed, and Clark's 1884 tax assessment dropped dramatically to $25,275.[42]

During the 1880s, circumstances for the Sheidley Company proved to be a nearly ideal. By running their herds on reservation land, Clark and Lemmon had access both to an excellent cattle range and a ready market for their beef and could avoid paying taxes at the same time. But while Agent McGillycuddy remained unconcerned about illegal grazing, some of the Indians at Pine Ridge began to show their displeasure. McGillycuddy's 1884 report stated (apparently without irony) that "there have been a few instances where evil-disposed Indians have, out of spite or revenge, maimed or killed their neighbors' cattle, but a prompt incarceration in the agency guard-house at hard labor is rapidly teaching them a respect for other people's property."[43] Despite these few unpleasant instances, McGillycuddy contended that during the annual roundup, "the Pine Ridge Indian now works in company with the stockmen of Nebraska and the Black Hills, assisting each other in gathering and returning their strays, so that where a few years ago each party preyed on the others' horses and cattle, now the most amicable feeling prevails, and the Indian is welcome in the settler's house, while the settler is welcomed when visiting the reservation on business or pleasure. As the future of the Indian will be his gradual adoption of the white man's ways and absorption into the general mixed population of the country, their friendly and neighborly intercourse should be encouraged."[44]

The relationship between white "neighbors" and the Oglala Sioux who lived near the Pine Ridge Agency was clearly not as rosy as McGillycuddy described, and the assertion that "the most amicable feeling prevails" was a stretch. For white cattlemen with large herds, however, the Indian agent's lack of action and the absence of any organized opposition from the Indians themselves served as a silent endorsement of illegal grazing. The Indians' perspective was irrelevant, so far as the cattlemen were concerned, as long as they did not start killing cattle or cowboys. A lost steer or two would do little to deter ambitious men like Dave Clark and Ed Lemmon, and their operations continued unchanged.

While Lemmon spent his twenties expanding his knowledge of the business side of open-range cattle ranching, he also began to hone his skill in managing cowboys. The Flying V inherited a number of cowboys from smaller outfits the Sheidley Company acquired in the mid-1880s. Four men, in particular, were top cowhands but also "independent men."[45] The man Clark initially selected to lead this group, Hugh Adair, could not control them, so Clark asked Ed to take the men into his crew, one by one, until he had them all. Ed had acquired a reputation as a popular manager; his obvious cattle-handling skill, love of storytelling, competence in difficult situations, and ability to overcome his physical infirmities earned him widespread respect. His four new cowboys were wild and unruly when they reached town, drinking, shooting, and riding their horses on sidewalks and into saloons, but "Oh, my," Lemmon later recalled, "what cow punchers they were!"[46]

Lemmon let local law enforcement handle the raucous crew when they reached city limits but kept them under control while in camp. This crackerjack gang may have caused trouble for sheriffs in Valentine, Chadron, Ogallala, and other railroad towns where the Flying V shipped cattle, but "they didn't know what the word 'quit' meant," and after Ed got them trained properly, "they needed practically no bossing." Eventually these new cowboys joined four of Ed's established crew in a topnotch unit he called his "eight killers."[47]

They received the moniker at a roundup on Hat Creek in present-day Fall River County, South Dakota, where they showcased their incredible skills. When the main roundup boss came out to check brands on the Flying V cattle, Ed told his crew to cut the herd of twenty-five hundred head "into five equal bunches and in so doing, slip through them carefully so as not to cut the cows away from the calves, and place them on that level spot in a circular position." The men completed the order to the letter in less than twenty-five minutes, causing the boss to remark, "Ed, how in [hell] do you get such results out of that bunch of killers?" Lemmon responded that "it required no effort at all for they knew my methods."[48]

Such was Ed Lemmon's style of management. He had a systematic approach to cattle handling, taught it to his men, and then stood back and let them work. Although he might not have appreciated the analogy, Lemmon orchestrated men like a symphony conductor, pushing each individual to use his own talents for the good of the whole. The ability to sort one hundred head per minute with an eight-man crew took equal measures of individual skill and group cohesion; Ed's cowboys demonstrated this high level of proficiency on several occasions. He may have urged people not to "judge me by my cowboy crews" while they were in town, but he knew how to motivate and inspire his employees.[49] In this respect, Ed's inherent understanding of cattle and horse behavior seemed to extend to people as well. Rather than trying to change his crews, he sought to mold them into the best cowboys they could be by harnessing their natural abilities. Lemmon did not rein them in to the point of rebellion, nor did he allow them to operate independently. He taught his men to work together and follow orders while bringing out the qualities that made them excel at working cattle. Much like the spirited horses in his remuda, the men of Ed's "killer" crew were headstrong and determined. His ability to tame them made Lemmon an unusually effective boss.

Strong cowboy crews were essential for the Sheidley Cattle Company in the mid-1880s because the Flying V outfit continued to expand. By 1885, the company had at least thirty thousand head on ranges spread over hundreds of square miles. Lemmon was a key contributor to their success, but he also spent time attending to other issues. In 1884 and 1885, he served as a commissioner for Fall

Bertha
Reno
and Ed
Lemmon.
Virginia
Grabow
collection

River County, his election likely supported by "many of the pioneer cattlemen" who afterward "considered Mr. Lemmon to be the best and most capable cattleman who ever lived in southwestern Dakota."[50] In 1886, Lemmon's brother Hervey died of injuries sustained in a riding accident, and later that year Ed married sixteen-year-old Bertha Reno in a small ceremony in Buffalo Gap, Dakota Territory.[51]

The exact cause of Hervey's death is unclear. In late 1885 or early 1886, he was thrown from a horse and likely sustained internal injuries. For two months in mid-1886, he sought a cure at the hot springs in Arkansas but saw little improvement. After lingering for several months, Hervey died on 20 August 1886. The Lemmon family buried him next to his mother Lucy in the Oak Grove Cemetery overlooking the Little Blue River in Nuckolls County, Nebraska.[52]

Hervey had been Ed's best friend and hero since early childhood. His older brother had helped Ed get his first job working cattle on J. W. Iliff's ranch, and Hervey's cowboy career in Texas served as a motivation for Ed to pursue similar work on the northern plains. Hervey participated in nearly every major event of Ed's young life and was doubtless his strongest role model. Both men had sustained severe injuries in accidents on horseback, and Ed must have dwelled on the fact that he survived both of his close calls while Hervey did not. Although Ed had lost his mother several years earlier, Hervey's death was likely the first (and perhaps the only) loss that caused him deep emotional pain. He never wrote about it, choosing instead to honor his brother's life and memory in dozens of stories dramatizing his bravery, cunning, and unmatched frontier skills.

Lemmon wed Bertha Reno on 25 November 1886, just three months after Hervey's death. Then twenty-nine, Ed was almost twice as old as his new bride, and their courtship was not lengthy. Women seemed to find his humor and easy demeanor charming—at least, he readily made friends with women and mentioned them often in his reminiscences—so a teenager like Bertha could easily have found him attractive. Ed was not overly compassionate, however, and was probably not a particularly loving or attentive husband. In fact, he once noted that love "is almost wholly out of my line."[53]

Lemmon likely tried to establish the same kind of relationship with his wife that he had with his cowboys. As the boss, he administered specific orders and expected their execution. Combined with their age difference and his indifference toward romance, the couple's situation was far from ideal, and the marriage would end in divorce. Ed's marriage never altered his work habits much; he lived for working cattle and spent most of his time engaged in activities on the range. In future years, he would display little devotion to his wife, cavorting with "painted ladies" and pretty girls in cow towns throughout the region on numerous occasions. The couple even took up residence at the headquarters of the Flying V outfit near the mouth of French Creek so that Ed could remain close to his men. Hervey's death may have caused Ed to think about his life and legacy and perhaps played a role in his hasty decision to marry. In any case, working cattle for the Flying V outfit continued to hold the greater portion of his attention.[54]

Lemmon became increasingly focused on business concerns in 1887, when passage of the General Allotment Act threatened the Sheidley Company's lucrative practice of grazing the Great Sioux Reservation. This legislation, known as the Dawes Act after its key sponsor, Republican senator Henry L. Dawes of Massachusetts, was an attempt to solve the "Indian problem" by replacing "tribal consciousness with an understanding of the value of private property."[55] Reservations would no longer be "owned" by the entire tribe. Instead, each individual or family would receive its own parcel of land—between 40 and 160 acres—for farming or raising livestock. Its proponents touted the Dawes Act as a step toward assimilating Indians into American society as well as a means of saving federal money and protecting Indians from whites who took unfair advantage of their lands. In practice, however, the law would substantially reduce the size of the Great Sioux Reservation yet again by opening "surplus" land for white settlement.[56]

A major selling point for the Dawes Act was the popular belief that the Indians were letting their lands sit idle while tens of thousands of whites were willing to "improve" these lands and use them "properly." As historian Frederick Hoxie argues in *A Final Promise*, much of the support for the Dawes Act came from private and commercial interests whose goal was "gaining entry to and reducing the size of tribal holdings."[57] Many whites who lived near the reservations saw them as barriers to prosperity that hindered local economic development. Settlers, railroad executives, businessmen, and politicians all clamored for Indian land and pushed to open up the reservations for settlement.

Not all whites supported opening the reservations, however, as the large-scale cattlemen had demonstrated five years earlier. Hoxie points out that throughout the 1880s "railroads with special privileges . . . and cattlemen holding profitable leases joined the tribes in opposing the settlers' demands" in other locations as well.[58] Although the Sheidleys had failed to obtain a legal lease for grazing on the Great Sioux Reservation, their opposition to the opening of the reservation was strong nevertheless. Unlike businessmen and potential homesteaders who saw Indians as a hindrance to progress, Clark and Lemmon saw Indians, or rather Indian lands, as the *key* to progress. The reservation contained thousands of acres that they could access at virtually no expense beyond wages and supplies for their cowboys, and the permeable boundaries between the public domain and the reservation—often just a small stream or dry creek-bed—offered a ready excuse when counties tried to collect taxes on their herds.

White cattlemen had other reasons to preserve the Great Sioux Reservation. The proximity to Indian agencies gave them access to a market without having to ship livestock to Chicago by rail. The Sheidley Company used the Chicago markets, but they had to trail thousands of cattle to shipping points on the Union Pacific Railroad at Ogallala, Nebraska, or on the Fremont, Elkhorn & Missouri Valley Railroad at Valentine or Chadron. Selling cattle to Indian agents saved a great deal of time and effort and prevented shrinkage that could cost the company considerable money. Less savory to contemplate but equally advantageous was the ease with which they could cheat the Indian market. Above all, the Great Sioux Reservation kept thousands of acres of open range free from white settlement. Were this land to be removed from the reservation, cattlemen would be forced to compete with homesteaders for the opportunity to use it. Because opposition from settlement interests had defeated their earlier attempt to acquire leases on the Great Sioux Reservation, the ranchers knew they could not win that battle in the long run. The reservation provided a settlement-free haven that they could use relatively undisturbed. Cattlemen in Dakota Territory were businessmen, first and foremost, and they understood that the opening of the reservation would reduce their profits.[59]

When Congress finally passed the Dawes Act on 8 February 1887, however, the threat it posed to white ranchers had already been temporarily surpassed by the winter of 1886–1887, which arrived in October and did not abate until March. It was the worst winter that many ranchers had ever seen. Fierce winds, bitter cold, and heavy snows ravaged cattle herds throughout the ranges of the Northern Great Plains. For fifty-six days, the temperature never rose above zero. "Thousands of cattle had already drifted in on the river," cowman W. H. Hamilton wrote, "and they had nothing to eat except willows and young cottonwood. Before spring there was not a twig left within reach. The range cattle began dying by the hundreds."[60]

Tens of thousands of cattle had arrived just before winter, exacerbating the problem. In August 1886, President Grover Cleveland had ordered more than two hundred thousand illegal cattle removed from Indian Territory in the southern plains; many of those animals appeared on the northern ranges that fall. These were joined by thousands more cattle driven up from Texas and other southern ranges that had been ravaged by drought. Underweight due to rapid travel and unused to the low temperatures of northern winters, the recent arrivals fared poorly. Some cattlemen lost 80 to 90 percent of their herds. Others, including Theodore Roosevelt, lost more than their cattle—they lost their ranches as well. The hard winter on overstocked ranges claimed so many animals that it became known as the "Great Die-Up."[61]

While hundreds of thousands of beeves perished in Dakota Territory, the Sheidley Cattle Company managed to survive with fewer losses than it sustained in the winter of 1880–1881. The company had sold most of its young stock the previous fall, retaining only animals that had spent at least one winter in Dakota. In addition, Clark selected a protected winter range that had not been grazed during the summer. As a result of Clark's planning and skill in choosing an adequate pasture, he and Lemmon had an above-average roundup, while many of their neighbors left the territory, never to return.[62]

The passage of the Dawes Act and the severe winter of 1886–1887 forced Clark and Lemmon to reexamine their operation. A number of large cattle companies left Dakota for good that spring, freeing up thousands of acres of prime range in the northern Black Hills. The area north of Belle Fourche, in particular, experienced a massive exodus, as most outfits saw winter losses of between 85 and 90 percent. Many cattlemen simply could not remain in business after such losses. In addition, the government finally began to take an interest in illegal grazing on the reservations. The agent at the Cheyenne River Agency, Charles McChesney, threatened to have all white cattlemen and their stock forcibly removed if they were still on the reservation after 31 May, and other agents quickly followed suit. With huge expanses of grassland available farther north and the United States government turning against them, Clark and Lemmon decided to move the bulk of the Flying V operation north to the Moreau River range they had begun to occupy three years earlier.[63]

The Sheidley Cattle Company's success in Dakota Territory came largely as a result of illegally using the Great Sioux Reservation as its own grazing land. Although Indians and whites had contrasting attitudes about land use, Ed believed that the Indians did not mind having the cattle on their land and that there was no reason not to take advantage of the situation. Still, he conceded, "We, the cattle owners, [were] really contributing very little to the support of the country."[64] They avoided paying taxes when they could, grazed the prairies to their breaking point, and did their best to make a profit. They were nineteenth-century businessmen who extracted as much as they could for as long as they could and then moved on— literally—to greener pastures. Nevertheless, these cattlemen began the development of the region's modern economy. Ed's participation would continue on an even larger scale in the coming years, when he would take a step not made by many men—leaving the ranks of the cowboys and becoming a full-fledged business owner and cattleman.

4 ROUNDUPS

After joining the Sheidley Cattle Company for good in 1880, Ed Lemmon had risen through the ranks to become one of the outfit's most important cowboys. By the spring of 1888, a few months after the disastrous "children's blizzard" that killed more than one hundred schoolchildren in Dakota Territory and Nebraska, Ed was serving as the roundup boss, organizing the gathering of the company's Flying V cattle from their old grazing lands on the Cheyenne River and driving them to a new range based 140 miles north on the Moreau River. Following the passage of the Dawes Act the previous year, the Flying V outfit had been moving its cattle off the Great Sioux Reservation— where they had been grazing illegally for seven years—and onto the federal government's open ranges near the Black Hills. The reservation had once provided cattlemen with thousands of acres of free grass, but when the Dawes Act opened it for non-Indian settlement, the days of open-range cattle grazing were numbered.

The eventual dismantling of the Great Sioux Reservation did not bring about an immediate end to open-range cattle ranching, nor did Joseph F. Glidden's invention of barbed wire in the 1880s. In fact, the changes were more gradual, and despite historian Walter Prescott Webb's contention that the entire Great Plains region from Texas to the Dakotas shared a unique system of development due to its "geographic unity" (treelessness, levelness, and semi-arid climate), the northern and southern plains were subject to distinct influences at different times.[1] The economic context in which the Sheidley Company operated had never been static, and resourceful cattlemen were no strangers to adaptation.

Following the Civil War, cattlemen on the southern plains had gathered herds of wild longhorns and driven them north to railheads in Kansas and elsewhere. The relatively mild winters on the southern plains made for moderate cattle losses but encouraged the spread of diseases such as "Texas Fever," a highly transmissible parasitic infection in cattle. Ticks carried the disease, which caused high fever, trembling and convulsions, lesions, paralysis, miscarriage in pregnant cows, and often death. Missouri, Kansas, Arkansas, and other states eventually banned Texas cattle due to the risk of Texas Fever. The problem would persist into the mid-twentieth century, when a federal eradication program finally managed to control the disease. The arrival of barbed wire on the southern plains split the cattlemen into two rival factions—the "free grass" men versus the "big pasture" or "fenced range" men. Barbed wire led to violent fence-cutting wars in Texas and was the first stage of what Webb called "the evolution of the range."[2] In his influential book *The Great Plains*, he outlined four stages involved in this transformation: 1) open range; 2) fenced range without windmills; 3) fenced range with windmills; and 4) farms. Webb also argued that the arrival of barbed wire forced cattle ranchers to operate under a system of fenced pastures, either leased or purchased; to improve their longhorn cattle with superior European breeds; to take a greater interest in the care of free-range animals, particularly in winter; and to replace traditional trail drives with shipment by rail. In short, he claimed that after 1885 ranching had been "converted from an adventure into a business."[3]

Several regional differences affected the development of the northern part of the Great Plains, including the lack of a native cattle herd; the delayed start of the cattle industry, which reduced the need for long trail drives because railroad shipping points were closer to the ranges; and especially the longer, colder winters that caused greater hardship for the cattle but reduced disease. Thus, many of the changes attributed to the expansion of barbed wire on the southern plains were already underway on the Northern Great Plains prior to its widespread use. The Sheidley brothers' decision to move their cattle operation from Nebraska to Dakota Territory in 1880 was a business decision, not a fanciful adventure. Their selection of the fine grasses in Dakota and their use of the Great Sioux Reservation for grazing offered the best possibilities for making money and a better opportunity to care for their cattle. Dave Clark's selection of the deep, protected draws in and around the Cheyenne River proved valuable on several occasions, including the Great Die-Up of 1886–1887.[4]

Moreover, as early as the 1870s the Sheidleys recognized the importance of crossbreeding Texas longhorns with heavier-muscled (but more expensive and less hardy) English breeds, such as shorthorns or Herefords, in order to produce a superior beef animal. While longhorns were cheap, they took four years or more to develop fully and had little muscling; some said they were all hide, horns, and hooves. Historian J. Frank Dobie summed up the "heroic" longhorn in this way: "The Texas steer stood with his body tucked up in his flanks, his high shoulder-top sometimes thin enough to split a hailstone, his ribs flat, his length frequently so extended that his back swayed. Viewed from the side, his big frame would fool a novice into a ridiculous overestimate of his weight, but a rear view was likely to show cat hams, narrow hips, and a ridgepole kind of backbone. His bones appeared to be heavier than they actually were."[5] In an attempt to correct these deficiencies, in 1876 the Sheidleys purchased nine hundred shorthorn cattle, which they trailed to their Nebraska ranges and started to breed with longhorns brought up from Texas. By 1884, the Sheidley Cattle Company had shorthorn-longhorn crossbred steers that weighed between one thousand and thirteen hundred pounds after just three years on the range—a significant improvement over the longhorn steers that took four years or more to weigh between eight hundred and one thousand pounds.[6]

The Sheidleys had also recognized the value of leased land several years before the arrival of barbed wire. In 1882, they had petitioned for grazing leases on the Great Sioux Reservation, deeming it far better to have control of the land than to rely on the whims of the federal government or an ambiguous relationship with the Sioux Indians. Likewise, the violent fence-cutting disputes in Texas were largely avoided on the northern plains, although incidents such as the 1892 Johnson County War in Wyoming demonstrated that the region was not without conflict.[7]

The timing of settlement likewise influenced the different development of the northern and southern plains. Homesteaders may have forced a change in the cattle industry in Texas around 1885, but at that time much of western Dakota Territory was still a part of the Great Sioux Reservation and not open for settlement. Outside the Black Hills, homesteading in the West River portion of what would become South Dakota did not occur in any significant numbers until after 1900, and even then much of the range remained. And while the presence of settlers ("dry farmers" who "invaded" a "flourishing range country," according to former ranchman John Clay) played a major role in the end of the open-range cattle industry, many changes, including a new preference for leased or purchased land over unsecured range, had already taken place prior to their arrival.[8] Widespread fencing would take longer to arrive on the northern plains, but the change was inevitable.

Even Lemmon, who despised wire and in later years lamented the loss of the range to farmers, had no choice but to follow the tide and fence a pasture for the first time in his life in 1902. The boundary fencing was required in the terms of his lease of more than 1,350 square miles on the Standing Rock Indian Reservation. When Lemmon secured this colossal lease, he changed cattle ranching on the Northern Great Plains. As a well-known cattleman highly regarded for his skill in open-range cattle handling, Lemmon symbolized the shift from range to pasture and implemented the progression seen in Texas years before.

Heedless of barbed wire's expansion on the southern plains, the Sheidleys had continued to modernize and streamline their operation in the 1880s without using wire. Dave Clark, the company's general manager and Lemmon's boss, spent a great deal of time in town conducting business, so the outfit's day-to-day operations fell to Ed. His responsibilities had been increasing for several years, and in 1888 they expanded even further when voters elected Clark mayor of Rapid City. This responsibility was not unusual for a cattleman, as several had taken leadership positions in cities throughout western Dakota Territory, including Spearfish mayor Milton C. Connors, who six years earlier had supported Clark's efforts to acquire grazing leases on the Great Sioux Reservation. As Clark took a greater role in politics, Ed's leadership became more and more important to the Sheidley Company's success.[9]

Lemmon led from the front, never asking his men to perform a job he would not do. He repeatedly put himself in physical danger but viewed personal risk as a necessary part of completing the task he set out to finish. Whether crossing deep rivers, exposing himself to the elements, gathering cattle at night, confronting wild animals, or any of a dozen other natural dangers on the open range,

Ed seemed to relish the opportunity to overcome a challenge. He demonstrated this willingness in the spring of 1888, while gathering cattle for a second drive to the Moreau River range.

Ed had already finished one 280-mile round-trip cattle drive and had given orders to collect several thousand more head for another. He situated his mess wagon south of the Cheyenne River, where most of the company's cattle had spent the winter of 1887–1888 in the region's deep, protective draws. One morning, he directed his cowboys to fan out north of the river in a wide circle to gather strays. They were to come back to the river that afternoon to return any cattle they found to the larger herd south of the Cheyenne. Ed and his men left early, and because the search took them several miles from their remuda of extra horses, their mounts were worn out by the time they circled back late in the afternoon. Meanwhile, heavy rains farther west had caused the river to rise until a stretch of nearly three hundred feet of deep water separated its banks.[10]

Lemmon's cowboys—most of whom probably could not swim— hesitated to cross the fast-flowing water on tired mounts, but Ed needed to return to camp so he could continue directing the roundup. While the cowboys pushed the cattle into the river, Ed prepared for the swim across. He would drive the cattle back to the main herd south of the river while the rest of the cowboys stayed on the north side to continue looking for strays. Leaving his clothes, saddle blanket, boots, and hat with the men on the north side, Lemmon grabbed the saddle horn and crossed the swollen Cheyenne on his favorite horse, named S. I. Bay, who "swam like a duck."[11]

Ed had kept his war-bag of extra supplies with him on the swim, but it contained only underwear—no pants or shirts. When he returned to his mess wagon with the cattle that evening, it took Ed's cowboys a moment to recognize their hatless, bootless, half-naked roundup boss. The river stayed high for three days, during which time Ed went without his regular clothes. He managed to borrow a pair of low-cut shoes and a pair of overalls, while the camp cook provided him an old straw hat with no crown that he had picked up on the prairie somewhere days before and that had recently adorned the wagon's brake lever as a souvenir. Ed's hobo getup concealed his identity well, and several cowboys from other outfits had a good chuckle when they came looking for the roundup boss.

Cattle branding on the Great Sioux Reservation, ca. 1887.
South Dakota State Historical Society

He eventually got his clothes back, but not before getting the mess wagon to the north side of a river that days earlier had been difficult to cross on horseback. The water had receded some, but to get the wagon across, the cowboys had to stabilize it with saddle ropes. They tied several together, attached them to the upper sides of the wagon, and then dallied them to their saddle horns to keep it from capsizing. Several men flanked the wagon at pretested places shallow enough to accommodate a horse, and they managed to get it across in one piece.[12]

Lemmon's decision to cross the river seems like an unnecessary risk in hindsight, but his main consideration was the efficient completion of the roundup, not his personal safety. As he later explained, "I had never yet fell down on a job, and I didn't propose to begin at that date [on account of] a little water."[13] Likewise, he probably never gave a second thought to crossing the Cheyenne without boots, a hat, or clothes. He knew that somehow he would get by. His ability to dismiss personal danger and inconvenience prompted others to follow his example and focus on tasks, not risks.[14]

On occasion, Ed demonstrated more than a bit of recklessness, but he also employed various techniques that reduced risk and accomplished tasks more efficiently. For instance, stray steers carrying another ranch's brand frequently got picked up with trail herds heading to market or to different ranges. Cattle outfits did not want to be accused of stealing another man's beeves, so they took great pains to make sure that steers carrying other brands were removed from their herds. Once strays started traveling with the herd, they became comfortable with the group and could be difficult to cut out, often rejoining the others within hours. Lemmon used a couple of techniques to prevent this problem. After an alien steer had rejoined his herd two or three times, Ed would rope him around the horns and drop him to the ground by tossing the slack over the animal's right hip and quickly turning his horse to the left. This action was extremely effective in pulling a steer down and not unlike the technique later used in steer-roping contests at rodeos. Once it was on the ground, Ed would rub sand into the steer's eyes, temporarily blinding the animal and often preventing it from rejoining the herd. If this method failed, Lemmon would rope and throw the steer down again and tie a knot in the extreme end of its tail. He would then wrap the knotted tail around the animal's right hind leg above the hock (knee), then lift the left leg and place the split hoof into the tail just above the knot. When the steer's left leg was suspended in this manner, he could hobble along and graze but could not move fast enough to keep up with the herd. Eventually the knot would fail or the steer would kick loose, but by that time the herd had usually moved on.[15]

After the Great Die-Up during the winter of 1886–1887, cattlemen on the Northern Great Plains worked to rebuild their herds. By 1888, cattle numbers in Dakota Territory had rebounded and then some, reaching more than 950,000 head—the highest level of the decade. The railroad played a significant role in the quick turnaround by providing ready means to ship cattle from the southern plains to the northern grasslands. In 1885, the Chicago & North Western Railroad had purchased the Fremont, Elkhorn & Missouri Valley Railroad and extended the line from Valentine, Nebraska, west to Chadron, and then north to Buffalo Gap in Dakota Territory. This line reached Rapid City the following year. The Sheidley Cattle Company headquarters was situated about ten miles from the Buffalo Gap railhead, providing a prime receiving location for new southern stock and an excellent shipping point for cattle that the company did not sell to the Indian agents on the Great Sioux Reservation.[16]

The destination for Sheidley Company cattle, like virtually every other beef animal shipped by rail from the Northern Great Plains in the 1880s, was the Union Stockyards in Chicago. Built in 1864 by a consortium of nine railroad companies, the stockyards covered several hundred acres southwest of Chicago and quickly became the country's largest livestock receiving point. Its more than twenty-three hundred pens could hold fifty thousand cattle at one time, in addition to two hundred thousand hogs, thirty thousand sheep, and five thousand horses. Between 1865 and 1895, nearly fifty million cattle arrived at the Union Stockyards, most of which were immediately transferred to the adjacent packing plants, known as Packingtown, for slaughter.[17]

When Sheidley Company cattle began arriving in Chicago in the mid-1880s, methods of livestock transportation and slaughter were undergoing a significant shift. Since the early 1870s, packing houses had integrated natural refrigeration into their operations. This technique used ice, usually large blocks cut from lakes and ponds in the winter, to keep meat cool during warm months. Prior to refrigeration, most slaughter took place from November to March, when the naturally cold temperatures would aid meat preservation; after refrigeration, livestock could be slaughtered at any time and stored until the carcasses could be further processed or distributed. At the same time, Gustavus Swift was among the first to use refrigerated railroad cars to transport chilled beef to cities on the east coast. In the 1880s, compressing machines that used ammonia as a coolant began to replace natural refrigeration as the preferred preservation method. This artificial refrigeration dramatically dropped cooling times—swine carcasses could be chilled in nineteen hours rather than sixty—which increased the number of animals that packers could process.[18]

Additionally, in 1888 an improved livestock car made its debut in Dakota Territory, reducing livestock shrinkage during rail shipment. The new car, built by the Western Stable Car Company, held twenty-one head and provided feed and water during the trip—a feature not available on earlier models. In addition, the new livestock car allowed for faster speeds. Trains pulling the updated cars could now make the run from Buffalo Gap to Chicago in forty-eight hours, a full day less than before. On one mixed-car shipment that year, cattle traveling in old-style cars averaged shrinkage of ninety-one pounds per head, while cattle on the same train shipped in the new cars lost just thirty-one pounds, a total savings of 1,260 pounds per car, or the equivalent of one large mature steer. This dramatic reduction in shrinkage was especially significant in 1888 because cattle prices in Chicago were excellent. One of the Sheidley Company's neighbors shipped a carload of large, heavy steers that earned $57.40 each in Chicago—a premium price when local steers sold for about $26.00 per head.[19]

Upon arriving at the stockyards, the cattle were transferred to pens assigned to individual owners. After being fed and watered, the animals were weighed—a crucial step in determining the sale price—before being inspected by a government official and then moved to another series of holding pens in preparation for slaughter. W. Joseph Grand described the slaughter process in 1896:

> A man stands on a board walk above, and with a well directed blow with a heavy sledge, stuns [a steer]. A door is raised as the steer falls, causing him to slide out upon the floor of the slaughter-house. A chain is now fastened to his hind legs and he is hoisted from the floor, his forelegs spread wide apart, and a sharp knife thrust into his throat by a man who does no other part of the work than this. As the knife strikes the throat the blood wells out in a torrent. This ocean of blood is washed down into a gutter leading to a tank, from which it is pumped into covered carts and conveyed to the fertilizer factory.
>
> The head of the steer is now removed. He is then lowered to the floor and laid upon his back, sticks set in the floor propping him up. The legs are now broken, the stomach opened and the hide skinned from the edges of the opening. A hook is then stuck behind each of the joints of the hind legs, and the steer hoisted up to a position convenient for the butchers,

whose subject he now is. The tail is cut off, the intestines removed and the hide pulled a little farther off. This done, the animal is hoisted from the floor. Above are two tracks on which are wheels with hooks hanging from them. These hooks are substituted for those previously put behind the joints of the hind legs, leaving the steer conveniently hanging from the wheels. The hide is now completely removed by two men pulling it and a third beating it and separating it from the flesh with a cleaver. When removed the hide is inspected and, if found intact, is sent to a cellar to be salted and folded and made ready for sale.

[Once] the hide is removed from the steer the carcass is halved lengthwise by means of a huge cleaver, the ragged edges being then trimmed by several men, who also wash and dry the meat very carefully. Numbering, tagging, weighing and hanging in the cooler now follow rapidly, the carcass being rolled rapidly along the tracks from man to man until the task is done. From five to eight minutes have elapsed from the time the steer was knocked on the head until placed in the cooler, during which time he has passed through the hands of forty-two men.[20]

In 1906, Upton Sinclair's novel *The Jungle* would expose widespread health and food-safety issues in Packingtown, triggering significant reforms. In the 1880s and 1890s, however, the Sheidley Cattle Company gave little thought to such concerns; its business was simply to turn cheap cattle and free grass into profitable beef.[21]

As one of the Sheidley Company's most important cowboys, Lemmon engaged in his principle passion—working cattle on horseback. By his early thirties, he had probably handled more than five hundred thousand head, worked for several different outfits, and taken charge of other cowboys, including his topnotch "killer" crew. Ed took great pride in his horsemanship, claiming, "I was almost continuously in the saddle and few indeed could out-distance me in long or continuous riding."[22] He thrived on the action and thoroughly enjoyed life on the open range. After he married Bertha Reno, Ed moved his bride to the company's range headquarters on French Creek so that he could be close to his cowboys. Living in a camp filled with more than a dozen single young men was probably an awkward situation for Bertha, a young, attractive woman. Ed continued to live the cowboy life—riding for long hours, sleeping near the mess wagon, taking a turn on night guard—even after the births of his sons. The eldest, named James Hervey after Ed's father and older brother, was born in 1888; the second, Roy Edward, in 1889; and the youngest, George Reno, in September 1894.

Ed also had a secondary passion—women other than his wife—even if he recounted his exploits in this arena with less enthusiasm and detail than his cattle-handling endeavors. From the 1920s to the 1940s, after he retired from the cattle business and began recounting his life for publication, Ed wrote about all manner of cowboy experiences—good horses, bad weather, exciting accidents, run-ins with Indians, ornery steers—as well as his knowledge of "painted ladies," the prostitutes he encountered during his regular visits to town. Ed generally refrained from publishing such stories in the *Belle Fourche Bee*, which printed hundreds of his reminiscences over more than ten years; his family and friends all read the *Bee*, so he likely sought to maintain appearances by avoiding the subject there. In a manuscript prepared by North Dakota historian Usher L. Burdick, titled "History of the Range Cattle Trade of the Dakotas," however, Lemmon described a large number of his various female acquaintances, both before and after his first marriage.

In fact, his chapter on the "Good and Bad Women of the West" reads like a who's who of the region's madams, dance-hall girls, and female gamblers and saloonkeepers: Calamity Jane, Poker Alice, Frisky Phyllis, Stepladder Jane, Kate the Bitch, Grace of Pimp Town, the Sage Hen, the Queen of French Creek, Mae of Hurdy Gurdy, Slippery Ann, Brockel-Faced Mary, Will o' the Wisp, and Monte Verde were all covered in detail. In this volume and other writings, he mentioned several other professional women he knew, including Mustache Maude, Connie Hoffman, Brockey Moll, Billy the Kid (obviously not the famous gunfighter), Nellie Bly (obviously not the famous journalist), Maude S., Addie Devier, and Dollie Varden. Even though Ed did not drink, he was clearly well acquainted with the saloons and gaming establishments in the cow towns where he shipped cattle to market.[23]

Lemmon exhibited a sense of humor in this vein, once describing a conversation with a respectable ranch wife, a Mrs. McMahon, about a man who had been a guest at her home. While she served dinner, this "fine gentleman" had told her about his cattle operation and the hog ranch he owned outside of town. Apparently she was unaware that "hog ranch" was a euphemism for the brothel that sat outside the city limits, beyond the reach of local law enforcement. A few days later, Ed stopped by the McMahon ranch for supper after selling some horses nearby. The conversation drifted to the man whom the McMahons had hosted earlier, a man Ed knew quite well. Mrs. McMahon remarked that he must be quite well off, for he owned a large hog ranch on the White River. Straight-faced, Ed replied, "Yes, Mrs. McMahon, if you will ask your husband I think he will tell you [the gentleman's] swine are of inferior breed and of little market value, especially in Chicago or Omaha markets, where there are so many of better value."[24]

Ed's interest in women was not limited to notorious frontier characters. He wrote regularly of the beautiful young ladies he met, describing one particularly lithe woman as "supple as a panther."[25] Among those who caught his attention were Mandy Shoemaker, whom he called the Sheep Girl; Jane Remington, the Belle of the Little Blue River; and Alta Steele, the Belle of Buffalo Gap. Miss Steele proved nearly irresistible for Ed, who described her as "hardly what would be classed a full fledged flirt . . . rather of the hands-off type that made the boys all the more anxious to possess her."[26] No doubt Lemmon was one of those boys. "She got to making her home very much with our family," he later recalled. "This was after I was married and living on the Flying V ranch on French Creek, she and my wife being very chummy, and possibly the same with myself, but just a fatherly adviser."[27] One can almost picture Ed, who was nearing eighty when he wrote this reminiscence, pausing and rereading the first portion of this passage before hurriedly including the last phrase to cover his true feelings. Alta Steele had clearly caught his eye.

Lemmon never described any sexual involvement with any of these women, instead focusing on their interactions with his cowboys. Clearly, he did not have a physical relationship with many of the women he named, including Calamity Jane, Poker Alice, and Stepladder Jane, whom he described as "too homely to hold a lover."[28] However, his stories are laced with innuendo ("her talents were much sought after"),[29] and he provided detailed physical descriptions of many women he admired ("a queenly style of a girl, slender, graceful with a large rope of dark hair").[30] Lemmon demonstrated a strong preference for young, beautiful girls, and on one occasion, he had one of his cowboys reassigned to a different part of the range so he could pursue a courtship uncontested. As he noted, "I never was much for company when trying to enjoy the company of a swell dame."[31] Yet women were far less important to Ed than the open range. As both of Lemmon's wives would discover, cattle, horses, and cowboys meant more to him than any woman ever could.[32]

As the Sheidley Company prepared for the 1889 spring roundup in Fall River County, perhaps half of its nearly thirty thousand cattle had been moved to the Moreau River range north of the Black Hills. The balance of the Flying V cattle ranged in Custer and Fall River counties south of the Hills. During the winter months, cattle tended to drift with the prevailing northwesterly wind at their backs, and cattle that began the winter in Montana or Wyoming could end up as far south as Nebraska. In the spring, all of these animals were rounded up and returned to their home ranges for summer grazing. Roundups also provided an opportunity to brand the young calves, who were generally born in March or April after about nine and a half months' gestation. Cows nursed their calves throughout the summer and early fall, weaning them before winter returned. The cows would need all their available energy to survive and carry next year's unborn calves through the cold months, and yearling calves born the previous spring either learned to care for themselves or perished.[33]

As soon as the grass began to green up and the meadowlarks appeared with the warmer weather, roundup bosses like Ed Lemmon began preparing for the spring roundups by sending their cowboys to gather all the horses that had been left to roam free over the winter. When a cattle outfit cut cowboys for the winter, it needed far fewer horses than it had used during the busy months, so some were turned loose to graze the open range unattended. After they were caught, some horses had to be rebroken to carry a saddle and rider. Because the cowboys were busy with a number of tasks— inspecting, fixing, greasing, and preparing the roundup wagons for duty; trimming hooves, manes, and tails; repairing and oiling harnesses, saddles, cinches, bridles, belts, and other tack—sometimes the rebreaking was not as thorough as it could have been. The battles between a half-broken horse and a cowboy with months of winter rust made for an amusing spectacle and sometimes led to "a man or two carted to town for repairs."[34]

Meanwhile, Dave Clark and the other general managers of the region's cattle enterprises met to determine where roundups would be held and who would boss them. They published notices of their upcoming roundups in all of the stock newspapers so other outfits would know when and where to send reps to collect the cattle carrying their brands. Under Clark's management, Sheidley Company roundups generally began on 25 May to allow for warmer weather. Even so, spring storms could emerge quickly and make roundups unpleasant. One cowboy recalled a morning that started off cloudy and warm, but "rain began falling before noon, the summery breeze became icy, and the rain changed rapidly to snow, blanketing everything—the makings of a blizzard growing by the hour!"[35] Some outfits chose to begin in early June, "the cattle being too weak to handle before that time," but after Lemmon took over he moved the start date forward to 15 May because he believed that a later roundup caused the cattle greater harm.[36] Ed handled cattle deliberately and with total control, and he realized that his penchant for rapid work could cause them injury. If the cattle had regained enough strength after the winter months to move quickly, the cowboys could easily push them to the point of overexertion. If handled ten days earlier, however, while still recovering from their winter atrophy, the weakened cattle simply could not move fast enough to injure themselves.[37]

Roundups were located on large, flat places near a river or stream so that water would be available for the dozens of cowboys involved. Each of the participating ranches sent a roundup outfit, which consisted of a chuck wagon, one or more bed wagons, and a group of cowboys. In addition to four extra horses per wagon, every cowboy brought a string of eight to ten mounts. For a large ranch with four wagons and a dozen cowboys, this arrangement meant traveling with a herd of more than 120 horses. The bed wagons hauled bedrolls and extra supplies and featured racks for carrying ropes used

A roundup, 1887. *South Dakota State Historical Society*

to picket horses and build makeshift corrals. Because nights on the northern ranges could be quite cold even in the summer (the average low temperature for Custer County, South Dakota, in mid-July drops to about fifty degrees Fahrenheit), Lemmon's cowboys would pack their bedrolls as heavily as they preferred or could afford. The chuck or mess wagon contained a dustproof wooden mess box about three and a half feet high with drawers for plates, cups, utensils, seasonings, and leftover food. The hinged lid doubled as a table. Meals consisted of fresh beef, baked or boiled beans, potatoes, biscuits, bread, canned tomatoes, corn, dried fruits, suet pudding, and occasionally a pie. Beneath one or both of the wagons was a cooney, a cowhide used to carry wood or cow chips to fuel the cooking fire. The cooney was just large enough to accommodate a small man and made a snug sleeping spot away from the ele-

ments; Ed took refuge in a cooney on more than one occasion. Both the bed and mess wagons carried boxes with horseshoeing tools, patching and mending equipment, and a crude first-aid kit with crutches, cloth bandages, and a bottle of horse liniment to be "used for man or beast, practically in the same proportions."[38] Lemmon's wagons also always carried enough water for at least three meals, so his crew could make a dry camp if they needed to. The roundup wagons served as a cowboy's home base throughout the summer and provided for all his needs.[39]

Roundup outfits had a distinct hierarchy, with different responsibilities and pay scales. In Lemmon's crews, the wagon boss was the outfit's leader and earned about eighty dollars per month. He directed the men and saw to their needs. Second in command was the cook, who had complete control of the chuck wagon and earned between fifty and sixty dollars per month. The wrangler cared for the horses during the day and occasionally relieved another cowboy from his two-hour guard responsibilities at night. The nighthawk cared for the horses after dark and drove one of the bed wagons during the day when the main camp moved; cowboys familiar with the country around the roundup area were selected to drive the other bed wagons. When the outfit reached camp, these men assisted the cook and wranglers in setting up the stove, pitching the tent, stringing the horse corral, gathering wood, peeling potatoes, carrying water, and other tasks involved in preparing the campsite. Once the roundup got underway, the cowboys worked under the direction of their wagon boss and the overall roundup boss. During the day, they gathered, sorted, moved, and tended the cattle; at night, every cowboy worked a two-hour guard shift between 8:00 P.M. and 4:00 A.M. An average day lasted more than eighteen hours, beginning when the cook rang the "come-and-get-her" call at 2:45 in the morning and ending at 8:45 in the evening.[40]

Roundups that Lemmon bossed always began with "circling," in which all the cowboys would ride in a wide arc from the central gathering point, collecting any cattle they found and driving them to the roundup grounds. Even though "Ed Lemmon slapped a roundup together fast," as cowboy Ike Blasingame recalled, circling could take several days, depending on the terrain and the number of cattle in the area.[41] Once the cattle were rounded up, they were sorted by brand. All the calves were branded and the bull calves castrated. The cattle were then driven onto their home ranges, with line riders keeping the stock on each outfit's individual range as much as possible. Additional "beef roundups" were held in the fall to gather cattle for shipment to market. After these year-end roundups, the cattle were once again turned loose on the range and then regathered the following spring.[42]

Every year, Lemmon looked forward to the "action, swapping experiences, [and] fun" of the spring roundups.[43] With his lifelong fondness for storytelling and constant desire for action, the annual roundups suited his personality perfectly. Unfortunately for Ed, he would miss all but one day of the 1890 roundup due to a severe injury. Since his last major accident fifteen years earlier—the 1875 fall that crushed his right leg, crippling him permanently—Ed had managed to avoid serious injury save two broken collarbones, the left in 1884 and the right in 1886. Neither of these accidents caused him any great inconvenience, although the fracture of his right clavicle forced the right-handed Lemmon to start roping his mounts left-handed. But his lucky streak ended on 11 May 1890, just a day after the start of the spring roundup.

For most of the day, Lemmon had been leading a circling party of eighteen men not far from Smithwick Station in Fall River County in the southwest corner of the newly admitted state of South Dakota, gathering bunches of cattle and sending them back to the main roundup grounds with pairs of cowboys. He had just directed his last two cowboys to return to the roundup site with three hundred head when he noticed a group of fifty to sixty cattle that apparently belonged to a nearby homesteader. As his men left for the roundup, Lemmon rode alone about three-quarters of a mile to check the brands on the small herd, intending to return any "rangers" to the main roundup. He spotted six rangers among the group and cut them from the main body but could not prevent one of the settler's steers from joining his cut. Ed kicked his mount—S. I. Bay, the same horse he had used to swim the Cheyenne River in 1888—to a gallop to remove the steer from his half-dozen, but as he did so the bay broke through a gopher tunnel on the edge of a hill, causing horse and rider to tumble forty feet to the bottom. S. I. Bay survived the fall uninjured, but as they rolled, the horse had flailed "all four of his ragged hooved limbs right in my face, digging it all to pieces, but nothing serious only as to looks."[44] In addition to the cuts and bruises on his face, Ed had once again broken his right leg severely and fractured his left shoulder as well.[45]

After the fall, he tried to get the attention of his two cowboys. They were still within view but had not witnessed the accident, and Ed's voice could not carry against the stiff wind blowing in his face. Once they passed out of sight, Ed began the agonizing process of trying to set the broken bones in his leg and shoulder, but his efforts proved futile. Because he could not mount his horse, he decided to make himself as comfortable as possible and wait for help. He assumed that as the roundup boss, he would soon be missed and riders would come out looking for him. Getting comfortable was a difficult proposition, however, because in addition to the excruciating pain in his leg and shoulder, a light dusting of snow had fallen the previous night and had not yet melted in the chilly air. Ed was wearing only a thin shirt; his heavy flannel jacket and waterproof "slicker," or overcoat, were tied to the saddle and out of reach, and he "soon became so chilled," he said, that "I could only utter a guttural sound."[46]

Unbeknownst to Ed, the cowboys at the roundup thought nothing of his absence. They assumed that he had gone to Smithwick Station to post the letters he had written the previous evening. For more than four hours Ed shivered in the snow and wind, waiting for his men. Help finally arrived when the homesteader came to check on his cattle. The man retrieved Ed's slicker from his horse, wrapped it around him, then mounted the bay and rode for Smithwick. Within thirty-five minutes, the homesteader had returned with a wagon and three men. They placed Ed on a cot in the wagon "without hurting me in the slightest" and headed for town.[47] At Smithwick, someone went to the telegraph office and sent a wire to Buffalo Gap, sixteen miles north, requesting a doctor, who arrived on a train just half an hour later. Despite his lengthy exposure and the severity of his injuries, the resilient cattleman was moving around on crutches within a month. Ed claimed that he was "not the least bit worse crippled than before,"[48] but one of his cowboys noted that this third break "handicapped to quite an extent his riding and horse breaking activities."[49]

Lemmon's accident prevented him from rejoining the 1890 roundup, but instead of staying with his wife and sons at the Flying V headquarters on French Creek, he spent the next several months at his father's farm in Thayer County, Nebraska. Ed's older brother Moroni had died on 27 February 1888 at only thirty-two, and Ed had not gone home for the funeral. He may have returned to Nebraska to pay his respects and to visit his sister Alpharetta and her husband, who lived nearby. In addition, according to Ed, his father James had been "clamoring" for him to "quit the range and come back to our old Nebraska homestead and settle down before I got killed chasing the longhorns."[50] After breaking his right leg for a third time, Ed finally heeded his father's suggestions and returned home for the remainder of the 1890 cattle-handling season.[51]

Roping a steer, ca. 1887. *South Dakota State Historical Society*

Lemmon appears to have made a genuine effort to give up his cowboy life. He loved everything about the open-range cattle business, but he was only thirty-three years old and had already suffered several severe injuries. Perhaps he began to question how long his body could hold out, given the physical demands and inherent dangers of his profession and the fact that both of his older brothers had died in their thirties. What seems clear is that concern for his wife and sons played little part in his decision. Ed did not spend his time away from the Flying V playing with his children, showering affection on his teenage wife, or sitting at the ranch headquarters deciding what to do next. He spent it building an independent cattle business.

This venture was not Ed's first foray into business; he had been buying and selling cattle to supplement his regular wages since 1878. That fall, he had purchased his first sixteen Texas yearlings for $180, then added fifteen head to his herd and sold the lot to George Green for four hundred dollars. Ed continued buying cattle through 1885, when he bought more than two hundred quality shorthorn cattle, later selling them for $6,750. Between 1886 and 1889, he purchased no livestock, instead loaning his money out at a rate of 2 percent per month. After his 1890 accident, however, he began buying steers in South Dakota, driving them to his father's land in Nebraska, and selling them to local settlers as feeder cattle. He marketed more than one thousand head that year, netting an average of five dollars apiece.[52]

While Lemmon tended cattle in Nebraska in 1890, two additional accidents made him rethink his decision to leave the open-range cattle business. He owned a string of purebred shorthorn cattle that he grazed on a ten-acre area of corn stubble within a larger cornfield. The cut section was "fenced" on its boundaries by the tall, uncut corn stalks. Ed cared for the animals himself, and on one occasion, as the cattle attempted to cross into the standing corn, he spurred his horse into a gallop to head them off. As he raced across the field, his horse stumbled and fell, throwing Ed from the saddle. He landed face-first into the cut stalks, with one of the sharp edges making a deep cut near his left eye. Placing a hand over his right eye, he brushed the blood out of his left and squinted "to see if daylight would appear, showing my eye to not be gouged out, and to my delight daylight appeared."[53]

Later that winter, Lemmon had the steers in what he called a "river feed lot," with the steep banks of the frozen Little Blue River forming the southern barrier of his makeshift corral.[54] To make the most of his investment, Ed also owned a hog for each one of his steers. Because corn kernels would often pass through a steer's body undigested, he ran these hogs in the same pasture to clean up the waste grain, maximizing the cornfield's profitability. The river ice was relatively thin; it could hold the weight of a hog, but not a steer, so while the cattle remained north of the river, some of the hogs crossed to feed on the south side. The nearest bridge was a mile and a half away, so it took Ed quite some time to ride to his wayward animals, gather them, and return.

On one occasion after he had collected the hogs and driven them back across the river, he decided to try to take his horse the few hundred yards across the ice rather than make the three-mile return trip. The choice was perhaps the quintessential example of Lemmon's controlled recklessness. He rode to a shallow wagon ford two hundred yards upstream from his feed lot, dismounted, and limped out onto the ice to test its strength. The ice was solid except for a ten-foot-wide section in the middle kept open by the current. Using a stick to test the depth of the open section, he found the river only four feet deep. Ed decided that he would lead his horse out onto the ice, mount the animal, spur him into the current, and force him to climb the ice on the far side, thus saving a half hour of riding time.

His plan did not go as expected. Lemmon's horse made an awkward plunge into the frigid river, dragging him in head-first. He had not removed any clothing, not even his heavy overcoat, and this poor decision combined with his crippled leg and the ice-cold water to render him nearly helpless in the swift current, which carried him downstream. Luckily, one of his father's hired men was working near the Little Blue and heard his call for help. The man threw him a rope as he passed by the house and dragged Ed, soaked, freezing, and probably embarrassed, from the water.[55]

Lemmon survived this latest near-death experience with no long-term effects—he even managed to retrieve his expensive Stetson hat—save one. As soon as he reached the house and met his father, Ed "did not hesitate to make it plain to him that no matter where a person was they encountered about equal dangers, and in the spring I certainly would go back to the open range, and longhorns, which I did."[56] This single incident, which took place within the space of perhaps a few minutes, clarified Ed's thinking about his future more completely than the months he had spent in Nebraska. After Moroni's death, Ed probably sensed his own mortality and reasoned that if he wanted more time on earth, he ought to choose a safer way of life. Any semblance of a new approach vanished, however, after his river rescue. Once again, Ed felt free to pursue his life's work without guilt. He decided that if he was going to die, he might as well die doing what he loved. Ed loved working cattle. Never again would he question his gut instincts.

Lemmon did not wait until spring to return to the range; he departed in December 1890, just as tensions between Lakotas and the federal government reached their boiling point. Ever since Custer's 1874 Black Hills expedition had discovered gold, the Lakotas had seen more and more of their territory fall to white expansionism. They had signed the 1868 Treaty of Fort Laramie expecting to retain the entire western half of present-day South Dakota in perpetuity. Instead, they lost the Black Hills to gold seekers in 1877 and survived the 1887 Dawes General Allotment Act only to see their remaining territory nearly halved on 10 February 1890. The Sioux would be limited to the newly created Standing Rock, Cheyenne River, Pine Ridge, Rosebud, and Lower Brule reservations, while the remaining Great Sioux Reservation lands, approximately nine million acres, became available for non-Indian settlement.[57]

This radical reduction in territory, combined with the near-extermination of the bison by hide and sport hunters, poor food rations at the agencies (exacerbated by the ranchers' unscrupulous practices at the weighing pens), insufficient winter clothing and other supplies, and rampant disease, pushed the Sioux to their breaking point. It was not surprising that by December 1890 many Lakotas embraced the teachings of a Paiute medicine man named Wovoka, who said that by performing the Ghost Dance, Indians could bring back the buffalo, banish whites from the land, and restore their previous way of life. The new religion flourished on the Standing Rock, Pine Ridge, Cheyenne River, and Rosebud reservations, taking on what historian Robert M. Utley described as "an increasingly militant and alarming aspect."[58] Sitting Bull, the famed Hunkpapa chief and a revered leader among all the Lakota tribes, encouraged the Ghost Dance and worked to prevent Indian agents, missionaries, schoolteachers, and others from disrupting the ceremonies. When Indian police sent by agent James McLaughlin on 15 December to arrest Sitting Bull met with resistance from his followers, gunfire erupted, and the great chief was among those killed.[59]

A few days later, Lemmon, still in Nebraska, heard rumors about Indian activity near the Sheidley Company cattle herds wintering near the southern Black Hills. Since he had purchased a large group of steers ranging on Lame Johnny Creek in Custer County to sell to homesteaders in Nebraska, he took a train to Buffalo Gap to see about his investment. When he arrived at the station, he received news that seven Flying V cowboys had lost their horses to a band of raiding Indians. Concerned for their safety, Lemmon gathered several saddle horses and rode out to meet his dismounted men the next morning.[60]

Meanwhile, a contingent of Hunkpapa Sioux had fled Standing Rock for the Cheyenne River reservation after the death of Sitting Bull. There they joined the Miniconjou chief Big Foot, and a portion of the mixed group left for the Pine Ridge reservation to seek guidance from Red Cloud. On 28 December, the Seventh United States Cavalry—Custer's old regiment—intercepted Big Foot's band near Wounded Knee Creek in present-day Oglala Lakota County, South Dakota. The next day, Colonel James W. Forsyth ordered the Sioux to surrender their weapons, and when two soldiers tried to disarm a reluctant Indian, his rifle discharged. The tense situation erupted instantly into a confused and protracted firefight. The soldiers, more numerous and better armed with both rifles and light artillery, continued shooting for more than three hours and killed more than 250 Indians, including dozens of women and children.[61]

Lemmon had not yet reached his stranded cowboys when he received word of the massacre at Wounded Knee. He decided to investigate further when he heard rumors that one of the seven, a cook named Isaac Miller who had worked with his "Eight Killers" crew, had been killed. On 4 January 1891, he gathered two men and rode for General John R. Brooke's camp on the White River, about thirty-five miles southeast of Buffalo Gap and twenty miles northwest of Wounded Knee. As they neared the general's headquarters, they saw several groups of soldiers and Indians, including a large group camped near a stream that Lemmon knew as Grass Creek. When they arrived at Brooke's camp, a man named Bob Pew met Lemmon and asked for his assistance in gathering a herd of 420 cattle and driving them fifteen miles south to Pine Ridge for distribution at the agency. If he agreed, Ed would command a crew of trusted Indian cowboys who would help him with the job.[62]

Well aware of the recent hostilities and seeing firsthand the Indians roaming the countryside, Lemmon was reluctant to make the drive. He said, "Bob, do you know the body of those government issue cattle are ranging right back against the hostile camp, against that bad land bluff of Grass creek?" Pew, who knew little about cattle and was anxious to pass on the task, replied, "I don't believe the Indians will hurt you as you have always been their friend and your helpers will all be Indian boys."[63] Lemmon was skeptical, but he agreed to boss the herd, although he wanted a detachment of cavalry to protect it. He spoke with Captain Almond B. Wells and had just secured the cavalry's protection when a courier arrived with a message from General Brooke, who requested that Lemmon lead a military and civilian delegation through hostile territory to a safe location in the northwest corner of the Pine Ridge reservation, roughly forty miles from Wounded Knee. The delegation had been documenting the scene of the massacre and included men sent to investigate Colonel Forsyth's actions to determine whether he had acted appropriately. Glad to be rid of a foolhardy mission driving cattle that were not his responsibility, Ed made Captain Wells promise to explain the situation to Pew and left to guide the delegation.[64]

The group that Lemmon guided on 5 January consisted of Captain Frank D. Baldwin, Lieutenant Edward W. Casey, and several other cavalry officers; a teamster's wagon hauling seven Cheyenne Indian scouts, an interpreter, and the baggage; and "a Harpers Bazaar artist, who was appointed to sketch the Wounded Knee battle field."[65] Ed guided the party to the safe camp without incident, earning praise from Captain Baldwin for his prudent travel route. He left the group the following day to continue the search for his missing men, all of whom he later found except for Isaac Miller, who had indeed been killed. Although Lemmon did not know it, the artist he had escorted was almost certainly the famed painter and sculptor Frederic Remington, whose illustrations of cowboys, Indians, and western landscapes later earned him worldwide fame. Remington left South Dakota the next day after a staged holdup by six Cheyenne Indians arranged by Captain Baldwin, who viewed him as an unnecessary burden and a liability. Remington's sketch "The Opening of the Fighting at Wounded Knee" appeared in the 24 January 1891 issue of *Harper's Weekly*. Had Lemmon realized the connection, he would have mentioned it in his reminiscences, for he never let brushes with famous individuals pass without mention. Because Ed's one-day stint as a military man ended when the delegation arrived at camp, he may never have heard the artist's name. A few days later, Lemmon would visit the battle site for himself, but the bodies had long since been buried and there was nothing to see.[66]

For Ed, General Brooke's request to lead a group through dangerous country was an endorsement of his leadership qualities and skills as a navigator. He was proud of this assignment and in later years would use it as an example of his knowledge of Indian tactics and behavior. His reputation for efficiency in managing cowboys, bossing roundups, and handling cattle had begun to spread throughout the region; Ed was widely considered a man who could get a job—any job—done well. Lemmon had demonstrated an ability to handle any situation that came his way, and this knack for adaptability would serve him well later in 1891, when Dave Clark's sudden death provided Lemmon the opportunity to manage the outfit he had served for more than a decade.[67]

5 CATTLEMEN

During the late nineteenth and early twentieth centuries, thousands of cowboys worked on the open ranges of the Northern Great Plains, tending millions of beeves for dozens of large cattle outfits. Often financed by backers in Europe or the eastern United States, these companies sought to capitalize on the incredible opportunities available on these grasslands, which stretched from the Nebraska sandhills to the Canadian prairie provinces and from the Missouri River into Wyoming and Montana. With millions of acres of federal or Indian land available for livestock grazing at virtually no cost, returns could be enormous. If all went well, cattlemen such as Ed Lemmon, Cap Mossman, and Murdo MacKenzie would raise their cattle using public grass, sell the mature beeves to local Indian agents or ship them by rail to markets in Chicago, and reap huge profits. In contrast, the cowboys who spent long, hot days on horseback caring for herds of stubborn steers rarely became rich from their efforts. Some spent a lifetime riding the range and ended up worse off than they began— penniless, with broken-down bodies and few prospects for the future. Others trailed cattle for a few years during their teens and twenties, trying to earn enough money to purchase a farm or ranch of their own. Among cowboys, perhaps one of the most popular ambitions was to become a wealthy cattleman. Yet few of those who fantasized about running their own spread ever saw their dreams come to fruition. Ed Lemmon was the exception.[1]

From the time Lemmon began working for the Sheidley Cattle Company in 1880, Dave Clark had been the outfit's general manager. Clark led with authority, skillfully choosing cattle ranges and earning the respect of Lemmon and his other cowboys. As general manager, he had a one-fifth stake in the company and was its overall superintendent but relied heavily on Lemmon and others to manage the day-to-day operations during his absences, which were frequent. In addition to serving as mayor of Rapid City and president of various cattlemen's organizations, Clark was elected in 1890

Ed Lemmon (left) with fellow cowboy Jim Hudgins.
South Dakota State Historical Society

to the South Dakota state senate. A respiratory ailment had plagued him for some time, and he traveled to Florida after the November election in the hopes that the warm sunshine would prove easier on his lungs than the frigid northern plains winter. When the legislative session opened in January 1891, he spent much of his time in the Missouri River city of Pierre, South Dakota's capital. During the session, Clark worked to pass legislation favorable to cattlemen, but on 8 March he succumbed to his disease and died. He was only thirty-three.[2]

Following Clark's death, George and William Sheidley turned the general manager's duties over to Lemmon, who had served as range manager since 1880. Ed was also thirty-three, and Clark had been grooming him for the position for years. As the general manager, Ed now had the opportunity to weave the various systems he had developed for handling men and livestock into the fabric of the entire enterprise. In Lemmon's estimation, the position of general manager required a different skill set than that of range manager. A cowboy was an expert in roping, cutting, branding, and handling cattle, while a cattleman managed cowboys, displayed sound judgment, and selected choice ranges. As he said of W. P. Philips, the general manager of a different outfit: "He was one of the most thorough cow men I ever worked for, but in the true sense of the word he was never a real cowboy. What I mean, he could scarcely rope his own saddle horses or successfully cut a cow, or count a herd, but was a wonderful manager and trail and range boss."[3] Likewise, skill in handling open-range cattle did not necessarily equate to success in making a profit for the company, which was the general manager's primary responsibility. Ed had already earned widespread respect as a cowboy; since the general manager was also entitled to a 15-percent ownership stake in the company, he now sought to prove himself as a cattleman.[4]

Lemmon's transition from cowboy to cattleman was not a clean break from one set of responsibilities to another. Whereas Clark usually supervised the outfit from his office in Rapid City, Ed took a hands-on approach and managed from the saddle. While other managers used a buggy and team to cover broad expanses of territory, Lemmon always rode horseback, just like his cowboys. Working on the range came naturally to him, and he was more comfortable sitting in the saddle than behind a desk. Despite his various injuries and the dangers associated with life on the open range, Lemmon felt at home there for reasons he could not always articulate. He had intrinsic abilities in many aspects of cowboy life, which contributed to his rapid rise in the industry. In addition to his inherent knowledge of cattle and skill in cutting animals from the herd, for instance, Ed was renowned for his remarkable ability to discern directions on the open range at night. After galloping with a stampeding herd that changed direction multiple times, many cowboys had difficulty finding their way back to camp. For Lemmon, the ability to keep one's bearings "seemed to come to me by nature as to the homing pigeon."[5] After one stampede when he was just nineteen, Lemmon separated from the rest of the cowboys and headed for camp alone because the other men thought it lay in a different direction. He was sound asleep in his bedroll when they arrived after riding around in the dark for many miles. When asked how he knew to find his way, he recalled: "I could not tell them, I confessed I kept no track of the different directions the stampeded cattle had taken, but by some instinct knew how to go for camp."[6]

Cowboys soon learned to follow Lemmon's lead at night, especially when clouds covered the stars or there were no other navigational aids. Company managers also gained confidence in his abilities. As Ed later noted, his natural instincts were "a very strong factor in my advancement in the business."[7] The trust of his cowboys played an important role in Lemmon's ability to lead, but skill alone did not make him a great leader. Many successful managers are unable to understand why their subordinates cannot function as efficiently or as skillfully as they can. This shortcoming did not affect Lemmon, who never berated a cowboy for lack of ability but compensated for weaknesses by implementing methodical systems for virtually every aspect of cattle handling. Ed fused his skills with clear organization to create a system that took much of the uncertainty out of working cattle. His crews were more successful than other outfits, in part because everyone worked from the same rubric and knew the overall plan. They capitalized on the tremendous ability of a well-organized, well-managed group to get things done. As Lemmon later said about his fabulous "killer crew," "It was results that we were after and results was what [we] got."[8]

Trail drives required as much organization as roundups, and Ed employed a specific structure for his drives, which in the 1890s averaged about twenty-five hundred head. Following the Civil War, trail bosses tended to use one cowboy for every hundred head of longhorn cattle because the animals were wild and difficult to handle. Charles Goodnight even selected a man to kill any calves born on the trail because they disrupted the progress of the herd and were not worth the trouble. As more docile crossbred cattle increased in numbers in the 1880s and 1890s, bosses increased the ratio to three hundred head per cowboy. Lemmon's crews usually consisted of eleven men: a trail boss, a cook, a horse wrangler, and eight cowboys. Two cowboys, known as point men, rode in front of the herd and were usually the most experienced hands deemed best at holding the cattle together when crossing rivers or corralling stock. About one-third of the way back from the pointers rode two swing men, one on each side of the herd. Two flankers rode one-third of the way behind the swing men and were followed by two drag riders who brought up the rear. The cowboys "handling the drags," or the slowest animals in the herd, were given specific instructions to "weave back and forth, rounding the corners and . . . keeping the hind center full, and in a manner always moving forward the hindermost animal, and never under any circumstances crowding an animal or your horse up into the herd, which causes the cattle to tromp on one another's heels making bruises or cracked and chafed heels."[9] Riding the drags was dusty and unpleasant, so the most inexperienced cowboys usually drew this assignment.[10]

Lemmon wanted a trail herd of twenty-five hundred head to spread out for three-quarters of a mile and average between thirteen and fifteen miles per day. Each day the cowboys would push the herd off at about 6:00 A.M., traveling perhaps eight miles before breaking for lunch. Ideally, this plan left a shorter drive for the afternoon, when warmer temperatures caused greater weight loss. The trail boss tried to select a night camp near water, if possible, and bedded the cattle on high ground where evening breezes would keep insects away and cowboys would be less apt to encounter a river or stream if the herd stampeded. To prevent stampedes, Lemmon liked to bed the cattle with plenty of space so that a steer could rise and turn over without disturbing the animal sleeping next to it. The eight cowboys divided the night guard into four two-hour shifts, with the first pair beginning at 8:00 P.M. The night guards rode around the herd in opposite directions, singing or humming a lullaby to calm the animals. Lemmon's chuck wagon carried a dozen lanterns, one of which was always hung inside the wagon cover at night to act as a beacon to guide the cowboys to camp in case of a stampede. The night guards each carried a lantern as they rode around the herd. During a stampede, they used them to signal other cowboys and to slow or stop the rushing cattle, which looked on them as a familiar sight. Lemmon's system extended to every aspect of the trail drive, from the design and staking of the rope horse corral (which held the remuda of sixty-three horses) to a detailed list of the chuck wagon's utensils and tools. His methods of "drifting or slow trailing, over good grass and watered regions," brought results. Herds handled this way, he noted, "should land at destination with a gain in flesh, and very few sore footed."[11]

Goodnight and Lemmon differed in their opinions on how best

to conduct certain aspects of cattle handling, largely due to geography and personal preference. For instance, on his trail drives, Goodnight advocated sending stampeding cattle "into a mill" by having one cowboy race to the front of the herd and turn the animals to the right. When the leaders circled in this way, they eventually reached the tail end of the herd and began milling about, putting an end to the stampede. Ed viewed this technique as a last resort because it could injure cattle and endanger cowboys. His disciplined crews avoided the hazards of these nighttime dashes by working together and following his methods. Ed's approach proved a success. Although he participated in innumerable stampedes during his half-century on the range, he never had a cowboy or horse seriously injured during one.[12]

The seasoned cowboys also differed on the relative quality of their gear. Lemmon believed that Texas trail equipment, including the chuck wagons Goodnight had invented and the sourdough keg they usually carried, were "inferior to our northern equipment."[13] In the mid-1890s after the Sheidley Cattle Company purchased the NUN ranch in Texas, one of Ed's hands, Othe Arndt, ridiculed an adjacent outfit's cowboys about their sourdough keg, "which had a tight hinged cover, with felt around the cover edges."[14] The design kept out air and dust, but "with the shaking and jostling the dough would ferment and gather gas until it was known to blow up and cast off the lid with a loud roar and it always smelled near as strong as a skunk."[15] One night, Arndt and a Texas cowboy were on night guard together when a herd of thirty-five hundred yearling cattle stampeded for no apparent reason. After the cattle had quieted down, the Texan asked Arndt, "Now what the [hell] do [you] suppose stampeded them yearlings?" "Be damned if I know," Arndt replied, "unless it was the lid blowed off that sour dough keg."[16] The actual differences in quality between northern and southern equipment were largely a matter of opinion, but the cowboys enjoyed ribbing each other about the perceived deficiencies of their respective outfits.[17]

Lemmon and Goodnight probably never met, but they would have enjoyed arguing over different methods of handling cattle and likely would have shared a mutual respect. Goodnight's reputation for producing quality cattle was well known, and Lemmon raved about his skill as a cattleman, calling him the "greatest builder up of stocks of breeding cattle the world ever knew."[18] During the 1890s, Lemmon demonstrated this belief by purchasing thousands of JA-branded cattle with genetics developed by Goodnight. Without question, the men would have agreed on one element crucial to successful cattle handling: it was essential to have a plan. Goodnight and Lemmon both used their systems to great effect and owed a portion of their success to teaching cowboys the intricacies of their techniques.[19]

In addition to adhering to his system, Lemmon's cowboys were expected to use good judgment and adjust to changing circumstances. Their boss led by example. In May 1891, Ed boarded a train for Amarillo, Texas, to begin his first cattle-buying trip as general manager. He had overcome the shame of his crippled condition years before but believed that his unsightly leg, slight build, youthful looks, and range attire would detract from his ability to negotiate a good price. Instead, he put on his best clothes and borrowed a fine gold watch and chain in order to "look the part of a full-fledged business man."[20] After purchasing thirty-seven hundred cattle for the Flying V ranges in South Dakota, he arranged to ship them to Buffalo Gap by rail. A number of other outfits were attempting to load at the same time, and the shipping yards were crowded. Ed volunteered to load in the early morning hours of 18 May and asked permission to sort some of his cattle into the holding pens the night before. Seasoned Texas cattlemen frowned on the practice because in the early days of cattle shipping wild longhorns often damaged the corrals or injured themselves when penned overnight. Lemmon supervised the penning of several carloads of cattle and then went to supper, where he met a sixty-year-old cattleman who questioned his decision, saying, "Whenever a man in my employ pens a bunch of cattle the evening before loading, he ceases to be in my employ." Ed, who took exception to the condescending statement, replied, "When a man in my employ won't vary from any set rule to fit circumstances he ceases to be in my employ."[21] After both men calmed down, they bonded by swapping stories about working with former Colorado cattleman J. W. Iliff.

Lemmon appreciated adaptability in his cowboys and did not look on them solely as cogs in the wheel of his cattle-handling machine—he truly enjoyed spending time with them. He was lenient during their infrequent trips to town, usually giving cowboys "their regular three days to lush up and [then get] sober and be ready to move with the outfit."[22] This attitude was similar to that of the saloon owners and businessmen of Chadron, Ogallala, Valentine, Belle Fourche, Rapid City, Buffalo Gap, Smithwick, Evarts, and the other towns Lemmon's outfits visited. Since the men "spent their money freely, it was [commonplace] . . . to allow the cowboys the freedom of the town as long as they rode down no ladies or old [decrepit] men."[23] Lemmon let his cowboys enjoy themselves, and they appreciated it. "Everyone liked him," as cowboy Ike Blasingame said, because he lived in cow camp with his men, told stories, played practical jokes, and in general made his camps congenial places to be.[24] Unlike some managers, Lemmon understood that a "cowboy's life was a lot of hard work with little time for recreation or gunplay," so he and his men made the most of their opportunities to have fun.[25]

Sometimes the men in Lemmon's outfit got a laugh over the most commonplace events. His chuck wagons carried extra tobacco, bullets, and other conveniences that cowboys could purchase, since several weeks could pass without an opportunity to buy such items in town. One of Ed's wagon bosses, Ves Merritt, kept a "day book" in which he recorded purchases that cowboys had charged against their monthly pay. Merritt recorded each man's charges with a list of the items, followed by the word "ditto" for repeat purchases. At the end of the month, he confirmed the charges with each cowboy before subtracting them from their pay. Bill Boggs, an excellent cowboy but a man with limited education, once racked up a large bill for Durham and Climax tobacco and pistol cartridges, having "smoked up every town or roadranch he struck." Merritt's ledger for Boggs looked something like this:

1 box cartridges	$1.00
Ditto	1.00
Climax	.50
Ditto	.50
Durham	.60
Ditto	.60

When Boggs reviewed the charges, he exploded in anger. "Yes, I got those cartridges, the Climax and Durham all right," he thundered, "but I never got a damn 'ditto.' In fact I never used any in my life and I positively won't pay for them." Lemmon and the other men joked at Boggs's expense but appreciated his outstanding cattle-handling skills. Ed called him "the second best cowboy I ever saw."[26]

Although Lemmon enjoyed being around people and got along well with them, he probably did not have many close friends. He almost certainly did not confide in either of his wives, and with his brother Hervey's death in 1886, Ed lost the person who knew him best. He considered George Sheidley "the best friend I ever had," a telling statement because Sheidley was almost thirty years older, lived in Kansas City, and only interacted with Lemmon on an extended basis during the winter months, when they held business meetings in Chicago.[27] Still, Ed got along well with a wide range of personalities and made a point of getting to know his hands. His penchant for spending time with the cowboys rather than with his wives placed a tremendous strain on his marriages and doubtless was the main reason Bertha divorced him. But the wishes of his wives had little influence on Ed, who actively sought the company and conversation of cowboys. Even when he became the outfit's general manager, his men viewed him as one of them—a cowboy. Dave Clark's men had held him in high esteem, but they also viewed him as a boss, a cattleman. Lemmon's men both respected *and* liked him, which probably made his crews even more successful.

By 1892, Lemmon had become comfortable with his position as general manager of the Sheidley Cattle Company and was viewed by many as a leader in the industry. His management paid off handsomely for the Sheidley brothers, who reaped average annual profits of 12 percent under his leadership. In April, just as the Johnson County War in Wyoming erupted, Lemmon began working with other large operators to address a problem that was taking a toll on their profits: cattle rustling. Theft had been a nuisance for cattlemen on the Northern Great Plains from the beginning of the industry, becoming problematic in the late 1870s with the arrival of thousands of gold miners and prospectors in the Black Hills. The newcomers needed meat, and there were plenty of men willing to steal cattle and sell them in the gold camps. As one early South Dakota rancher noted, "the little fellow never thought of killing one of his own steers for beef but always picked on a brand belonging to some big outfit or a neighbor who lived quite a way off. . . . A lot of cattle were butchered in lonely little draws."[28]

Lemmon differentiated between thieves who stole cattle for profit and homesteaders who pilfered them to feed their children. As he put it, "We never had seriously objected to the small cattlemen and settlers butchering our cattle for winter beef when the whole carcass could be saved and consumed, but woe be to the man we could catch butchering and peddling it."[29] Although he was a businessman first and foremost, Lemmon was benevolent by nature and sympathized with needy families. His father James had demonstrated generosity in several instances, such as his profitless sale of wheat to hungry Mormons in the 1850s. Ed's munificence manifested itself in numerous other ways after he founded the town of Lemmon, including offering charitable land deals to poor ranchers and gifts of candy to children.[30]

During the 1870s and 1880s, cattle companies in Wyoming, Montana, and Dakota began organizing associations for, as one group succinctly put it, "the protection of stock and the detection and punishment of stock thieves."[31] Although some individuals, such as Montana pioneer Granville Stuart, organized vigilante groups and shot or hanged suspected horse and cattle thieves, most ranchers preferred organized deterrence over murder. These groups levied a self-assessment, usually between two and five cents per head of cattle and one or two cents per head of horses, to pay for brand inspectors and livestock detectives. A few such organizations included the Black Hills Live Stock Association, later known as the Black Hills Stock Growers Association, of which Dave Clark served a term as president; the Western Dakota Stock Association; the Fall River County Stock Growers Protective Association; the Montana Stock Growers Association; and the longstanding Wyoming Stock Growers Association (WSGA), which had been founded in 1872. Cattlemen in Dakota, including the Sheidley brothers, had been involved with the WSGA for years, and the organization maintained brand inspectors at Pierre, Deadwood, and Custer and at the Pine Ridge, Cheyenne River, and Rosebud agencies. The WSGA had sent brand inspectors into the Black Hills as early as 1876, when it was still part of the Great Sioux Reservation. As Bob Lee and Dick Williams noted in their history of the South Dakota cattle industry, "The prospectors were there illegally and so were some of the cattle, having been rustled from the nearby Wyoming ranges."[32]

The West River half of South Dakota had many individual associations designed to protect the cattlemen, but there was no overarching body covering the entire region. Large outfits like the Sheidley Cattle Company sought to organize a single, unified organization because they believed a majority of their losses were due to small ranchers who rounded up cattle they found on the range and marked them with their own brands. Small operators tended to form their own associations, and the big outfits believed these groups existed as a front to conceal theft. Lemmon contended that small operators were more prone to this activity than were large outfits, because the big ranches "had their hands full caring for legitimately acquired cattle, while the smaller owners had more time to look for mavericks or large unbranded calves old enough to wean."[33] He claimed to have known of several poor newcomers who arrived in the territory with a handful of cows and within a few years had built up herds larger than they possibly could have acquired through natural reproduction.

The poor relationship between large cattlemen and small-scale ranchers came to a head in Wyoming in April 1892. Many of Wyoming's largest ranchers were members of the wsga, and the wealthiest of these operators financed the Cheyenne Club, a prestigious social organization in the state's capital. The wsga held a great deal of political power and was the prime organizing body for annual roundups; it also established cattle-shipping schedules and employed a team of brand inspectors. In some areas, wsga ranchers had banded together and used their combined power to control large swaths of public range land, which prevented smaller cattlemen and homesteaders from using it for grazing. In retaliation, some of the smaller operators branded the mavericks they found on the range, an act the large cattlemen considered stealing. When the wsga declared war on the "rustlers" in 1890, the uneasy relationship between the two sides grew even more strained. Over the next two years, several alleged rustlers from small ranches were lynched, continuing the tradition set by Cheyenne's Vigilance Committee twenty-five years earlier. In 1891, the small-scale ranchers in Johnson County attempted to counter the WSGA by forming their own group, the Northern Wyoming Farmers and Stock Growers' Association. The WSGA blacklisted the members of this new group, which planned to hold its own roundup in the spring of 1892. It also created a list of alleged rustlers and hired twenty-three gunmen from Texas to track them down. The hired guns received five dollars per day, plus a fifty-dollar bonus for every rustler they killed. On 12 and 13 April, the WSGA and their hired men faced off against two hundred to three hundred small ranchers and their allies, with several men killed in the ensuing gunfight. Though a number of the WSGA organizers were arrested for conspiring to kill innocent men, none were prosecuted for their part in the Johnson County War.[34]

In South Dakota, there were some instances in which large operators attempted to remove small ranchers from the range, such as when the Sheidley Cattle Company and others petitioned the federal government to open the Great Sioux Reservation for grazing leases in the early 1880s. There were also occasions when large operators pushed off other outfits that violated the "rules" of the open range by infringing on another's established range. In one such instance in the 1890s, several Flying V cowboys organized a late-night roundup to remove thirty-five hundred "trespassing" cattle from the Sheidley Company's Moreau River range. A half-dozen other outfits followed suit and pushed the herd from their ranges as well; within a week the cattle ended up more than one hundred miles southwest of where they started. As Lemmon remarked, such activities ensured that the "code of the open range usually was very strictly observed."[35] He preferred to handle disagreements with other cattlemen personally, but through subtle hints such as running off a trespasser's cattle rather than direct confrontation, since hot tempers could cause itchy trigger fingers. Lemmon also found this course far easier and much more effective than involving the legal system.[36]

Dakota cattlemen also managed to avoid the violent confrontations of Wyoming because of the region's environmental characteristics. In the ponderosa pine woodlands of the Black Hills, many of the smaller operators grazed their cattle in the mountain meadows that dotted the forest. These meadows were relatively small and thus unfit for grazing thousands of cattle, so larger operators tended to run their herds on the adjacent grasslands, leaving the wooded areas to the smaller ranchers. Individual homesteaders were far more likely to take the time and effort to round up their cattle in the woods than the larger cattlemen like Lemmon, who found such activity a waste of time and resources. Anything less than one hundred head was not even a "herd" as Ed termed it, but "merely a bunch or lot" and therefore not worth the trouble.[37] It proved far easier to leave the mountain meadows to ranchers with just a few head and graze the open ranges of the public domain or the Indian reservations. This relative lack of competition, combined with illegal grazing on the Great Sioux Reservation, where all white cattle ranchers regardless of size were trespassers, differed from the situation in Wyoming and helps to explain why major conflicts like the Johnson County War did not erupt in the Dakotas.[38]

Still, problems with rustlers remained. The WSGA provided large Dakota operations some protection, but with its difficulties in 1892 many cattlemen, including Lemmon, began to realize that South Dakota needed its own organization. On 21 April, just a week after the showdown between the WSGA hired guns and the small ranchers, Lemmon and Frank Stewart boarded a Rapid City-bound train at Buffalo Gap to attend an organizational meeting of the Western South Dakota Stock Growers Association. When they reached the station, Lemmon, Stewart, and several other men set out for the Harney Hotel in a street car pulled by a plodding white horse. The hotel was not far away, and the driver, a black man carrying an umbrella, set a steady pace that would not strain the animal. Lemmon could never stand traveling any slower than at top speed, and as a cowboy riding with him recalled, Ed "grabbed the umbrella and beat the nag until he had him on the run." The group had a laugh over this characteristic Lemmon move and "pulled up in front of the Harney in great style."[39] Among the meeting's attendees were the most influential cattlemen in the region, including Rapid City mayor J. M. Woods and James ("Scotty") Philip, the visionary rancher who would earn international recognition as "the man who saved the buffalo."[40]

The Western South Dakota Stock Growers Association immediately became the most influential cattlemen's organization in the state. In 1893, the year historian Frederick Jackson Turner famously announced the closing of the frontier at the World's Columbian Exposition in Chicago, the Stock Growers added seventeen companies to its original membership of fifteen-plus cattle outfits; by 1902 the organization counted 677 members. Eventually all the smaller associations in western South Dakota would disband or merge with the Stock Growers, just as its organizers had intended. The association issued assessments on cattle and horses, employed a seasoned stock detective, Sam Moses, to investigate losses and catch rustlers, and became the principle organization for brand registration in South Dakota. Within a dozen years, the association's brand inspectors had recovered nearly forty-three thousand stolen cattle valued at $1.5 million. The Stock Growers printed their first brand book in 1893; within two years it listed brands belonging to 271 different owners. In the late nineteenth and early twentieth centuries, the Stock Growers became involved in the political process as well. They pushed for the establishment of a state brand board, implementation of statewide brand registration, and laws that continued to enable them to use "the range country in the only practical way it can be used to increase the assessed valuation of this country," that is, cattle ranching.[41] Lemmon would remain actively involved in the organization for the next two decades, serving as an elected member of its executive committee from 1892 to 1914. Although fellow members repeatedly asked Lemmon to run for president of the Stock Growers, he turned them down each time. Despite his remarkable ability to connect with people on a personal level, Lemmon appears to have suffered from stage fright. Because he could not confidently address an audience, he never ran.[42]

As the primary procurement officer for the Sheidley Cattle Company, Lemmon spent a great deal of time traveling around the country searching for low-cost, high-quality cattle to fill the Flying V ranges. After his first visit to Texas in 1891, he returned several times over the next four years, purchasing thousands of JA-branded Hereford/shorthorn/longhorn-cross cattle from Charles Goodnight's ranch in the Texas panhandle. This approach worked well for the Sheidley outfit. Buying cattle in Texas and shipping them by rail to the company's South Dakota range for fattening proved a sound business model that paid its investors handsomely. Throughout the decade, Ed also bought tens of thousands of cattle in New Mexico, Arizona, Kansas, and other states. The expansion of the national rail network facilitated Lemmon's trips and fundamentally changed the way the Sheidley outfit acquired and marketed cattle. Before the railroad reached Dakota Territory, the Flying V had to trail cattle up from Texas, a process that could take months and required hiring large numbers of cowboys. With the expansion of the rail system, the same number of cattle could arrive from the southern ranges in less than a week, with minimal additional labor. This important development was a major factor in the Sheidley Company's 12-percent annual returns.[43]

While most Flying V beeves traveled by rail to Chicago for marketing, some were trailed the old-fashioned way and sold to local Indian agencies. In 1890, the five reservations created out of the former Great Sioux Reservation—Cheyenne River, Lower Brule, Pine Ridge, Rosebud, and Standing Rock—purchased almost thirteen million pounds of beef, or roughly thirteen thousand steers, for the twenty-one thousand-plus Indians living there. The Indian agents encouraged the tribes to take up stock raising, though they continued to struggle with white trespassers.[44]

In 1892, the Pine Ridge Agency impounded three thousand head of cattle grazing illegally on the reservation. The agent announced a hearing on the issue, and although the bulk of the Flying V cattle had been moved farther north and Lemmon had no impounded animals, he attended as an interested observer. During the proceedings, a government official asked Red Cloud what he knew about trespassing cattle. As he scanned the crowd, Red Cloud saw Lemmon and pointed him out, saying, "My friend, Crooked Rump, over there used to have thousands of them grazing on my reservation, but I did not object, for he always, when rounding them up, fed me and mine bountifully, and the cattle really did us no harm for they were not near our settlement farms."[45]

Lemmon still believed that because the Indians were not using the reservation grass for their own livestock, white cattlemen should take advantage of it. Even so, he understood the potential problems in getting caught and continued the company's recent practice of grazing exclusively on the public domain. In the fall of 1894, with the majority of the Sheidley Company cattle on the Moreau

River range, he arranged to ship their beeves to market from Belle Fourche, the town founded by Black Hills lawman Seth Bullock and then the country's largest cattle-shipping point. That year alone, cow punchers loaded and shipped more than forty-seven hundred railroad cars there—upwards of ninety-four thousand cattle. Belle Fourche served southeast Montana, northeast Wyoming, and the western halves of North Dakota and South Dakota, which had been created out of Dakota Territory in 1889. Following the closing of the Great Sioux Reservation and the arrival of the Chicago & North Western Railroad in 1890, the city had seen a tremendous increase in stock numbers.[46]

The Belle Fourche stockyards offered a ready location for marketing Flying V cattle, another aspect of the industry at which Lemmon was adept. Each year, the Sheidley Cattle Company produced fifteen thousand mature beeves for the Chicago markets, so Lemmon aimed to ship about thirteen hundred head per week during the usual 10 August to 10 November shipping season. Most beef shipments took place in the fall to coincide with the natural reproduction cycle of the cattle and because severe winter weather could impede later transport. Lemmon employed four active crews during the shipping season, three to trail the cattle to the railhead and load them at the yards, and one to gather beeves from the range and bring them to a central location near Sand Creek in present-day Harding County for "shaping" (sorting the mature animals and preparing them for market). Ed preferred to finish shaping the herds by "slow trailing" the animals, covering the seventy miles to Belle Fourche in a full seven days, several miles per day slower than normal trailing. He wanted to oversee this work personally because proper shaping was essential to add extra pounds to the beeves, earning the company larger profits. Ed's determination to shape every herd the company sold necessitated long rides back to the range after he finished loading each week's shipment. He recalled that "sometimes I would be as late as 9 P.M., getting shipped out and supper and a change of horses, when I would pull for the cheese factory, 22 miles out, where I would remain for the balance of the night, and make Sand creek and my herd by the following day, . . . a 70 mile ride."[47]

Shipping from Belle Fourche required meticulous organization, in part because the livestock agent in charge of the shipping schedule had to accommodate dozens of cattle companies. Each outfit had a predetermined time for loading based on the quantity and quality of its cattle. Outfits that did not sort their beeves and had poorer-quality animals loaded in the pre-dawn or dusk hours. Most cattlemen, including Lemmon, sorted their animals according to quality to ensure high prices once their beeves reached Chicago, so they followed a daytime loading schedule that was strictly enforced. If an outfit exceeded its loading time by more than thirty minutes, it lost its loading rank for the next day and fell to the end of the line. Almost all of the larger companies, including the Sheidley operation, had agents in Chicago who helped determine the number and grade of beef marketed on a particular day.

During the peak of the shipping season, Lemmon loaded cattle five days per week: Monday, Tuesday, Thursday, Friday and Saturday. The Monday shipments included the highest-quality animals because the men buying for the packing houses in Chicago looked for the best beeves on that date. The quality decreased throughout the week, with the worst animals ("poorly fattened and trashy") sold on Saturday.[48] Lemmon did not ship on Wednesdays because the New York beef buyers who competed with the purchasing agents in Chicago did not buy cattle that day. When live cattle bought in Chicago on a Wednesday were slaughtered and shipped as beef later that week, the shipments did not arrive in New York until late Saturday or early Sunday. When sold to retail outlets on Monday, these animals were termed "stale beef" and brought a lower price.

Shipping five days per week pushed the limits of Lemmon's stamina, but to the thirty-seven-year-old this hard work was the best part of being a cowboy. In the final weeks of the season, he recalled getting so chilled that he had to roll around on the ground for "several minutes before circulation got enough restored to balance me on my feet, but I was soon in camp shoveling hot beef steak and tea down me, and the affects were hardly noticeable when remounted on one of my splendid cutting horses and [chasing] after a fat beef, for there is certainly something fascinating about cutting and shaping prime beeves, such as our free open ranges produced."[49] To Lemmon, the open range represented freedom and provided value beyond the free grass necessary to feed beef cattle at a profit. As he reflected years later, "The facts that the ranges were free were not the only redeeming features for the fact of them being open, was a still greater pleasure."[50]

Lemmon understood the value of the open range for making a profit, but he also prided himself on the Sheidley Company's marketing system, which in the mid-1890s brought solid returns. He estimated the company's average costs for buying, raising, transporting, and selling its stock at $32.75 per head, including death loss—younger or weaker animals that fell victim to disease, perished in the cold, or were killed by wolves, coyotes, or other predators—and cattle lost to rustlers. Average sale prices were $4.00 per hundredweight (hundred pounds of live weight) on twelve-hundred-pound steers, which grossed $48.00 and generated a return of approximately $15.25 per head. With the company marketing fifteen thousand head per year, it could earn profits of almost $250,000.[51]

Despite advancements made in rail transportation, shipping cattle from Belle Fourche to Chicago via the Fremont, Elkhorn & Missouri Valley Railroad still took sixty hours, a long trip for cattle unaccustomed to rail transportation. The resulting shrinkage (up to ninety pounds per head) caused unacceptable losses, in Lemmon's opinion, and he sought a better option. In 1895, Lemmon split a herd of twenty-seven hundred head in two, half of which he trailed 120 miles east to the rail terminus at Forest City, across the Missouri River from the Cheyenne River Indian Agency, and the other portion 70 miles southwest to Belle Fourche.

Forest City had constructed a rail line that merged with the Chicago & North Western Railroad line seventeen miles east at Gettysburg and promised reduced transport times to Chicago. Lemmon gathered 1,350 mature beeves and headed east to try the untested yards, employing his best slow-trailing techniques en route. They arrived on the west bank of the Missouri without difficulty, only to find that the meager holding pens had been hastily built on a sand bar prone to flooding. He also discovered that the only means of getting the cattle across the river was via two small boats that could hold a total of thirty head. For three and a half days, Lemmon and his men "worked like slaves" to move just half of their cattle across the river.[52] Frustrated with the prospect of spending a week loading the 1,350 head—a process he could normally accomplish in a day—Lemmon, who never commanded deep reserves of patience, decided to swim the balance of his herd across the wide Missouri River. He bought an old halter-broke steer from a nearby farmer to lead the herd, tied him to a canoe, and pushed the cattle into the water.

Urged on by additional hired help and a fleet of support canoes, the beeves had begun to swim across nicely until someone on the far side used a mirror to flash a light into the faces of the leading animals. The frightened cattle spun around and headed for shore, trampling and killing seventeen head when they reached the bank. Lemmon suspected one of the boat owners of causing the melee in order to continue profiting from the numerous trips. In spite of these challenges, Lemmon managed to swim the cattle across the Missouri for loading into railroad cars and shipment to the Union Stockyards. Rather than the sixty hours required to reach Chicago from Belle Fourche, the trip from Forest City took only thirty-one hours. The shorter travel time reduced shrinkage considerably, and his cattle averaged forty pounds heavier and sold for twenty cents more per hundredweight than the other 1,350 head shipped from Belle Fourche. Despite the slightly better returns, the trouble involved with shipping from Forest City far outweighed the additional profits, and Lemmon never shipped from Forest City again.[53]

By 1896, the Sheidley brothers had been operating in Dakota for sixteen years, earning strong returns due to the region's excellent grazing lands and the company's sound managers—both on the range and at company headquarters in Kansas City. Ben, George, and William Sheidley had started in business together shortly after the Civil War, with George overseeing the cattle operation following Ben's death in 1883. The Sheidleys also had interests in manufacturing, banking, and real estate, and George relied heavily on two key advisors, Richard C. Lake and Thomas B. Tomb, to assist in managing the cattle business. While Dave Clark and Ed Lemmon had handled the on-the-ground activities of the Flying V, Lake and Tomb had guided its long-term development. Lake was a thriving entrepreneur who had started to make his fortune in the Black Hills in 1876 as a hardware store owner. After profiting from selling tools and equipment to the throngs of gold miners, he invested in cattle and soon diversified into banking. By the early 1890s, Lake was the wealthiest man in the Black Hills, having a net worth approaching $1 million. Part of this wealth resulted from investments in the Sheidley Cattle Company, of which he was a partner along with Clark, the Sheidley brothers, and Thomas Tomb. Like Clark and the Sheidleys, Tomb hailed from Tiffin, Ohio, and brought banking experience to the company. He had invested in the Northern Great Plains cattle business early, having registered brands with the Wyoming Stock Growers Association in the 1870s. Tomb had also spent time working in Chicago; his personal connections in the Chicago livestock markets and banking industry contributed much to the Sheidley Cattle Company's success.[54]

Since 1895, Lake and Tomb had been urging George Sheidley to expand their cattle operation by purchasing a ranch in Texas. The Sheidleys had sold all of their southern holdings when the business moved from Nebraska to Dakota Territory in 1880, relying on the open ranges of the public domain and the Indian reservations to graze their stock. But after the breakup of the Great Sioux Reservation and its opening for settlement, Lake and Tomb began to realize that the days of open-range cattle grazing were numbered. They sought to add a measure of security to their operation by buying a ranch in the Lone Star State. The proprietors of the NUN ranch near Lubbock ran seventeen thousand head of cattle, owned fifty-four thousand acres, and were looking to sell. Lake and Tomb also identified 306,000 acres adjacent to the NUN that they could lease, which would give them 360,000 acres in Texas from which to initiate a new management system developed in conjunction with Lemmon. They planned to stock the Texas land almost exclusively with breeding animals, taking advantage of the milder weather to reduce winter death loss and ease spring calving. In the spring, the company would ship its weaned calves north to South Dakota, grazing them on the quality grasses of the open range. Early in 1896, George Sheidley assented to the purchase; on 2 March, the sixty-three-year-old had a stroke and died.[55]

Lake and Tomb continued to implement their plans following George's death, arranging to drill wells, erect windmills, and install tanks at forty locations on the newly acquired Texas lands. George's shares in the cattle operation passed to his brother William and sister Sarah, both of whom played no active role in the company's management. For Lemmon, Sheidley's death meant the loss of his best friend, but it is unlikely this event affected him greatly. Ed had lost his only confidant, his older brother Hervey, ten years earlier and never shared the same closeness with anyone else. Shortly after George's death, Lemmon headed south to direct the initial setup of the NUN operation. Meanwhile, Lake and Tomb continued to broaden the scope of the company's cattle business. To accommodate the growing herd, they arranged to move some stock from the Moreau River range in South Dakota to a new location on the Big Dry range northwest of Miles City, Montana, near present-day Jordan.[56]

With no Sheidley family members actively participating in the cattle segment of the family's various business ventures, Lake and Tomb encountered no opposition when they proposed to develop the Texas and Montana portions as a separate enterprise. They organized their interests as Lake, Tomb & Company, marking their twenty thousand cattle with the Reverse L7 brand (ᒍⲅ). The pair continued to remain involved with the Sheidley Cattle Company, however, as did Lemmon, who served as general manager of both operations and retained his ownership stake. The Sheidley Cattle Company continued using the Flying V brand on its forty thousand cattle and printed new letterhead with Lemmon's name prominently centered. Sheidley Cattle Company wagon boss Bird Rose (in Lemmon's words, "the best technical cow man I ever knew") moved to Lake, Tomb & Co., becoming range manager of the NUN operation in Texas, while Sam Sheffield, Lemmon's range boss since 1891, remained with the Sheidley Company.[57]

For Lemmon, Lake, and Tomb, the future seemed bright. On 6 November 1896, just days after that fall's presidential election, Lemmon wrote, "We . . . all feel very Jubilant over our success."[58] He referred to Republican William McKinley's victory over Democrat William Jennings Bryan, but he could have been describing the trio's attitudes toward the cattle business. Lake and Tomb had already earned hundreds of thousands of dollars selling beeves; their Texas-Montana venture had begun to take off; and with Lemmon handling the day-to-day operations, all three had abundant cause for optimism. The following year, Ed had another reason to feel

Sheidley Cattle Company letterhead.
Betsy Sheidley Fletcher collection

jubilant when he successfully bossed one of the country's largest cattle roundups.[59]

Because of Lemmon's unquestioned cattle-handling skills and renowned organizational talents, other cattle outfits often looked to him to boss their spring roundups. In late June 1897 on the Peno Flats east of present-day Wall, South Dakota, five hundred cowboys gathered fifty thousand head during the largest cattle roundup any of the participants had ever seen. This huge undertaking marked the convergence of four separate roundups, consisting of twenty different crews and sixty reps charged with inspecting the brand on every cow, calf, and steer on the grounds. The roundup was considered a "general cleanup" for the entire region, stretching from the Cheyenne River on the north and west, east to the Missouri River, and south to the Nebraska border. A skilled roundup boss named George Jackson had initially been tasked with managing the event, but as cowboy John Anderson recalled, "As Jackson viewed the situation, 50,000 cattle, 20 wagons, 500 men, 4000 saddle horses—he felt himself pitifully small for the job."[60] Jackson turned the management responsibilities over to Lemmon, saying, "You have worked more cattle than I have ever seen. You can handle men better than I. I wish you would take over." Lemmon replied, "If that is the way you feel about it, all right. Let's get to work."[61] He implemented an innovative system of organization, forming several bunches of five hundred head each, spaced in a circular orientation. Ed instructed all of the bosses to move the cattle counterclockwise in order to reduce the chances of head-on collisions when sorting them back into larger groups. After giving his orders, Lemmon rode to a small butte with a view of the entire roundup grounds, occasionally riding down to give instructions. Incredibly, the five hundred cowboys managed to work five cattle herds each day, finishing the entire cleanup of fifty thousand head—a job that could have taken two weeks or more—in only four days.[62]

For Lemmon, the Peno Flats roundup marked one of the high points of his life. He had put his twenty years of cattle-handling experience to the test and passed with unquestioned success. Physically, he was short and crippled, but when working cattle in the saddle he towered above other men. He may not have looked as natural on a horse as Buffalo Bill Cody, but no one doubted his remarkable skill. Lemmon's success stemmed largely from ambition and an intense desire to demonstrate that his infirmity was no match for his determination. Natural talent, combined with a tendency to outwork every man in camp, paid off in the widespread recognition of his abilities. He believed he had bossed the world's largest roundup—taking over for a man who did not feel up to the task—and in so doing earned the respect and admiration of other cowboys. Lemmon had always felt comfortable on the range, but handling a group of fifty thousand cattle confirmed his belief in his own abilities. Now forty, he was in his prime and making a name for himself. As Anderson recalled in a 1950 interview, "Ed Lemmon, who handled this Roundup, was always considered to have been easily the best all-around cowman in South Dakota. His ability to work a large group of men to get best results, his knowledge of cattle, always knowing just what they were thinking about—was phenomenal."[63] Ed could not have asked for higher praise.

Expansion of the Sheidley enterprises continued in 1898, even as one era in the company's history came to a close. William, the last of the original company founders, passed away that year; like his brother George, he willed his shares in the cattle operation to Sarah Sheidley. Lemmon also transferred his company stock in 1898, selling it to range foreman Sam Sheffield. Ed wanted to free up capital so he could buy into another of Lake and Tomb's ventures, a livestock enterprise known as the Lake, Tomb & Lemmon Company. The new company continued its relationship with the Sheidley family and marked its cattle with the Reverse L7 brand.

Since 1880, Lemmon had worked for various cattle outfits owned or controlled by the Sheidleys, including D. H. Clark & Co., the Sheidley Cattle Company, and Lake, Tomb & Company. He continued that relationship with Lake, Tomb & Lemmon, for although the exact accounting of these businesses is unclear, the Sheidley name was affiliated with them all. Ed's decision to sell out of the Sheidley Cattle Company was probably motivated by a desire to participate more fully in the business portion of the cattle operation, an aspect previously controlled almost entirely by managers in Kansas City. It also made sense financially, as Lemmon would eventually earn a 15-percent ownership stake in fifty-three thousand head.[64]

His interest in the fiscal management of Lake, Tomb & Lemmon was probably heightened during their annual business meeting in Chicago, which continued a tradition the Sheidley brothers had started years before. Each year since becoming general manager of the Sheidley Cattle Company, Lemmon had met Lake, Tomb, George and William Sheidley, and the other partners for several weeks of winter meetings. They reflected on the season's results, arranged marketing opportunities with potential buyers, and discussed plans for the coming year. Ed usually took a room at the Great Northern, an expensive hotel downtown at the corner of Dearborn Street and Jackson Boulevard. After several weeks in the noisy city center, he longed for the calm and quiet of the open range and sought cheaper lodgings on west Thirty-ninth Street, not far from the Union Stockyards. Throughout the 1890s, Lemmon spent months in Chicago but never truly felt comfortable there. He disliked the "adulterated air," congestion, and artificiality of city life.[65] Lemmon was a man who always preferred the "$6 California trousers" cowboys wore to the three-piece suits of the company's financial backers.[66] He also never quite got over the fashion of wearing pant legs over boot tops. An intensely practical man, Lemmon found it difficult to "pull my trouser legs out of my boot tops and . . . let them drag under my heels, gathering up all dust and refuse on the streets."[67]

Ed attended the annual Chicago meetings by himself, always leaving his family back in South Dakota. In 1891, Lemmon had moved Bertha and their three sons, James, Roy, and George, from the Flying V headquarters outside of Buffalo Gap to a small house in north Rapid City, possibly on what is Lemmon Avenue today. On 13

February 1896, the family moved into a modest home at the corner of Quincy and Seventh streets near the city center. If anything, Ed visited his wife and children even less frequently when they lived in Rapid City, since the town was ninety miles from the Flying V's range on the Moreau River. Life on the Great Plains was fun, exciting, and fulfilling for Ed, and he demonstrated little desire to spend time with his family. By the late 1890s, about the time the United States reaffirmed its national manhood by winning a "splendid little war" against Spain, Lemmon suffered a blow to his honor that challenged his dominion over his wife. Fed up with his lack of attention, womanizing, and overall indifference, Bertha—only in her twenties—divorced him. Even though he had done little to deserve her loyalty, Lemmon strongly resented her for the rest of his life. As with his mother Lucy, Lemmon is almost completely silent about his first wife, mentioning her only a few times in his more than eight hundred pages of reminiscences. When he did write of Bertha, he did not call her by name but referred to her only as "my wife" and, in one strikingly cold reference, "the mother."[68]

Characteristically, Lemmon did not quit seeking companionship after his divorce. At the January 1900 National Live Stock Association annual meeting in Fort Worth, Texas, he became envious of cattleman Scotty Philip's "lady escapades."[69] Philip had earned a substantial fortune in cattle and buffalo ranching and he spent lavishly on food, drinks, jewelry, and lace stockings for women at the convention. As a result, Lemmon recalled, Philip "added many notches to his gun stock, but not for the killing of men, but palpitating hearts."[70] Lemmon was chagrined by these developments, which rendered him "rather on the scrub order."[71] He redeemed himself two months later when he married Rosella B. Boe at Edgemont, South Dakota, on 4 March, the day of her twenty-fourth birthday. Rosella was six years younger than Bertha and almost twenty years younger than Ed, who would turn forty-three in May. The similarities between Lemmon's marriages were striking. Both women were young and attractive, possessed limited financial resources, and married following a brief courtship. They also shared a complete lack of understanding of Lemmon's character. But Lemmon was a well-known, respected cattleman, on solid financial footing and with strong prospects for the future—qualities that appealed to

Rosella. He could also be charming, an attribute that enhanced his ability to make a lasting first impression and probably helped to win over both of his wives. Lemmon's charm faded with time, however, and like his marriage to Bertha, his relationship with Rosella would end in divorce.[72]

After suffering through a decade of childrearing with virtually no assistance from her husband and years of loneliness caused by his extended absences, Bertha likely would have fumed over the way Lemmon indulged Rosella in their first few months of marriage. He bought expensive gifts, catered to her desires, and treated his new bride and two sisters-in-law to a five-day honeymoon trip to Chihuahua, Mexico. The couple thoroughly enjoyed themselves, touring a brewery (where Ed failed to finish the only two beers he ever tasted), visiting a factory where they watched workers weave exquisite rugs ("of course, we then had to buy one"), witnessing a cockfight, gambling in the casinos, and attending a bullfight ("the most exciting performance I ever witnessed").[73] When they returned to South Dakota, Ed secured a house for Rosella in Spearfish, fifty miles north of Rapid City in the northern Black Hills. Lemmon's new "home" was closer to the Flying V range on the Moreau River, but being outside of Rapid City also made it far easier to avoid accidental encounters with his ex-wife. This concern disappeared the following year after Bertha married Joseph Pitt in a small ceremony at her Rapid City home. No doubt anxious for a fresh start away from Ed, the couple moved the boys six hundred miles southwest to Palisade, Colorado, a short time later. For the next eight years, Ed would have limited contact with his sons.[74]

During the 1890s, Lemmon's reputation for cattle-handling skill, widespread knowledge of the region's topography, and ability to get along with a broad range of personalities made him a popular cattleman. It also placed his services in high demand. As general manager of the Flying V, he traveled the country on cattle-buying trips, building up the Sheidley Cattle Company's herds to as many as sixty thousand head. In the spring, he regularly served as boss for many of the region's general roundups, and in the fall he guided the "shaping" of nearly every beef animal his outfit shipped to Chicago. As a cattle buyer, roundup boss, and general manager, Lemmon worked tens of thousands of animals per year. His experience

working with large herds, efficiency in leading roundups, and tremendous longevity enabled him to work an incredible number of
cattle during his open-range days. Within a few years, Lemmon
would be recognized as having saddle-handled more cattle than
any other cowboy—perhaps a million head. But the days of open-
range cattle ranching were numbered, as Lake and Tomb foresaw;
they addressed this potential change by purchasing the NUN ranch
in Texas and acquiring the Big Dry range in Montana. By the beginning of the twentieth century, Lemmon held a respectable share in
the burgeoning cattle enterprise of Lake, Tomb & Lemmon, fulfilling the dream he had envisioned as a common range cowboy more
than a decade earlier. Still unsatisfied, he began looking for an opportunity to secure a tract of land for cattle grazing that could fore-
stall the end of the open range for a few more years. Lemmon found
his opportunity in a familiar place: an Indian reservation.[75]

6 THE LARGEST FENCED PASTURE IN THE WORLD

Ed Lemmon was no stranger to grazing cattle on Indian lands in western South Dakota, having illegally ranged beeves on the Great Sioux Reservation from the Sheidley Cattle Company's arrival in Dakota Territory in 1880 until the reservation was divided into the Standing Rock, Cheyenne River, Pine Ridge, Rosebud, and Lower Brule reservations in 1890. Although Lemmon's Flying V outfit ran its cattle outside of reservation boundaries for most of the 1890s, many other white cattlemen continued to trespass. In the early 1900s, federal officials in the Department of the Interior, including Commissioner of Indian Affairs William A. Jones, began to investigate the possibility of leasing Indian lands in South Dakota to white ranchers. The Standing Rock Indian Reservation, which straddled the North Dakota-South Dakota state line just west of the Missouri River, emerged as a focal point in the battle between the country's pro-grazing and anti-grazing forces; it also became home to a privately controlled lease larger than the state of Rhode Island, an extensive enclosure Lemmon called "the largest fenced pasture in the world."[1]

The Standing Rock reservation, bordered on the south by the Cheyenne River Indian Reservation and on the north and east by the Cannonball and Missouri rivers, covered more than two million acres of Northern Great Plains grassland. The reservation received its name from a stone formation resembling a woman with an infant strapped to her back located near the agency headquarters at Fort Yates, North Dakota. The Standing Rock Sioux included several bands: the Hunkpapa and Sihasapa Lakota; the Hunkpatina and Cuthead Dakota; and the Yanktonai Nakota. These bands tended

William A Jones.
*Wisconsin Historical
Society, 30884*

to live in separate locations, with the Dakotas and Nakotas residing primarily on the North Dakota side, the Hunkpapas in the central portion, and the Sihasapas in the south, next to the Cheyenne River reservation. Some Sihasapas also lived at Cheyenne River, along with members of the Miniconjou, Itazipco, and Oohenumpa bands. The settlements on Standing Rock were located near water sources such as the Grand River, which flowed west to east through the reservation, leaving vast areas with no permanent structures.[2]

Leasing out land on Standing Rock had several advantages from Jones's perspective, and in seeking to establish leases he was doing what he considered to be in "the best interests of the Indians."[3] Born in 1844 in Wales, Jones emigrated to the United States with his parents at age seven. He grew up in Wisconsin, becoming an educator and serving as superintendent of Iowa County schools from 1877 to 1881. He then moved into banking and business, founding the First National Bank of Mineral Point, Wisconsin, and investing in a zinc-mining company in the same city. He resigned his positions in both endeavors in 1897 when President William McKinley appointed him commissioner of Indian affairs. Jones took office ten years after the passage of the Dawes General Allotment Act, which had opened the Great Sioux Reservation to non-Indian homesteaders and resulted in a significant loss of Indian land. As commissioner, he dedicated himself to making Indians responsible for their own welfare, following a "well known policy of doing away as fast as possible with tribal funds."[4] A devoted Republican, he sought to cut government spending on the reservations and believed that raising livestock offered the greatest opportunity for Indians on South Dakota's reservations to become self-sufficient.[5]

By 1901, Jones knew the tribes did not have enough cattle to become self-reliant but thought grazing leases could solve this problem and others plaguing the reservations. He was keenly aware that white cattlemen had illegally used reservation grass in western South Dakota for years. Dozens of large and small ranchers ran thousands of head—perhaps as many as fifty thousand animals on the Cheyenne River reservation alone—inside the reservation boundaries without compensating the tribe. Illegal grazing was difficult to track, and because trespassing cattle that had been forcibly removed from the unfenced reservations could easily return within days, it was even more difficult to stop. George H. Bingenheimer, the Indian agent at Standing Rock, did not have a clear understanding of the policy regarding illegal grazing, asking Jones, "Have I the right to impound these cattle and horses for trespass and hold them until a reasonable settlement has been made, or can they only be turned back across the line?"[6]

This ambiguity was partly a product of Bingenheimer's inexperience—he had been the agent only since 1898—and partly the result of a lax federal policy that took no great pains to punish trespassing ranchers. In addition, the prevalence of "squaw men"—white men (such as Scotty Philip) who married Indian women and thus acquired legal access to reservation grasslands—threatened to undermine Jones's vision of the future on these reservations. These men grazed thousands of their own cattle on the reservations and sometimes contracted with outside ranchers to utilize the grasslands for their stock as well, depriving Indians of a key potential source of income. The commissioner found it "manifestly unfair and unjust . . . to permit a few intermarried whites and progressive mixed-bloods to monopolize practically all the common lands, . . . whereas, if the lands were leased for the benefit of the tribe, all would share alike in the financial results."[7]

Jones began developing a plan for leasing a portion of Standing Rock that would include several conditions to address these problems. He wanted to limit the number of cattle on the range so the prairie would not lose its productivity through overgrazing. To accomplish this goal, he expected the lessee to erect a fence around the entire pasture, which would become the tribe's property once the five- or ten-year lease ran out. The fence would protect Indian crops and settlements from intruding livestock and prevent white ranchers from trespassing once the lease ended. The profits would finance tribal purchases of cattle, thus eliminating all or most of the government's obligations to care for the Indians. With a number of cattle outfits looking to expand their holdings and increasing numbers of new homesteaders threatening to end the era of open-range grazing, Jones figured that a secure, long-term lease would be an attractive alternative for many cattlemen and lead to high bids. Jones saw leasing Standing Rock as a cost-saving measure that addressed illegal grazing, one of the key challenges facing Indian self-sufficiency on the reservations of western South Dakota.[8]

Federal officials were not the only parties interested in leasing land on the Standing Rock reservation to white ranchers. The Chicago, Milwaukee & St. Paul Railroad had arrived on the east bank of the Missouri River in 1900, terminating the line at a small, ramshackle community called Evarts. The Milwaukee sited Evarts across the river from the north-south line dividing the Standing Rock and Cheyenne River reservations, hoping to capitalize on the cattle grazing there and anticipating an opportunity to extend the railroad west across the Missouri. Although initially not much more than a haphazard collection of crude wooden buildings, Evarts thrived as a livestock shipping point because the railroad made several investments to ensure its success. It erected a large stockyard in town and constructed substantial holding pens across the river to the west. Hired men dug "dipping" facilities—channels filled with lime, sulfur, and other anti-parasitic solutions in which cattle were immersed as a means to eradicate diseases like scabies (a contagious skin disease) and the widely maligned Texas Fever. The Milwaukee also built a pontoon bridge and later provided a ferry service so ranchers would not have to chance swimming their cattle across the river—a dangerous activity that could result in the deaths of cattle and cowboys.[9]

To facilitate trailing cattle across the reservations to Evarts, the railroad reached an agreement with officials in charge of the Cheyenne River Indian Agency, securing the use of a six-mile-wide section of land in the extreme northern portion of the reservation. This parcel, known as "the strip," was a fenced thoroughfare extending from the reservation's western border eighty miles east to the Missouri River, with the northernmost fence running along the Standing Rock reservation's southern boundary. The fence featured gates to allow access to the trail, and eventually the six-mile-wide right-of-way contained several stock dams for watering cattle. By arrangement with the cattlemen, sheep were banned from the strip, and the Sioux Indians on Cheyenne River received twenty five cents for each beef animal trailed there.[10]

The existence of the strip and the large number of cattle grazing in western South Dakota both on and off the reservations helped to make Evarts one of the largest livestock shipping points on the Missouri River. In 1904 alone, the Milwaukee line shipped almost forty thousand head from the Evarts terminal, many of them Reverse L7 cattle owned by Ed Lemmon. The railroad wasted no time looking to expand on these profits and as early as 1901 began undertaking surveys to extend the line across the river. The Milwaukee also sent agents into the region to test the Sioux Indians' reaction to the possibility of opening the reservations for cattle grazing. As George Kennan, a correspondent for the New York City magazine *The Outlook*, noted, such an arrangement "would be profitable to the stockmen, and . . . increase the business of the railroad."[11]

The Sioux on the Standing Rock and Cheyenne River reservations found that the questions surrounding grazing leases had no

125

*Largest
Fenced
Pasture
in the
World*

easy answers. As historian Peter Iverson has demonstrated, reservation Indians in the first decade of the twentieth century were still posing fundamental questions about their altered existence. How should they make a living? How should they use the land? And if "outsiders asked for access to lands that few or no one occupied or used," they said, "then perhaps we can agree to it. However, if it is truly our land, do we not have the right to say no?"[12] These difficult questions had no clear answers, particularly when they involved a government that many Indians had ample reason to distrust.

In May 1901, Agent Bingenheimer held two councils at Standing Rock to present a proposal for charging white cattlemen to graze their animals on the reservation. The Milwaukee Railroad also sent a representative, a man named Hunter, to encourage the Indians to lease out their lands for grazing. The plan called for the development of a permit system, whereby white ranchers would be charged one dollar per head per year for cattle already grazing on the reservation. While this approach fell short of Jones's vision, he believed it would be more palatable to tribal members because it did not greatly change the current arrangement except to generate financial returns; after all, thousands of cattle were already grazing illegally, so their owners might as well pay for the privilege. Hunter told the Indians that the arrangement "is for your interest and ours. It will give you a dollar a year for every critter and for every calf that is branded. It will give us the hauling of these 10,000 cattle every year."[13] In addition, the permit holders would pay fifty cents per ton for all the hay they cut themselves and a higher figure for any hay the tribe provided. "At present," he stated, "you will get nothing for this land that lies useless."[14]

A small contingent of Sioux, members of the Returned Students' Association, supported the proposal. These generally younger Indians had left the reservation to attend boarding schools such as Hampton Normal and Agricultural Institute in Virginia or Carlisle Indian Industrial School in Pennsylvania and returned to the reservation after graduating. Considered by Bingenheimer to be the tribe's most progressive members, they recognized the economic advantages of the plan and urged its passage. This group was in the minority, however. Representatives of the older generations stated that they already had fifteen thousand head of their own cattle and seventy-five hundred horses grazing on the reservation and that dividing ten thousand dollars between the thirty-seven hundred reservation residents would do much less good than selling their own stock. Rather than reducing illegal grazing, many tribal members believed the permit system would lead to even more cattle trespassing on the reservation. Despite the urging of the Returned Students' Association members, most of the Sioux on Standing Rock were skeptical of any new agreement with the federal government and rejected the plan.[15]

Jones was disappointed with the decision but undeterred. He continued to press for reservation leases, writing, "I would like very much to have the surplus lands [on the Standing Rock and Cheyenne River reservations] used for grazing, but cannot do so without the Indians' consent, and it seems, at present, that we are unable to secure it."[16] At the time, Jones operated under an interpretation of federal law that required approval from three-fourths of all males over the age of eighteen to approve the plan. Throughout the summer of 1901, Jones worked with Bingenheimer to try to convince the men on Standing Rock that charging ranchers for grazing rights would benefit the tribe. The Milwaukee Railroad continued to encourage leases as well. In June, an unidentified man who may have been employed by the railroad—possibly Hunter—stopped at rancher William Wade's home in south-central North Dakota. The man stated that he was "looking over" the reservation with the expectation of leasing it.[17] Wade had situated his small ranch just north of the reservation boundary, and since his cattle trespassed there, he had a strong interest in keeping its grasses available for his herd. In an effort to convince Wade to support the reservation leases, the man told him that Commissioner Jones was involved in acquiring them. In the coming months, this innocuous statement would provide the tinder for a fiery debate.[18]

That September, as the fall cattle-shipping season began to heat up, President McKinley traveled to Buffalo, New York, to attend the Pan-American Exposition. On the afternoon of 6 September, he was greeting the public at the Temple of Music when an anarchist named Leon Czolgosz fired two shots, severely wounding him. Although McKinley initially appeared to be recovering, an infection set in, and he died on 14 September 1901. His forty-two-year-old vice president, Theodore Roosevelt, took the oath of office that afternoon and became the youngest president in United States history. Born in 1858 into a wealthy New York family, Roosevelt was a sickly child who spent much of his time reading and studying nature. As a young man he embraced exercise and a "strenuous life" as a means to overcome his physical limitations. He graduated from Harvard University in 1880 and served in the New York State Assembly. In early 1884, his wife and his mother died within hours of each other; later that year, disillusioned by party politics at the Republican National Convention, he sought respite at a remote ranch in western North Dakota. Roosevelt lost most of his cattle herd during the severe winter of 1886–1887 and returned to New York, where he reentered politics, serving as New York City police commissioner and assistant secretary of the United States Navy. After leaving his post to volunteer for duty in the Spanish-American War, Roosevelt was elected as New York's governor in 1898 and became McKinley's running mate in the 1900 presidential election. His succession to the presidency in 1901 played a key role in Lemmon's acquisition of the Standing Rock lease.[19]

On 4 October, Secretary of the Interior Ethan Allen Hitchcock wrote to Commissioner Jones granting him permission to implement the "permit system of taxation for resident cattle and the permit system of pasturage for outside cattle on the Standing Rock reservation."[20] Within a month of Roosevelt taking office, the administration—possibly due to Jones's urging or, perhaps, at the behest of the new man in the Oval Office—adjusted its interpretation of federal law, allowing Indian agents to charge white cattlemen for grazing on the reservation without a vote of the Indians living there. Jones notified Bingenheimer of the decision, and the agent spread word to railroad officials and area ranchers, including William Wade and Ed Lemmon, that the Standing Rock reservation would be opened legally for cattle grazing in the spring of 1902. Bingenheimer called a council and explained to the Indians that white ranchers would now have to pay for grazing cattle under terms similar to those outlined five months earlier. He also described a new provision that would require Indian families who owned more than one hundred cattle to pay a one-dollar tax on each additional animal. The limit was designed to prevent "enterprising squaw-men and mixed-bloods" from using more than their share of the range, but it imposed a burden many Indians thought unfair.[21] Given the new legal interpretation, Jones and Bingenheimer took little notice of their objections and "did not contemplate securing the consent of the tribe for [the system's] inauguration."[22]

129

*Largest
Fenced
Pasture
in the
World*

The following month, Jones began to explore options for implementing a grazing plan more extensive than the permit system outlined in October and similar to his initial ideas for leasing Standing Rock. The permit system would generate about ten thousand dollars annually, but Jones believed the reservation had the potential to produce far greater returns. No accurate surveys of Standing Rock had been finished, and his reservation maps were incomplete, but it appeared to Jones that roughly two million acres could be leased with minimal impact on the tribe. He estimated that the range could support one cow for every forty acres, a low stocking rate that would allow grazing for up to fifty thousand head. The lessee (he rightly believed that leasing to one outfit rather than several would make administration easier) would fence the area to protect Indian settlements and to ensure that the stocking rate was not abused. Jones estimated that a lease of three cents per acre would bring in about sixty thousand dollars per year—$1.20 per head, and six times more than the permit system. Over five years, it would generate enough revenue to buy an impressive cattle herd and move the Standing Rock Sioux one step closer to self-sufficiency.[23]

Jones had no experience in managing a livestock enterprise, however, and overestimated the feasibility of his plans. On 23 December, he published notices in the major stock newspapers of Chicago, Omaha, and Kansas City announcing that bids for grazing leases on a large tract in the western two-thirds of the Standing Rock reservation would open on 10 January 1902. He also wrote personal letters to cattlemen and railroad officials announcing the opening. John J. Roche, secretary-treasurer of the Omaha Cattle Loan Company and a friend of Jones, responded that the proposed conditions "knock me out." The cost of such a lease was far higher than his company could afford. Furthermore, he did "not believe that you can get reasonable parties to lease the land at the figures you name, and, in addition to this, pay for fencing it and then give the fencing away at the end of five years to the Indians."[24] As Jones would soon learn, Northern Great Plains cattlemen were shrewd businessmen who would not pay high rates for land they had been using at no cost for more than twenty years.

Three days after the commissioner published the lease offering, 771 of the 983 adult male Indians on the Standing Rock reservation (seventy-eight percent) voted to authorize a five-year grazing lease on the reservation's "unoccupied portions."[25] The document, which the Sioux considered an agreement subject to their approval, included a number of additional stipulations, including a rate of one dollar per head per year; proper fencing to be built, paid for, and maintained by the lessee(s), which the tribe would own after the lease ended; and provisions to address disease control. The tribe, "fearing that the 'permit system' would be worse for us than the regular mode of leasing," adopted the plan under the condition that a committee of three Indians and Agent Bingenheimer would mark the boundaries of the tract to be leased.[26] Tribal leaders and Bingenheimer apparently agreed verbally to the latter provision because it was not included in the written document the Indians signed, which "covered only the bare fact of their consent to the leasing of lands."[27] To help achieve this favorable vote, the Milwaukee Railroad had secretly employed Louis P. Primeau, a mixed-blood Sioux who served as an interpreter, to help persuade his fellow Indians to support opening the reservation for livestock grazing. As compensation for his lobbying efforts, Primeau received five hundred dollars and an annual pass on the Milwaukee Road.[28]

At the time of the vote, Jones believed that he did not need the consent of the Standing Rock Sioux to institute the lease. The United States attorney general had determined in October that the federal government held the final say in the terms of any reservation lease, and Jones operated under that assumption. A few months later, when the nature of the lease came into question, the commissioner claimed a different interpretation, noting

It is . . . pointed out that the terms of the leases as drawn do not agree with the tribal consent, intending to convey the impression that the Department had entered into an *agreement* with the Indians relative to leasing their lands and had then broken faith with them.

Nothing could be further from the truth. The council proceedings are in no sense an *agreement*—unless it be an agreement among the Indians themselves, to which this Department is in no degree a party. The law provides that surplus tribal lands "may be leased by authority of the council speaking for such Indians . . . in such quantities and upon such terms and conditions as the Agent in charge of such reservation may recommend." The law, therefore, does not contemplate that "the council speaking for such Indians" shall do more than give its consent to the leasing; the quantity of land to be leased and the terms and conditions are to be left to the Agent in charge, subject of course, to the directions of the Department.[29]

Regardless of his future reinterpretation, as Jones viewed the situation in December 1901 the tribe had clearly voted in favor of leasing, which simply reinforced his authority. The commissioner believed that the attorney general's opinion gave him, through Agent Bingenheimer, full discretion for determining the size, location, stocking rates, leasing price, and all other relevant details of a lease on the Standing Rock reservation. All Jones needed to complete his plans were willing ranchers.[30]

One of the cattlemen interested in the Standing Rock lease was Ed Lemmon. For several years he and his partners, Thomas Tomb and Richard Lake, had recognized that the days of open-range cattle grazing were coming to a close. Newcomers with their small herds had hindered the expansion of large-scale operations on the Northern Great Plains since the late 1880s; by the twentieth century, most cattlemen were taking steps to address the situation. When settlers began homesteading sections of land and fencing off the range in western South Dakota during the 1890s, Lake and Tomb purchased land in Texas and secured additional grasslands in Montana. Leasing Standing Rock offered a unique opportunity to continue their operations with few significant alterations. Lemmon, Lake, and Tomb met in Chicago that winter—as they had for a number of years as employees of the Sheidley Cattle Company—and probably discussed the challenges and opportunities involved with a reservation grazing lease. Over time, the trio had come to know a number of railroad executives in the Windy City, including those of the Chicago, Milwaukee & St. Paul, which had its headquarters there. Ever since the Milwaukee founded Evarts, the railroad had expressed strong interest in stocking greater numbers of cattle on the Standing Rock and Cheyenne River reservations. Lemmon, Lake, and Tomb knew the Milwaukee had participated in discussions with the Sioux on Standing Rock in May and likely consulted with its executives to gain insight into the negotiations on the lease. It was probably during their time in Chicago that the partners in the Lake, Tomb & Lemmon Company decided to try to acquire a lease on Standing Rock.[31]

Lemmon and Lake arrived in Washington, D.C., on 8 January 1902 to submit a bid. Their strategy called for Lemmon to seek the lease in his name, with Lake and Tomb providing financial support. Lemmon met Commissioner Jones the following day and became one of six parties, including William Wade and Omaha cattleman W. I. Walker, to submit bids. Walker, who had known Lemmon for several years, had also traveled to Washington to see about the lease. In the advertisement, Jones had announced that more than 2.1 million acres would be available, with the rate determined on a per-acre basis. By January, he realized that his faulty map had caused him to overstate the available acreage by nearly twofold. Jones subsequently notified the bidders that the actual tract included roughly 1.25 million acres—the entire western two-thirds of Standing Rock—for which he hoped to receive a minimum bid of three cents per acre.[32]

Commissioner Jones opened the sealed bids on 10 January and Lemmon and Walker quickly emerged as the frontrunners. Two other parties had submitted higher bids, but they were inconsistent with the terms of the advertisement soliciting proposals, and Jones rejected them. The highest offer came in at 3.75 cents per acre but included provisions allowing the outfit to trail cattle to the Evarts railhead over the eastern third of the reservation, which was not included in the lease. The two companies whose bids were rejected could afford to submit higher bids because their shareholders anticipated a dramatic expansion in acreage as they trailed their beeves to market over the course of "a month or two."[33] This approach was probably not unlike the shaping technique Lemmon had used on the ranges northeast of Belle Fourche, where his cattle spent most of the grazing season far out on the range before being moved to a special location for finishing on the drive. The rejected proposals also would have allowed the companies to avoid using the strip to bring their cattle to Evarts. If these outfits could circumvent the twenty-five-cent per-head toll on the strip and access grass outside of the actual lease boundaries, their ventures could prove profitable even with higher bids. Jones objected to the notion of grazing outside the set boundaries because trespassing had caused him to propose the lease in the first place. He saw these requests as a continuation of the former practice.

133

Largest
Fenced
Pasture
in the
World

Lemmon and Walker submitted the next-highest bids. Both had proposed an identical figure of 3.05 cents per acre and complied with all the provisions outlined in the advertisement, including a deposit of 5 percent of the entire bid amount. Since both men were present during the bid opening, they discussed the matter with Jones and agreed to divide the 1.25 million acres into two portions, with Lemmon receiving an L-shaped tract of roughly 780,000 acres in the extreme north and west and Walker taking the remainder, a rectangular section of 460,000 acres. Lemmon's lease would include Standing Rock's relatively unoccupied areas and allow for watering on the Cannonball and Grand rivers. Walker's portion was closer to Evarts but had fewer acres and included several settled areas, and its only significant water source was the Grand River. Jones found this agreement satisfactory, particularly because it would result in the construction of an additional fifty-four miles of fence, which would revert to the Indians when the lease expired in 1907.[34]

The proposed Lemmon and Walker leases came under scrutiny almost immediately. On 13 January, three Standing Rock chiefs, Thunder Hawk, Walking Shooter, and Weasel Bear, sent a telegram to Democratic senator James K. Jones of Arkansas, a former chairman and current member of the Senate Committee on Indian Affairs, requesting an investigation. They asserted that four hundred families opposed the leases because the cattle would overrun their crops and farms. In addition, the Indian Rights Association (IRA), a Philadelphia-based advocacy group, asserted that the leases violated treaty obligations and that the cattle would damage Indian crops planted along the rivers. The IRA would later make a number of other objections, contending that the Indians were not consulted prior to making the lease; the lease price was too low; the amount of land was too great; the land should not be leased at all; and the railroad was the driving force behind the issuance. In response to these charges, Senator Jones requested a hearing to explore the circumstances surrounding the proposed Standing Rock lease. The Committee on Indian Affairs held its first hearing on 16 January.[35]

During the inquiry, Commissioner William Jones explained his actions over the previous year, outlining the extent of trespassing on Standing Rock, describing the attorney general's opinion regarding the leasing of Indian lands without their consent, and clarifying how he had arrived at the terms of the proposed leases for Lemmon and Walker. The commissioner also read a letter from former Standing Rock Indian Agent James McLaughlin, in which he offered strong support for grazing leases. Because McLaughlin had a reputation for honesty and fair dealings with the Indians—even though he and Commissioner Jones shared the paternalistic attitudes that characterized many white leaders of the day—his determination that the lease was "in the interests of the Indians" carried great weight with committee members.[36] In addition to the commissioner's testimony and McLaughlin's letter, questionable statements from Senator Robert J. Gamble of South Dakota, who suggested offering concessions to smaller ranchers trespassing on the reservation, convinced Senator Jones that something had to be done to address illegal grazing. By the end of the hearing, he seemed ready to allow one or two grazing leases on the western portion of Standing Rock. The committee adjourned without reaching a decision but planned to reconvene the following week.[37]

While the Senate committee in Washington, D.C., debated the merits of grazing leases, in south-central North Dakota William Wade penned a letter that further exacerbated the situation. He had heard rumors that the Milwaukee Railroad had acquired the lease on Standing Rock for the unbelievable price of just 1.3 cents per acre. Incensed at having lost the lease to a lower bidder, Wade wrote to Senator Jones on 16 January—the same day as the committee's first hearing—denouncing "the wrongs being done the Sioux Indians" on Standing Rock. Ignorant of the facts and recalling his conversation with the unidentified railroad employee six months earlier, Wade claimed that the lease had gone "to a company in which the

Commissioner of Indian affairs is connected" and asserted that "a thorough investigation will show up some dark objects only slightly under cover."[38] In the coming weeks, Wade's accusations would lead to an intensive investigation of William Jones.

The Senate Committee on Indian Affairs met again on 23 January but took no definite action in regard to the lease. Not content to stand by and see how the congressional committee would address the issue, Lake and Lemmon requested assistance from South Dakota's junior senator, Alfred B. Kittredge, who favored the leasing of Indian lands. Senator Kittredge worked with the White House to arrange a meeting between Lemmon and President Roosevelt, which took place on 31 January. Roosevelt and Lemmon had much in common: both were intelligent, ambitious, and characterized by a restless energy that suffused their personalities. During the meeting, they discussed cattle ranching in Dakota, Lemmon's lifelong passion and a topic on which the president had some expertise, having spent portions of 1884–1886 at his Maltese Cross and Elkhorn ranches in the badlands of what would become North Dakota. Roosevelt apparently enjoyed talking with Lemmon, for the meeting "resulted in Roosevelt's order to Secretary of the Interior Hitchcock to approve my lease," the cowman stated.[39] The president also met with a delegation from Standing Rock that included chiefs Thunder Hawk, Walking Shooter, and Weasel Bear, as well as interpreter Louis Primeau. The Indians had begun to reconsider their position regarding leases on the reservation's unoccupied areas, and during the meeting Roosevelt and the delegation agreed that both the Lemmon and Walker leases would be approved.[40]

The following day, 1 February 1902, Lemmon signed a five-year lease granting him an L-shaped tract of 788,480 acres in the northern and western portions of Standing Rock at a rate of 3.05 cents per acre annually. Lemmon's lease would cost the Lake, Tomb & Lemmon Company about twenty-four thousand dollars per year, less than half the revenue Jones had hoped to generate, but more than twice as much as the proposed permit system. Walker's 460,800-acre lease was also initiated but could not be finalized until he secured a bond. In this regard, the financial backing of Tomb and Lake proved invaluable, as it ensured the rapid approval of Lemmon's lease. He could not place cattle on the tract until 1 June but would be allowed to start fencing it in March because the lease terms required that the roughly two hundred miles of fence be entirely completed by 1 June 1903. Lemmon's lease called for the posts to be spaced two rods (thirty-three feet) apart, which would necessitate setting approximately thirty-two thousand posts and stringing them with three strands—six hundred total miles—of barbed wire.[41]

For a brief moment, Commissioner Jones might have believed the questions regarding leases on Standing Rock to be over. Congress had held hearings with no finding of fault; the president had given his blessing; and the Indians appeared to be in favor as well. But any feelings of satisfaction probably ended when he received a subpoena to appear once again in front of the Senate Committee on Indian Affairs on the evening of 4 February. The committee called the hearing to investigate an issue the Standing Rock Sioux had raised regarding the specific boundaries of the Walker lease. Most tribal members—including a majority of the Hunkpapas and Sihasapas living in and around the lease—did not object to the boundaries of the Lemmon lease, which encompassed the reservation's relatively uninhabited areas. Many, however, strongly disapproved of the boundaries of the Walker lease, which included several settlements as well as farms belonging to Indian families. The delegates contended that Walker's cattle would ruin their crops and expressed a desire to determine the lease boundaries for themselves, as they had outlined in the December 1901 agreement granting permission for the leases. The Sioux believed they had reserved the right to determine the extent of the tract; now they wanted Congress to affirm that right. If they could not select the boundaries, the Sioux would not support the Walker lease.[42]

To the commissioner of Indian affairs, this demand was troublesome but irrelevant. He had just brokered a deal to lease the entire 1.25 million-acre tract and still believed he had the right to determine its extent without the Indians' consent. Despite the relative inaction of the Committee on Indian Affairs thus far, most of its senators believed otherwise. As Senator Jones remarked, "So far as I am concerned . . . the law requires that these Indians shall consent to whatever lease shall be made . . . [and] I do not [propose] leaving it to you to say that they shall agree to a lease that they have not consented to."[43] The commissioner's reluctance to let Indians choose the boundaries was both a matter of pride and also a product of logistical concerns. Jones recognized that the Walker lease had several problems that could not be overcome if the Indians altered the boundaries as they proposed. By fencing out the settlements—which were located near the Grand River and other important waterways—cattle would have reduced access to water or would have to travel further to reach it. The decreased acreage, lack of water access, a complicated fencing structure, and questions about who would pay for the additional fencing and be responsible for its upkeep created numerous challenges that Commissioner Jones found insurmountable. He knew that if the Indians set the Walker lease boundaries, the tract would not be viable for grazing and the financial returns would prove far less than he anticipated. Once again, the committee hearing ended without definite action.

Over the next few months, third-party critics of the grazing leases continued to voice their opposition in forums both public and private. The IRA increased its involvement, publishing several articles attacking the leases and likely providing the funding for attorney William M. Springer to contest them in court. The IRA's antagonism reflected its members' understanding of the situation on the western cattle ranges, namely that "the Indians' cows never have calves, whereas the white man's always have twins," implying that leases granted to outsiders would "lead to a dwindling away of the small herds of the Indians."[44] Reporter J. A. Truesdell of the *Philadelphia Ledger* also expressed his concerns, asserting collusion between Commissioner Jones and the Milwaukee Railroad and stating that the leases had "the color of fraud."[45] George Kennan wrote two lengthy articles on the subject for *The Outlook*, claiming that the commissioner showed a complete "disregard for the interests of the Indians."[46] The Standing Rock reservation's Christian missionaries and schoolteachers wrote letters to the committee opposing the lease arrangements, which, they predicted, would result in overgrazing and destruction of the range within two years. In addition, details began to emerge regarding Louis Primeau's arrangement with the Milwaukee Railroad to convince the Sioux to accept the proposal. Luckily for the commissioner, the free passes he and his wife received to travel on the Chicago & North Western Railroad did not become public, nor did his letter to the company's general freight agent, Thomas S. Rattle, assuring him that the Office of Indian Affairs had no intention of changing its freight shipping contracts from the North Western line at Forest City to the competing Milwaukee Road at Evarts. Had this correspondence surfaced, Jones may have faced even more difficult questions about his decision to award the leases.[47]

The arguments made by the IRA, Truesdell, Kennan, and other opponents of the Standing Rock leases were largely a product of idealistic visions and personal philosophies, not facts. They tended to ignore the problems illegal grazing caused and focused instead on theories that painted the leases as yet another conspiracy to steal Indian lands. Their contentions were not without some merit, of course; the railroads and the cattlemen who sought to acquire the leases had earnings in mind, not the Indians' welfare, and tried to secure deals that ensured a profitable outcome. But William Jones understood the prevalence of illegal grazing far better than his opponents did, and he developed a concrete proposal for ending it. While the commissioner sought to implement grazing leases without the Indians' consent, he did so out of a firm belief that his course of action was the one best for the tribe.

Jones corresponded with the railroads, even accepting free annual passes, but he did not conspire with them to defraud the Sioux. He also recognized the reservation's environmental limitations. The semi-arid climate was not conducive to growing crops, but it was ideal for producing grass. He believed that raising cattle offered the most promising long-term solution for Indian self-sufficiency; as he saw it, it was the best possible outcome for a people displaced from their traditional lands, shunned by white Americans, and victimized by unscrupulous ranchers, a people with few possibilities for advancement and subject to waning public interest and financial support. Jones and the idealists in the IRA viewed the situation from different perspectives. Where the IRA saw virgin grasslands prime for grazing Indian stock, Jones saw wasted resources poached by opportunistic whites; where the IRA advocated Indians raising and selling their own stock, Jones observed unfulfilled potential because the tribes had not fully embraced stock raising as a profession. From the beginning, Jones and his opponents had the same objective in mind—creating a better situation for the Indians living on Standing Rock. They simply had differing ideas for how best to reach that goal.

The controversy over grazing leases on the reservation also coincided with a national debate over use of the public domain. Beginning in the 1880s, large-scale ranchers from Texas to the Dakotas had begun fencing off portions of the open range to prevent homesteaders from breaking up the sod. Shortly after taking office, President Roosevelt had ordered the cattlemen to remove the fences. In December 1901, in response to pressure from large cattle companies whose leaders believed that obtaining leases was the only way to stay in business, Congress passed a bill allowing cattlemen to lease (and fence) the public domain. In April 1902, Roosevelt met with Bartlett Richards and William Comstock, owners of the two-hundred-thousand-acre Spade Ranch in Nebraska; Murdo MacKenzie of the large Matador outfit, and future namesake of Murdo, South Dakota; A. S. Reed, president of the Western Nebraska Stock Growers Association; and several other influential cattlemen to discuss fencing on the range. The president refused to reverse his decision, stating, "Gentlemen, the fences will come down."[48] This declaration caused a heated exchange between Roosevelt and Richards, with the former vowing to get the situation under control. The president subsequently vetoed the "lease law" and throughout 1905 and 1906 followed up on his promise by arresting and/or fining a number of cattlemen, including Richards, who had erected barbed-wire fences on public lands. "Roosevelt's Roundup," as it came to be called, demonstrated the president's willingness to back up his policies with action. It also made cattlemen more interested in seeking grazing leases on the reservations as a means to avoid the encroaching homesteaders.[49]

As the weather on Standing Rock grew warmer and the 1902 spring roundup season approached, the status of grazing leases on the reservation remained uncertain, in part because the Sioux Indians living there were not unified in support or opposition. The members of the Returned Students' Association favored the Lemmon lease, but it is unclear how they felt about the proposed Walker tract and its inclusion of several settled areas. Some objected to Lemmon fencing his lease while the matter was still being contested (he had hired men, including a number of Standing Rock Sioux, to

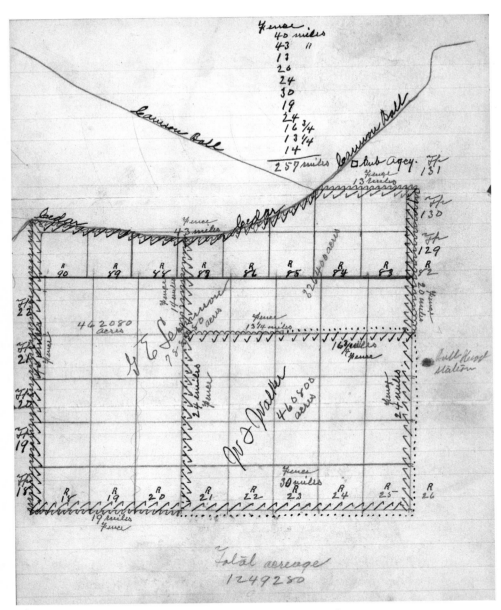

An Office of Indian Affairs sketch showing the proposed
Lemmon and Walker leases. *Wisconsin Historical Society*

start work on the project in March). Others continued to assert that the tribe should determine the boundaries of the Walker tract and supported leasing it under those conditions. A few opposed leasing any ground under any circumstances, but this minority was far overshadowed by those who believed leasing offered new opportunities. Many of the Sioux who supported grazing leases did so based on the belief that the proposed system represented the best deal they could get. Actions of the federal government in the past had jaded a number of the tribe's members, including most of its leaders, and the fear that they would lose even more land helped push them toward accepting—if not necessarily approving of—at least one of the leases.[50]

By early May 1902, the controversy over Lemmon's lease had faded to the point where he felt comfortable taking a buggy out to survey his new empire for the first time. When he reached a tall butte near Leaf-on-the-Hill Creek and looked out across the prairie, he reported not being able to "see the end of my domain," because it extended twelve miles to the north, twenty-eight miles to the south, sixteen miles to the east, and forty miles to the west.[51] Lemmon reveled in the expanse of his new kingdom, which offered a near-perfect situation—enough acreage to employ his favored open-range grazing techniques, but with the advantage that "when fenced no man could trespass on me."[52] Ed no doubt missed the irony of his statement, for he had been a trespasser on Indian lands for decades and, in the eyes of some, his lease was simply a continuation of the former practice.

To address this perception, in late May Roosevelt named his friend and fellow conservationist George Bird Grinnell as a "Special Confidential Indian Agent" and sent him to Standing Rock to rectify the situation with the Hunkpapa and Sihasapa Sioux. It appears the president chose Grinnell, a man he trusted completely and who had ample experience with Indians, over Commissioner William Jones as a gesture of good faith to the Sioux, who naturally viewed Jones with skepticism. Grinnell and former Indian Agent James McLaughlin held several councils with tribal leaders to correct any misperceptions regarding Lemmon's lease and to negotiate adjustments to accommodate some of their objections. On 23 May, the day of his forty-fifth birthday, Lemmon—whom the Standing Rock

Sioux called Taspaze ("Yellow Apple")—signed an agreement to fence off an occupied portion of his lease along the Grand River in exchange for additional unoccupied acreage in the northeast corner. The Sioux viewed Taspaze's willingness to compromise as an encouraging sign. This simple gesture, which even gave Lemmon a few additional acres, helped to ease tensions. For months, he had been the subject of dozens of complaints, particularly in regard to his early fencing of the lease. With the final agreement and Lemmon's hiring of dozens of Indians for fencing and freighting jobs, most of the objections subsided. Over the next five years, Taspaze would treat the Standing Rock Sioux with liberality, just as he had done with the Oglalas on Pine Ridge, and would come to enjoy an amicable relationship with the tribe.[53]

While Lemmon's acquisition of the huge five-year lease became the high point in his career as a cattleman, for Jones the Standing Rock conflict marked one of the lowest of his tenure as commissioner. Despite the Indians' acceptance of the Lemmon tract, the controversy surrounding the Walker lease had not subsided. The Sioux continued to insist on the right to mark its boundaries, and the Senate Committee on Indian Affairs agreed. The myriad challenges of trying to lease the pasture under such conditions proved too much for Walker and Jones, and since the secretary of the interior would not approve the Walker lease without the consent of the tribe, they failed to finalize it. Jones's vision of generating revenue on 1.25 million acres of Standing Rock grass would not come to fruition.

In addition to this professional failure, the commissioner's personal character had been called into question. Rancher William Wade's accusation that Jones had colluded with the Milwaukee Railroad had become public, and several opponents of reservation grazing cited Wade's letter as a sign of the fraudulent circumstances surrounding the leases. Senator James Jones, who received the letter and overlooked its negative portrayal of the commissioner, had sent it to a reporter, which resulted in its widespread publication. The senator apologized to Commissioner Jones for the oversight and vowed to clear his name. On 26 May, he called a meeting of the Senate Committee on Indian Affairs to review Wade's claims and determine the extent of Jones's involvement with the railroad. The senator subpoenaed Lemmon, Lake, Walker, Wade, Truesdell, and the commissioner and thoroughly examined the issue. Under testimony, it became clear that Wade's accusations had no basis in fact and that "Commissioner Jones had no connection, direct or remote, with the leases in question, and that his conduct in connection with them was entirely unselfish."[54] One week after the hearing, Wade sent a letter of apology to the commissioner, begging his pardon for acting without all the facts. Jones probably did not get the letter for several months, having embarked on a well-deserved retreat to the Pacific Coast.

For Jones, the stress and controversy surrounding the Standing Rock leases had not been worth the result. As he later wrote to J. W. Davis, a member of the Boston Indians Committee, another Indian advocacy group, "If I had understood the conditions at Standing Rock as I do now, I should not have recommended the approval of the leases."[55] The commissioner's actions damaged his reputation and caused him tremendous anxiety, but he understood the situation of illegal grazing perfectly well. Before, during, and after the public outcry, he believed that leasing Indian lands where white trespassers roamed indiscriminately was a sound approach. His hesitancy to state his position to Davis likely came from the fact that he could not fathom such strong public opposition to a plan that seemed to make a great deal of sense. He simply could not believe that anyone would oppose generating income from a practice that had already been taking place for decades. Addressing this apparent lack of common sense represented only a small portion of the challenges Jones and the Department of the Interior faced in regard to the "Indian question."

Given the varied viewpoints and disparate feelings about how to work with the tribes, the commissioner of Indian affairs found it difficult to please all of the interested parties, as did the Indian agents who answered to him. As George Bird Grinnell remarked in a letter to President Roosevelt, "I sometimes think that I would hesitate to recommend the angel Gabriel for the position of Indian agent, a place where temptation, opportunity, worriment and insufficient pay combine to break a man down."[56] Indian agents were generally believed to be ill-qualified political appointees, and many of them earned the reputation. In 1903, Roosevelt sought to rectify this situation on Standing Rock by replacing Bingenheimer with someone having "more patience, judgment, tact and interest in Indians than he possesses."[57] The Standing Rock leasing controversy no doubt played a key role in Bingenheimer's dismissal. It also taught Commissioner Jones to be wary of other efforts to graze the reservations

of western South Dakota. In August 1902, just two months after the final Standing Rock hearing, Jones received a request to lease a portion of the Pine Ridge reservation in southwestern South Dakota. Not wanting to repeat the controversy at Standing Rock and in spite of support from several parties, including the Milwaukee Railroad, he refused to pursue the matter. Even with this minor setback, white ranchers would continue to graze cattle on Indian land for years to come.[58]

Early in the summer of 1902, the founders of the Lake, Tomb & Lemmon Company began the process of occupying their new lease on the Standing Rock reservation. Ed and Rosella Lemmon sold their home in Spearfish and moved to a boarding house in Fort Yates, North Dakota, but as usual, Ed spent the vast majority of his time on the range. To help manage the operation, the company brought in Bird Rose, the seasoned wagon boss they had selected to oversee the NUN ranch in Texas six years earlier, as a partner in the enterprise. Rose would serve as Ed's right-hand man during the entire period of the lease. There was no shortage of work to be done. In addition to conducting the annual spring roundup, Lemmon and Rose needed to drive perhaps thirty thousand cattle from their existing range near the forks of the Moreau River to the reservation, a distance of about seventy-five miles. To provide additional stock for the new lease, the outfit arranged to send sixty-five hundred NUN yearlings north via rail, in addition to their annual purchase of about seventeen thousand southern cattle. They also had to oversee the construction of a perimeter fence, the length of which seemed to grow daily.[59]

After signing the initial 788,000-acre lease in February, Ed added additional acreage through the 23 May agreement, but he had also expanded his fencing responsibilities to include several settlements along the Grand River. Further, the inaccuracy of the reservation surveys Commissioner Jones had used in determining its size meant that Ed had even more land than anticipated. All told, the increases put Lemmon's total lease at 865,429.5 acres, probably the world's largest fenced pasture at that time. In the 1880s, the XIT outfit in Texas had enclosed more than three million acres with barbed wire, but by the turn of the twentieth century this huge expanse had been subdivided into more than ninety smaller pastures, leaving the title of "world's largest" to Lemmon's lease.[60]

145

Largest
Fenced
Pasture
in the
World

The expanded territory and additional fencing around the settlements came to a total of roughly 270 miles of three-wire fence, which required 810 miles of barbed wire and more than forty-three thousand fence posts. To get the necessary supplies to Standing Rock, Lemmon employed sixty Indian freighting crews. He paid the freighters one cent per mile per one hundred pounds of cargo, which earned each team between seventeen and twenty dollars during the course of the five-day round trip. The freighters seemed pleased with their pay, which proved higher than their other primary wage-earning jobs, scouting and police work. Lemmon, whose father James had instilled in him an intimate knowledge of freighting, appreciated their skill, claiming, "They at all times did good work along these lines."[61] To reward their efforts and foster good will between his outfit and the Sioux, following the completion of each large delivery Taspaze would butcher a steer or two and hold a feast, just as he had done for Red Cloud and Young Man Afraid of His Horses almost twenty years earlier at Pine Ridge. In addition to the freighters, Lemmon hired more than three hundred Indians—almost one-third of the adult males at Standing Rock—to build the fence, which they completed in 1903.[62]

During the congressional hearings regarding the lease, James McLaughlin had called the 1.25-million-acre territory "the best virgin range of any tract of similar area in the Northwest . . . capable of maintaining 100,000 head without impairing the range or exhausting it."[63] Thousands of cattle had grazed that portion of the reservation for years, so it was hardly "virgin range" in the way that the southwest portion of the Great Sioux Reservation had been when the Sheidley Cattle Company arrived in Dakota Territory in 1880. Likewise, McLaughlin's suggested stocking rate of twelve acres per animal far overestimated the range's carrying capacity (the number of cattle the range could sustain indefinitely), which was probably closer to half his figure. Including the cattle that grazed on the NUN ranch in Texas, the Lake, Tomb & Lemmon Company owned about fifty-three thousand head at the end of the 1902 shipping season, with perhaps forty thousand of those grazing on the 865,000-acre Standing Rock pasture. The resulting stocking rate—almost twenty-two acres of grass per animal—marked the upper margins of the lease's carrying capacity. In short, Lemmon pushed the limits of his pasture but probably did not graze it to exhaustion. He later claimed that "at the end of my five year term of lease . . . the tract was as good as when I took possession."[64]

Although he and Rose each owned a 15-percent stake in the outfit, the equivalent of eight thousand head apiece, Lemmon remained a relative outsider in regard to the business dealings of the company. He knew how to put pounds on beeves, but he "never gave thought to the source our monies were to come from for the [next] season's new investment."[65] Further, because of the tremendous capital outlay needed to purchase 270 miles' worth of fencing materials and seventeen thousand cattle, as well as to provide wages for three hundred fencers, Lemmon owed Lake about ninety-six thousand dollars in 1902. Yet with cattle bringing roughly twenty-four dollars per head in Chicago, he had great confidence in his ability to make the lease pay off and called this period "the pinnacle of our supremacy."[66]

Lemmon's acquisition of the lease may have staved off encroachment by homesteaders and other cattlemen, but it could not defend against Mother Nature. A severe winter in 1902–1903 took a heavy toll, with the company losing more than ten thousand cattle, or 25 percent of its Standing Rock herd. Remarkably, the loss did not have a debilitating impact on company finances, as most of the animals were of poor quality or had been purchased far below market value. The bigger loss, from Lemmon's perspective, came with the death of his father James on 22 March 1903, at the age of seventy-two. Aside from his brother Hervey, James had been Ed's most important role model. With his father's passing, Ed's sister Alpharetta became his only living immediate relative. They interred James's body in the Oak Grove Cemetery, alongside his wife Lucy and sons Hervey and Moroni. A short time later, Alpharetta sold the Thayer County farm, severing Ed's last direct tie to Nebraska. Throughout his life, the country surrounding the Little Blue River in south-central Nebraska held a special place in Ed's heart. At Liberty Farm, he had survived Indian raids, followed the Pony Express, met Wild Bill Hickok, and witnessed the country's westward migration firsthand. James's funeral marked the last time Ed would visit his favorite childhood home.[67]

As he did with every major challenge, Ed quickly returned to the business at hand. That summer, he oversaw the completion of the perimeter fence and in the fall guided several herds of cattle to Evarts for shipping to market. As he trailed his animals to the strip, Ed likely gathered some of his "strays" and included them in his shipments. Although the eastern half of the reservation did not come under the lease, cowboy Ike Blasingame noted that before the fence was complete, "many L7 cattle drifted over into this Indian land" and had to be turned back onto the lease by the Standing Rock Sioux.[68] Ed also constructed a new log home on the Grand River and moved his wife Rosella out of the North Dakota boarding house. That winter, he traveled to Chicago for the company's annual meeting and survived another near-death experience while traveling home during a blizzard shortly after Christmas, relying on luck and a dependable team of wagon horses to guide him to shelter.[69]

By the spring roundup of 1904, the Lake, Tomb & Lemmon Company had settled into ranching within the confines of a pasture. Lemmon had adjusted his open-range system to conform to the realities of a fenced enclosure, plowing fire breaks, cutting hay, and purchasing oats for winter feed. His roundups had changed as well. Since the vast majority of his Reverse L7 cattle now ranged inside a three-wire fence, branding, castrating, and sorting them into bunches by age took the place of reading brands and cutting into groups based on ownership. Despite the changes, the forty-six-year-old demonstrated that he had not lost a step when it came to handling cattle. On 2 May, Lemmon and two other men, "Coon" Glover and John Ivy, cut almost twenty-seven hundred individual animals from the main herd, an average of nine hundred head per man. This incredible feat—which Lemmon called "the greatest cutting of cattle in one day to my knowledge"—added to his reputation as the region's best all-around cowboy.[70]

National recognition of Lemmon's achievements came the following January at the National Live Stock Association annual meeting in Denver, Colorado. In a corridor of the Brown Palace Hotel, Association Secretary Charles Martin, who made it his "business to find out such things," recognized Lemmon for having saddle-handled more cattle than any man who ever lived—over one million head—and operating the world's largest fenced pasture.[71] Lemmon's accomplishments stemmed from tasks like trailing, roping, cutting, and branding that were commonplace for cowboys, yet he performed them with unrivalled skill and enjoyed such remarkable longevity that he earned a place among the most accomplished men in the cattle industry. Even as he shook hands in the Denver hotel and basked in the glow of his success, Lemmon must have realized that his time as a cowboy, like the days of the open range, was rapidly drawing to a close. He was nearing fifty years old. After thirty years in the saddle, his crippled right leg stiffened up more frequently, he experienced the aches and pains of long-forgotten injuries with increasing regularity, and his renowned stamina started to show signs of fading. With his five-year lease set to end in mid-1907, Lemmon began thinking about his future—a future outside the cattle business.

Throughout 1905 and 1906, the Lake, Tomb & Lemmon outfit continued its usual operations while also preparing for the end of the lease in 1907. Each year, Lemmon purchased thousands of young southern cattle, shipping them to Evarts by rail and trailing them to the Standing Rock pasture for fattening. At season's end, Lemmon and Rose gathered the mature four-year-old beeves and drove them to the Evarts railhead for shipment to Chicago. In 1905, in order to comply with a new state law designed to control and prevent livestock disease, the men constructed dipping facilities and treated more than twenty-six thousand cattle. That year, the company also sold its NUN ranch in Texas, realizing a profit of one hundred thousand dollars on land they had owned since 1896. As the weather turned colder in the fall of 1906, Lemmon began to cut down his seasonal crews to a core group of winter cowboys. His outfit had hired more than two dozen hands that year, and settling their wages took a great deal of time. During the process Lemmon began to show his age, becoming "worn out from so much desk work." He blamed his fatigue on the fact that "a cow-puncher does not fit" behind a desk, but in reality his years on the open range—the broken bones, exposure to the elements, and the eighteen-hour days—had begun to take their toll.[72] Early the next year, Lemmon would sell his interest in the Lake, Tomb & Lemmon Company to Rose, ending the most successful and fulfilling chapter of his life.[73]

Pursuing the Standing Rock lease made so much sense from a business standpoint that Lemmon probably did not dwell on the broader significance of his decision. His entire career had been based on tenets learned in grazing cattle on the open range, yet he chose to operate within the confines of a fenced pasture. In making that shift, he changed how cattlemen on the Northern Great Plains approached the business. Lemmon's decision to forego the open range in favor of a lease with fixed boundaries was a product of changing circumstances, but it also represented a return to a familiar environment. Lemmon had been acquainted with Indians for nearly his entire life. Huste's years as a trespasser on the Great Sioux Reservation were marked by amicable relations with the Oglala Sioux who called Pine Ridge their home; although initially contentious, Taspaze's relationship with the Hunkpapas and Sihasapas also became one of mutual respect. As Lemmon later recalled, "All in all, my occupancy of the reservation for a term of five years, with practically thirty thousand cattle, was the very most pleasurable of my entire life, and I feel I founded a friendship with the Sitting Bull Indians that will endure for all time and then some, as evidenced by the fact that they call me to lead every function of note staged on their reservation."[74] For Lemmon, a man entirely defined by working cattle on the vast expanses of the Northern Great Plains, the simultaneous end of his career as a cattleman and the demise of the open range may have seemed like fate.

7 TOWN BUILDING

When the cattle shipping season closed in the fall of 1905, a large section of the Northern Great Plains remained relatively unsettled. A vast rectangular tract marked roughly on its corners by Bismarck, North Dakota; Pierre, South Dakota; Sheridan, Wyoming; and Miles City, Montana, contained a few dozen settlements and perhaps a handful of incorporated communities. This huge expanse covered a territory about the size of Indiana and included Butte County in South Dakota's northwest corner. The county spanned seventy-eight hundred square miles and would later be divided into three smaller counties: Perkins, Harding, and Butte, the state's second, fourth, and seventh largest counties, respectively. Fewer than four thousand people lived within its boundaries (a quarter of them in the town of Belle Fourche), making a population density of just over half a person per square mile—four times less than the threshold marking the end of the frontier, as historian Frederick Jackson Turner had declared thirteen years earlier. For decades, cowboys like Ed Lemmon had ranged beeves on the open range of Butte County and the rest of this sparsely settled region. During the next several years, thousands of homesteaders would make their way into the area, claiming free land from the federal government and seeking to capitalize on the promise of tremendous new opportunities.[1]

Homesteading west of the Missouri River came much later than farther east. In western North Dakota, only forty-seven thousand people—15 percent of the state's population—had settled there by the turn of the century. Between 1900 and 1915 more than one hundred thousand newcomers arrived in western South Dakota. After leaving the cattle business, Lemmon, who had for years tried to stifle settlement and preserve the open range, worked equally hard to *encourage* settlement. He helped found several towns, started a land company, held posts in city and county government, established a bank, and organized numerous small businesses.[2]

Ed Lemmon's contributions to town building began during the

winter of 1905–1906, when he helped the Chicago, Milwaukee & St. Paul Railroad chart its route across the Missouri River, spawning dozens of new communities and attracting flocks of settlers to the region. That winter, he traveled to Chicago for the Lake, Tomb & Lemmon Company's annual business meetings. During the fifteen years he had met there with his partners, Richard Lake and Thomas Tomb, he had come to know a number of men who worked for the Milwaukee Railroad, including assistant general freight agent (and future president of the line) R. M. Calkins. Ed's relationship with these employees would prove fortuitous; during a special meeting of the Milwaukee's board of directors on 28 November 1905, the board authorized the company to begin constructing a rail line from Evarts to Washington State, where it would connect with the Pacific Railway.[3]

The Milwaukee Railroad had expanded greatly in the thirty-three years following its arrival in Dakota Territory. Its network extended throughout the territory's eastern half, reaching Yankton (the capital from 1861 to 1883), Sioux Falls, Mitchell, Aberdeen, Fargo, and dozens of smaller towns. The Milwaukee had two terminals on the east bank of the Missouri River: Chamberlain (which it reached in 1881) and Evarts (1900). During its three decades of expansion, the Milwaukee had faced constant competition from the rival Chicago & North Western Railroad, which also owned a large network in Dakota and operated two Missouri River stations, one at Pierre and the other at Forest City, the small railhead from which Lemmon had struggled to ship beeves in 1895. In the early 1900s, the competition intensified as both railroads set out to be the first to extend tracks from the Missouri to the Black Hills. The Milwaukee began building west from Chamberlain, while the North Western commenced construction at Pierre. Meanwhile, in an attempt to capitalize on the increasing bounty of western lands—grain, livestock, coal, timber, minerals, and precious metals—and better position itself against the North Western, in 1905 the Milwaukee Road purchased the Pacific Railway Company of Washington and used the acquisition as the impetus to expand its line all the way to the Pacific. The proposed fifteen-hundred-mile extension was a major step for the Milwaukee and pushed the company far beyond its traditional bases of operation. The road maintained thousands of miles of track in Wisconsin, Illinois, Iowa, and other midwestern states; the acquisition of the Pacific Railway signaled a strong, determined push toward the West Coast.[4]

One of the immediate logistical obstacles to building the transcontinental line was finding a feasible route across the Missouri River, the largest natural impediment east of the Rocky Mountains. The Milwaukee had investigated the possibility of westward expansion for at least five years and conducted a number of surveys from Evarts in order to site a bridge at the location. Its topography and geology made this proposition quite difficult, however. The bluffs on the river's west side rose between one hundred and two hundred feet above those on the east and featured a rough, broken landscape that would require significant and expensive cutting and grading prior to laying the track. Further, rock formations beneath the water may have been insufficient for supporting a bridge. The steep grade, additional costs, and poor foundation would make running locomotives at that location impractical. As a result, the Milwaukee's engineers had been searching for an alternate site.[5]

Calkins mentioned this difficulty during the winter of 1905–1906 while Ed was visiting his friends in the railroad's construction department. "Our engineers have run a total of eighteen preliminary surveys west from Evarts," Calkins lamented, "none of which have been successful."[6] Lemmon was an aging cattleman, not a trained engineer, but he had a strong familiarity with the landscape west of Evarts. As a brand rep, trail guide, roundup boss, and cattle buyer, Lemmon traveled extensively and developed an unrivaled knowledge of the western prairies. His unmatched professionalism meant that he made it a point to know every butte, knoll, wooded draw, buffalo wallow, and creek bed where cattle might seek shelter. He understood the country as only those who spent their entire lives on the plains could. With ranches separated by miles of open space, misjudging a location by only a fraction of a mile could mean hours on horseback or on foot before reaching help. Lemmon's quarter century of experience, coupled with four seasons of cattle handling on the Standing Rock Indian Reservation, meant that he was uniquely positioned to help the Milwaukee Railroad site a bridge across the Missouri River.[7]

Lemmon immediately recognized the challenges of proceeding

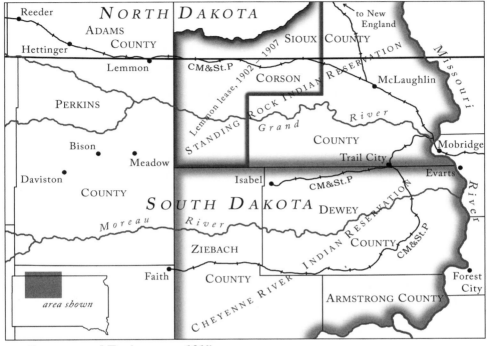

Lemmon and Environs, ca. 1915

west from Evarts and proposed an alternative. His route would start at Glenham, cross the Missouri at the mouth of the Grand River, travel up the west bank of the Missouri to the mouth of Oak Creek, and continue along the easier grade of the creek basin. The Grand River entered the Missouri twelve miles upstream from Evarts, so the route would require building several miles of new track, as well as leaving behind what had been one of the country's most lucrative cattle-shipping points. But Lemmon knew the flat bottomlands of the Grand would prove more workable for locating a bridge than the steep bluffs west of Evarts. He returned the next day with a map of the Standing Rock Indian Reservation, "upon which I penciled with a red pencil, a route beginning at the mouth of Grand River on the west bank of the Missouri River to the head of Flat Creek near the present site of Reeder[, North Dakota]." A short time later, the Milwaukee Railroad sent engineers out to survey the route and deemed it "thoroughly practical and feasible."[8]

The railroad quickly set to work. In 1906, the Milwaukee completed the twelve-mile line from Glenham to the east bank of the Missouri River. As work crews and materials began accumulating in preparation for bridge construction, a settlement sprang up. A white sign along the tracks labeled the location "MO. BRIDGE," and workmen soon began calling the town Mobridge. That fall, the Milwaukee announced its proposed route to the Pacific. The line would pass through the Standing Rock reservation over land obtained pursuant to a 2 March 1899 act allowing railroads to acquire rights-of-way through Indian reservations. The tracks would follow the North Dakota-South Dakota border, arc northwest into Montana, and cut across to the town of Butte—650 miles from Mobridge—where the Milwaukee Road would connect with the Jawbone Railroad and continue west to the Pacific Coast.[9]

While the Milwaukee began construction in earnest in 1906, Lemmon raced to take advantage of an incredible, but closing, window of opportunity. Because he had helped the railroad plan its route, Ed received assurance from Calkins that he would be "given an opportunity of knowing beforehand its exact location by legal government description."[10] To capitalize on this information, Ed purchased roughly thirteen hundred acres worth of scrip, which he intended to trade for land adjacent to the proposed rail line. The

Bridge builders at Mobridge, South Dakota, 1908.
South Dakota State Historical Society

scrip Lemmon bought cost him $8.50 per acre and consisted of doc-
umented paper vouchers for land. The federal government had issued a vast array of scrip for numerous purposes: as compensation
to soldiers who could not homestead their full allowable acreage;
in exchange for private property appropriated through eminent domain; as lands that railroad companies could sell to generate capital for constructing their lines; and several others. In many cases,
the scrip's original owner could not or did not care to exchange it for
lands located elsewhere, so he sold it to dealers for cash. The dealers would then resell the scrip to individuals who often exchanged
several different types for larger, consolidated tracts of land. Lemmon used this approach, along with his knowledge of the railroad's
route, to set about building a fortune. In 1906, he "scripped" land
along the proposed routes at several different sites.[11]

In early 1907, Milwaukee Railroad officials contacted Lemmon
and asked him to return to Chicago. As a token of appreciation for
his assistance, the railroad offered to establish "a major town site

west of the Reservation line" on one of the tracts for which Lemmon had filed his scrip.[12] He initially suggested a level piece of ground four miles west of Standing Rock, but the railroad objected to the location because it was in North Dakota. In 1889, the state constitutions of both North Dakota and South Dakota had included language prohibiting the manufacture or sale of "intoxicating liquors." The citizens of South Dakota voted to remove their prohibition clause in 1897, but North Dakota remained dry. Railroad officials believed that "in order to make it a real boom town, the saloon with its attendant evil would have to be tolerated," so Lemmon's townsite would have to be situated in South Dakota.[13] Ed had another tract that straddled the North Dakota-South Dakota state line four miles west of his first site. He had purchased this parcel hoping to establish a town that would serve as the seat of government for two counties—one in each state. The second location proved acceptable, and the railroad purchased a portion of Lemmon's land for the site. E. D. Sewall, assistant to the president of the Milwaukee Railroad, told him, "We will name the proposed city 'Lemmon,' and it will be up to you to make it a thriving and successful city."[14]

A short time later, Ed sold his shares in the Lake, Tomb & Lemmon Company, receiving perhaps $192,000 from the sale—a substantial return on the more than thirty years he had invested in becoming a successful cowboy and cattleman. He left the cattle business to focus his energies on developing the new community of Lemmon, South Dakota. These efforts, too, proved successful. As Ed later recalled: "There immediately sprung up one of the oddest and thriftiest of squatter settlements ever known to the prairie country of the west. It was known as 'tent town' and while there were a number of lumber shacks and shell-like frame structures, it was principally a tent town and as such attracted attention far and wide because of its novelty and 'wide open' spirit of the place."[15] Lemmon became the first town established—in either North Dakota or South Dakota— in the vicinity west of the Standing Rock reservation. As a result, "a great many would-be businessmen who wanted to get in on the ground floor in the anticipated boom" asked Ed for permission to build on his land, adjacent to the tracts he had sold to the railroad.[16] While the tent town thrived and awaited the arrival of the railroad, forty miles up the proposed rail line Ed worked to establish another community in southwestern North Dakota.

His ambitious plan to make Lemmon a dual county-seat town depended on redrawing county boundaries in both states. Butte County, South Dakota, would need to be reorganized, as would the adjacent Hettinger County, North Dakota, which included present-day Hettinger and Adams counties. The goal was not unreasonable, as numerous counties in the region were founded or redrawn during this time. Ed's strategy called for establishing another town along the Milwaukee Road in the western half of Hettinger County, which would become a separate county with his new town as the seat. The arrangement would then make Lemmon the prime candidate to serve as the seat of a second North Dakota county formed out of the eastern half of Hettinger and the western portion of present-day Sioux and Grant counties. With this idea in mind, Ed purchased several sections of land along the proposed railroad route near present-day Reeder, North Dakota, probably using the remainder of his government scrip and funds from the sale of his Lake, Tomb & Lemmon stock. He lived near the future site of Reeder for more than a year, peddling his land to settlers and attempting to split Hettinger County in two. In temporarily relocating, Ed perhaps felt like West Virginia transplant W. H. Hamilton, whose "greatest regret in leaving So. Dak. was in parting with my faithful old horse."[17]

As part of his efforts, Ed contacted other landowners along the proposed route, including the Hilton family, who owned land near his would-be county seat. He urged the Hiltons to sell to the railroad, but apparently the family had profited from a similar situation in eastern Dakota and "when approached by [Milwaukee Land] company officials . . . placed their price so high that the company would not pay it."[18] While negotiations there stalled, the town of Hettinger, North Dakota, launched its own promotional scheme. On 17 April 1907, when Governor John Burke split Hettinger County into northern and southern portions rather than east and west as Ed had hoped, the town of Hettinger—not Reeder—became the seat of the new Adams County. Lemmon's efforts did not go unrewarded, however. Governor Burke appointed him as an Adams County commissioner, a post he would hold for two years. During his term, he contributed further to the county's development, paying "out of my own pocket near all the labor bills on the Court House we were building" in Hettinger.[19]

As Ed threw himself into town development, the Milwaukee Railroad continued to expand. Unlike the Union Pacific's approach to construction in the 1860s, the Milwaukee did not lay its track from east to west. Building commenced at several locations along the intended route simultaneously, decreasing construction time and spawning towns that seemed to spring up in the middle of nowhere. Workers managed to span the Missouri River with a temporary timber-and-pontoon bridge in September 1907, two months before the first Chicago & North Western train crossed a completed railroad bridge at Pierre. The Milwaukee replaced its temporary structure at Mobridge with a 2,970-foot bridge the following year and began freight service to Miles City, Montana, on 30 August 1908. Ten months later, on 4 July 1909, the Milwaukee Railroad initiated full freight service from Seattle to Chicago via its completed transcontinental route.[20]

When the first Chicago, Milwaukee & St. Paul train reached the city of Lemmon in the fall of 1907, the burgeoning community hosted a tremendous welcome party. Platted on 24 September of that year, the town came to life on 3 October, the day of the lot sale. At least two thousand people attended to bid on more than two hundred lots. Following the sale, residents of the tent town rushed to move before winter. Within a short time, Lemmon featured "eight saloons, seven lumber companies, one half dozen general stores, one strictly clothing, three livery and feed stables, four blacksmith shops, one haberdasher store, two drug stores, three hotels and at least eight cafes, two photographers, four churches, two newspapers, three doctors, with offices, two dental offices, four barber shops, three with baths attached, five lawyers, with offices, five real estate and sale agencies . . . one club room, skating rink, [and a] general utility hall."[21] Ed purchased several lots for himself, intending to resell them to new businesses as the community expanded. He also offered to make "a Christmas present of a lot each" to ten of his relatives on the condition that they would move to South Dakota.[22]

While caught up in this whirlwind of development, Ed probably

"Tent town" at Lemmon, South Dakota, prior to lot sale on 3 October 1907.
South Dakota State Historical Society

did not stop to contemplate the dramatic ways in which his life had changed. For more than twenty-five years, he had tried to suppress settlement on the Northern Great Plains in order to maintain the open range for cattle grazing. Now he had removed himself from the cattle business and embraced the inevitability of settlement. For years, Richard Lake and Thomas Tomb had been preparing to exit the open-range cattle business due to shrinking access to grazing lands. Rather than hang on to a potentially losing enterprise, the ever-practical Lemmon refocused his efforts from hindering settlement to becoming an aggressive town builder. His father had taught him the value of entrepreneurship and encouraged him to take on new challenges. Ed believed his young community offered tremendous opportunities for success.

Lemmon's second wife, Rosella, probably relished the change in her husband's career. Since their marriage in 1900, he had moved his bride from a comfortable home in Spearfish to a temporary boarding house at Fort Yates and then to a rough cabin on the Standing Rock reservation. In 1906, prior to the formal establishment of Lemmon, he built her a large house on the western outskirts of town. The two-and-a-half-story structure—the city's first permanent residence—featured an open porch, bay window, detailed wood accents, and expensive fixtures. Ed must have spent a great deal on the home and furnishings because "no pains were spared in selecting the best."[23] Thirty-year-old Rosella enjoyed the new lifestyle that accompanied Ed's financial success and began to travel widely. In the coming years, she would visit Texas, California, Washington, Illinois, Wyoming, and other states, spending as much as sixteen hundred dollars per trip. His young wife's thirst for travel even forced Ed to trek across the country to Los Angeles in order to get her signature on the Lemmon townsite deed.[24]

Ed expanded his business ventures that year, purchasing a large interest in the First State Bank of Lemmon and serving as its president. The bank also doubled as headquarters for his land company. In addition to a number of lots in town, Ed bought and sold dozens of land parcels in North Dakota and South Dakota, totaling several thousand acres. He homesteaded and purchased land under his own name and under his wife's name, as the First State Bank, and in connection with the Moore Land Company, owned by M. E. Moore. Ed also attempted to start a cement-block plant with entrepreneur O. G. Bickford to capitalize on the local construction boom. From the remarkable exuberance he demonstrated, it appears that the fifty-one-year-old former cattleman had discovered a sense of satisfaction in his new endeavors. As when he worked on the open range, he kept a hectic schedule, refocusing his uncommon energy on the area's growth and development.[25]

Lemmon also increased his involvement in civic activities. During his ranching career, he had taken part in few organizations outside the cattle business, though he did serve one term (1884–1885) as a commissioner in Fall River County. His participation in the Western South Dakota Stock Growers Association had stemmed from a desire to reduce stock losses to rustlers, yet he would serve as a member of the organization's executive committee until 1914, seven years after he sold his Lake, Tomb & Lemmon Company shares. Ed's focus shifted once he embraced the role of town builder. In 1908, he funded a Fourth of July celebration that brought more than five thousand people to Lemmon. Such events were important for community-building in rural areas where weeks might pass before a homesteader saw his nearest neighbor. While adults shared a meal and discussed the events of the day, their children played games and made new friends. When families interacted at these celebrations, they forged bonds that strengthened the new community.[26]

Ed's support of such events, together with his cheerful demeanor, love of jokes and stories, widespread reputation for honest dealings, and penchant for giving gifts of candy to children at random, earned him respect and the community-wide appellation of "Dad." In addition to his duties as an Adams County, North Dakota, commissioner he chaired the Lemmon city council and was elected as a county commissioner in newly formed Perkins County, South Dakota. Apparently no one challenged his ability to serve simultaneously as a commissioner in two separate counties in two different states. Perhaps the fact that a portion of the growing community—called North Lemmon—had emerged on the North Dakota side of the railroad tracks played a role in this unusual circumstance. Yet even in this capacity Ed could not realize his dream of making Lemmon a county-seat town.[27]

In January 1909, Perkins County voters went to the polls to determine the new county seat. Their options included Lemmon, easily the county's largest town and most important railhead; Bison, a small settlement near the county center that featured four sod houses, a grocery store, and a post office; and Meadow, another tiny locale twelve miles east of Bison. Despite Lemmon's obvious potential, its location at the extreme northern edge of the county did not make it readily accessible to settlers in the southern portion sixty-five miles away. In a close contest, Bison edged out Lemmon as the new county seat, 1,001 to 987. Meadow received a mere fifty-six votes. Bolstered by the results, Bison began to attract settlers; in February, the town started constructing a courthouse and preparing to take the reins from Lemmon, where the county commissioners had met prior to the election. But a majority of the commissioners, including Ed Lemmon himself, had backed Lemmon as the county seat and refused to relocate. The Lemmon Commercial Club even appealed the results, but to no avail. On 27 April 1909, ten oxen pulling a heavy wagon filled with books, office equipment, and official records left Lemmon en route to Bison. Three weeks later, the final load left Lemmon, settling the question for good and ending Ed's dream of establishing his town as a county seat.[28]

While city and county organization commenced in western North Dakota and South Dakota, the Milwaukee Railroad continued its efforts to expand. Two years earlier, a national financial crisis known as the Panic of 1907 had shut down railroad construction in both states. The accompanying recession lasted for more than a year and resulted in Congress's creation of the Federal Reserve System. In 1909, with the recession over and its transcontinental line completed, the Milwaukee began exploring further development in the western half of both states. On 19 May, the board of directors voted to recommend the construction of "two lines of railway, one the Grand River Line and the other the Moreau River Line to a point beyond the Cheyenne Reservation as far as may be deemed necessary."[29]

Company officials had not forgotten Ed's phenomenal knowledge of the terrain and called upon his services once again to help chart a route from Mobridge southwest into the heart of western South Dakota. For eight days, he guided the "President's party"— a collection of railroad officials including President Albert J. Earling, two vice presidents, the chief engineer, the general livestock agent, townsite agents, and construction contractors—on a tour of the area "to take observations preparatory to the location of a branch line, now known as the Isabel branch."[30] During the trip, Ed showed them the practical routes; in return, they informed him that the lines would be constructed based on his recommendations. Ed gained a strong sense of satisfaction when others recognized his skill and accomplishments, and he never turned down an opportunity to showcase his talents. In fact, he enjoyed the experience so much that he refused to accept the eight hundred dollars railroad officials offered in return for his assistance. The following year, the Milwaukee commenced construction on two branch lines, the first a sixty-mile section running from a point just west of Mobridge southwest to what is now Isabel, and the second splitting off from this line at Moreau Junction (later called Trail City) and running to the present-day city of Faith. The new lines reached both communities in 1911. In 1910, the Milwaukee had also built a third branch from McLaughlin, South Dakota, northwest to the site of present-day New England, North Dakota.[31]

Part of the impetus for the railroad's expansion was the expected rush of new settlers to the region. On 29 May 1908, Congress had authorized the secretary of the interior to open more than 1.5 million acres of "surplus" unallotted lands on the Standing Rock and Cheyenne River reservations for homesteading. Milwaukee officials anticipated the arrival of thousands of newcomers in a rush similar to the openings on the Rosebud reservation in south-central South Dakota a few years earlier. Between 5 July and 23 July 1904, more than one hundred thousand people registered for the chance to homestead fewer than twenty-five hundred homesteads of 160 acres each. After the land drawing, settlers had filled the Rosebud country, triggering the appearance of numerous towns with shops, banks, eating establishments, and other businesses. Hoping to capitalize on would-be homesteaders on the Standing Rock and Cheyenne River reservations, the railroad began advertising lots in towns it had established along the line. Between 1909 and 1912, eleven railroad towns emerged in Corson County, the South Dakota portion of the Standing Rock reservation. The Milwaukee's North Dakota branch line to New England passed through another dozen communities spread over 132 miles. Fourteen more towns were platted in Dewey and Ziebach counties (which covered most of the Cheyenne River reservation) along the Isabel and Faith branches that Ed helped to chart in 1909.[32]

The opening of the reservations began a period of tremendous community development. For the Indians living on Standing Rock and Cheyenne River, however, history had repeated itself. This latest land grab likely jaded many, including the members of the Returned Students' Association who had advocated working with the federal government during the fight over the Standing Rock lease seven years earlier. The allotment of land once held in common forced the tribes to reassess their plans for the future and led to fundamental problems as they struggled to adapt to a system based on the individual rather than the group.[33]

The 1909 allotment also signaled an irreversible shift in the way the entire range country would be utilized. For decades, large cattle outfits, including the Matador, Flying V, Diamond A, Turkey Track, and others, had grazed cattle on open ranges both on and off the reservations. When homesteaders began to arrive en masse, fences appeared across the landscape, and plows tilled under some of the prairie grasses. Although stock raising, not farming, would eventually prove to be the most effective use of the grasslands in much of western North Dakota and South Dakota, this determination would come only after several years and scores of busted homesteaders. In 1911, South Dakota governor Robert S. Vessey signed a bill requiring stockmen to compensate property owners for crops damaged by cattle or horses. A 1907 state law had enacted this provision in all counties east of the Missouri River; West River counties were exempt unless voters in an individual county chose to implement it. The 1911 bill repealed this exemption, signaling a significant shift in the expected use of land in western South Dakota. As the editor of *Glenham State Journal* remarked: "The wide ranges of the past have gone forever; the thousands of cattle that once roamed in big herds; the South Dakota prairies farther than the eye could stretch are a thing of the past. Dotted everywhere are small homesteads; crossed by three lines of railroads; smaller but better kept herds already are commenced; and the big cattlemen shedding a tear for the old days, are silently adapting themselves to the environment brought about in the new and rapidly settling state."[34]

Ed Lemmon undoubtedly longed for days gone by—the familiar creak of saddle leather and the tug of the reins as he guided his mount; the sight of a large herd breaking a rise in the distance; the smell of horse sweat and singed hair around the branding fire; the nervous excitement of a nighttime stampede; the spectacular sunsets over endless prairies. For three decades, Ed had lived such a life, and now it was gone. Yet he not only adapted to the changing times, he thrived. In the coming decade, he would spend the bulk of his time—and his fortune—pursuing his new vocation of town builder.

Ever since Ed's first wife, Bertha, moved to Colorado with their three sons in 1901, the boys had experienced little contact with their father. In the fall of 1909, Ed's eldest son James, then twenty-one, moved to Lemmon to join him in business. James apparently harbored no ill will for his father's absenteeism. Part of James's reason for moving to town probably stemmed from the emergence of Lemmon as a thriving community. Since setting up the townsite in 1907, the Milwaukee Railroad had invested in it heavily, constructing a two-story depot and maintaining a busy rail yard with a main track and six sidings. The community continued to grow after 1909, when the nearby reservation land opened up; in addition to new settlers and businesses, Lemmon became home to the area's United States land office. By 1911, Lemmon had 1,255 residents, making it the largest town between Miles City, Montana, and Aberdeen, South Dakota, a distance of almost four hundred miles.[35]

Other developments helped to ensure that Lemmon would remain one of the region's principle business hubs. Once the railroad arrived in Faith in January 1911, neither the Milwaukee nor the Chicago & North Western made any significant expansions in South Dakota. Ed had helped to guide the routes for the only railroad lines that would ever enter northwest South Dakota and southwest North Dakota. In four short years, from 1907 to 1911, hundreds of miles of track had been laid and dozens of towns had been founded. These towns—most of them named by railroad officials—became the region's defining features and left a lasting legacy for their namesakes. On the main line, Indian Agent James McLaughlin gave a town his name, as did the McIntosh brothers, construction contractors for the Milwaukee. W. I. Walker, the Nebraska cattleman who bid against Ed for the large Standing Rock pasture in 1902 and then took it over after Ed's lease ended in 1907, also lent his surname to a townsite. The town of Thunder Hawk received its moniker from the Sioux chief who had opposed Ed's grazing lease several years earlier, while Wakpala, Mahto, and Watauga all came from the Lakota language. On the branch lines in South Dakota, Isabel, Timber Lake, Trail City, Faith, Dupree, Lantry, Eagle Butte, La Plant, and others grew at varying rates but would never reach the size of Lemmon. The North Dakota branch featured Maple Leaf (South Dakota), Selfridge, Shields, Leith, Elgin, New Leipzig, Mott, Regent, Havelock, and New England. Ed was not the driving force behind the founding of these towns, but the expansion of the Milwaukee Railroad and the simultaneous arrival of thousands of new settlers resulted in the rapid settlement of the region.[36]

As the second decade of the twentieth century opened, Ed continued to expand his investments beyond Lemmon. With assistance from James, he bought town lots and installed branch locations of his First State Bank in the small communities of Meadow and Daviston. Neither had a railroad, but both towns had two qualities that appealed to Ed: first, they were located in central Perkins County and could attract business from the county's southern settlers; second, they were not the town of Bison. As the county seat, Bison had far more business potential than either Meadow or Daviston, but Ed retained his scorn for the small collection of sod houses that had stolen his dream of establishing a county seat in Lemmon. He almost certainly avoided doing business there out of spite. He may also have retained a small glimmer of hope that Lemmon could still get the county seat if the Isabel railroad line continued its westward extension and bypassed Bison. Ed's resolution to refrain from doing business in the county seat—even though he served as a county commissioner—demonstrated a critical flaw in his business acumen: at times, emotion could coerce him into bad decisions.[37]

Entrepreneurs rarely lack confidence, and Ed spent vast sums on additional efforts to develop the Lemmon community. Throughout the 1910s, he engaged in various enterprises while James established himself in business. James initially worked as a clerk for the First State Bank, then rose to director and, by 1916, to executive vice president. In July 1912, he married twenty-year-old Della Donovan, a delicate young woman who had graduated from high school two months earlier. Also that year, Ed and three other Lemmon businessmen—Ole S. Quammen, F. A. Finch, and T. O. Ramsland—founded the Lemmon Brick & Tile Company. The company planned to utilize the area's abundant clay deposits, known locally as "gumbo," to make brick, tile, hollow blocks, and other products. These men were also actively involved in the Yellowstone Trail Association, a town-promotion and road-improvement organization founded in Ipswich, South Dakota, in 1912. The association sought to develop an improved road to accommodate tourists traveling to Yellowstone National Park by automobile. The Yellowstone Trail passed through Lemmon and would later become part of the national highway system as U.S. Route 12. In September 1913, Ed ended his association with the First State Bank, selling his shares to

Montana banker J. C. Kinney. Ed had served as its president since 1908, but he appears to have wanted to free up additional time and money for a different venture: land speculation.[38]

The land bonanza of the early 1900s had brought throngs of "honyockers" who settled on homesteads of 160 or 320 acres in western North Dakota and South Dakota. Homesteading east of the Missouri River, where productive soils and adequate moisture made farming profitable, proved to be far different from the West River experience. The semi-arid grasslands west of the one hundredth meridian received only half to three-quarters of the rainfall of areas farther east, making crop-raising difficult. Should a farmer manage to harvest his crop, the yields often proved far less than he could expect in Iowa, Minnesota, or eastern Dakota. Settlers who believed they could farm at a profit quickly discovered that most of the western prairie lands were better suited for grazing cattle or sheep. Recognizing these challenges, in 1909 Congress passed the Enlarged Homestead Act, which granted settlers 320 acres, double the amount offered in the original 1862 Homestead Act. Despite the additional acreage, settlers found in many instances that the land was simply not productive enough to support a family. In addition, once the five-year prove-up period ended and a homesteader gained title to the land, he became obligated to pay taxes on it. Lacking ready cash and unable to meet the tax burden, many newcomers petitioned for a "general leave of absence" of one year from their homesteads to find work in non-agricultural jobs so they could pay the taxes on their recently acquired lands.[39]

During the 1910s, thousands of acres in the region started passing through "final proofs," in which settlers acquired title to the lands they had homesteaded. In the Lemmon tax district alone, more than twenty-two hundred new tracts came up for taxation in 1911. Perkins County became one of three West River counties to "show an increase of a million or more dollars in their valuation figures on real estate."[40] The emergence of so many new taxable acres laid a heavy burden on the settlers; Ed, ever the businessman, stepped in to capitalize on the situation.

Ed began contacting tax-delinquent landowners, offering to purchase their land by paying off the back taxes. Within a short time, he acquired a number of parcels in North Dakota and South Dakota.

In several instances, the landowners transferred their property via quit-claim deed without an actual purchase. Because such a deed did not guarantee that the seller actually owned the land, Ed made some of these deals in good faith. In at least a few of his quit-claim deed transactions, he may have taken on the property intending to return it once the former landowner could afford the taxes. He probably agreed to such arrangements on a limited basis and with no expectation of making a profit, either as a favor to a friend or to help ensure the long-term viability of his community. In other instances, he was less altruistic and bought properties outright, planning to sell them at a profit. Exactly where the funds came from is unclear, but he probably bought land both with cash and on credit. Ed was not the only local land speculator, and he sold numerous parcels to other brokers. He made dozens of purchases and acquisitions during the 1910s, controlling thousands of acres on the county tax rolls. In order to earn the money needed to reacquire their homesteads, a number of former landowners left the area and sought work elsewhere. Many of these families did not return.[41]

This situation also pushed some of those who stayed toward political activity, in the hope of improving their circumstances through government action. Anticipating the 1912 elections and prompted by increasing progressive activities nationwide, area producers in 1911 formed a Farmers Equity Union to defend against playing "right into the hands of trusts and speculaters every time [we] have a good crop and lose hundreds of millions of dollars." The group planned to join with other farmers' organizations to form a "national union that will control shipments to the central markets sufficiently to prevent low, unjust prices."[42] Local producers believed in the potential of reform groups and sought to reduce the power of trusts, railroads, and grain speculators through organized activity. Although Ed was involved in land speculation, he did not draw the ire of the local union. As the town founder, he enjoyed an elevated standing within the community, and his business had little impact on the price that farmers received for their crops. His good nature and generosity toward children and adults also helped him avoid becoming one of the union's targets.

The Farmer's Equity Union had good reason to oppose the actions of railroad companies. Lemmon and the small town of White

Butte ten miles west were the only communities in South Dakota that did not benefit from a 1910 state law that cut express railroad shipment rates by 30 percent. Rates for all other South Dakota cities were reduced on long hauls, significantly easing a major burden for farmers, ranchers, and urban businessmen. Officials with the Milwaukee Railroad would not give discounts to these towns, claiming that the South Dakota law did not apply because the line traveled briefly through North Dakota before reaching Lemmon. This interpretation naturally displeased area citizens, who argued that "it makes no difference to the company whether their rates are just or unjust so long as they can collect them."[43] The Milwaukee eventually reduced its rates, but only four years after it had helped to establish the town, the railroad found Lemmon's citizens galvanized against its practices. While the community avoided many of the more radical aspects of the larger agrarian movement then emerging across the nation, its progressive inclinations led voters to approve citywide prohibition in 1912 (an ironic development, since the town owed its existence to the fact that South Dakota allowed alcohol and North Dakota did not) and later that fall to join their fellow South Dakotans in supporting trust-busting Teddy Roosevelt in his ill-fated bid for reelection to the presidency.[44]

By the time World War I broke out in 1914, Ed had established himself in various businesses in and around his hardscrabble community on the North Dakota-South Dakota border. Yet for all his efforts, his enterprises were not doing well. The concrete-block factory failed to take off. The brick and tile company could not manufacture a viable product from the local soil. Further, Ed began to lose money on his land purchases because he could not find buyers willing to pay his asking prices. His newfound wealth came with numerous expenses as well. He supported his youngest son, George Reno, who had also moved to Lemmon and would live there until 1936. He covered the labor bills for construction of the Adams County courthouse and threw an expensive Fourth of July celebration for his fledgling community. He had built a large home, and Rosella furnished it at no small expense. She traveled across the country, spending casually and conspicuously. Ed paid burdensome tax bills on various pieces of unsalable land. Little by little, his fortune was slipping away.

Despite his money troubles, Ed's health remained remarkably intact, even after a series of automobile-related accidents. The first occurred in early 1913, when the fifty-five-year-old broke his right wrist while trying to start his "flivver." As he turned the crank to engage the motor, the engine backfired, spinning the handle and fracturing his wrist. For those who knew his approach to motor vehicles, this event was not unexpected. When the town of Lemmon began to grow, Ed had traded in his saddle for a horseless carriage. Technological advancements could not change a lifetime of acquired habits, however, and he handled his new mode of transportation with the same vigor and recklessness as he did his strong-willed horses—and always at breakneck speed. Ed's aggressive driving led to numerous accidents. Following the 1913 incident, a local newspaper noted, "The day is coming when Ed will probably acknowledge that a broncho no matter how wild and untamable, is the safer instrument of transportation."[45]

Two years later, Ed's car turned over on him near Meadow, breaking his right leg in two places. This accident marked the fourth time Ed had broken the leg, and he spent a month on crutches. In 1922, as he cranked his wife's flivver, the clutch engaged and the car ran over him, injuring his left shoulder. The broken shoulder blade healed badly, and five months after the accident Ed took a train to Aberdeen to have a physician rebreak it and set it properly. In 1929, he experienced yet another mishap when the sixteen-year-old girl driving his Ford tipped it over, breaking his right shoulder. And in 1930, when Ed tried to dislodge his stuck Model A Ford, the car rolled backward and pinned him underneath. After two hours of "scraping with my hands and finally with my pocket knife," he managed to free himself.[46] Through it all, Ed still had "health . . . to spare," although he admitted, "I present rather an ungainly figure."[47]

In contrast to her husband, Rosella complained that her health had begun to deteriorate. She claimed to suffer from "neuritis and rheumatism," which rendered her "not physically able or fit to do any work or engage in any occupation."[48] To relieve her suffering, Rosella continued to indulge in extended trips, taking lengthy treatments at sanitariums. In addition to traveling widely, she also spent her time redecorating their home, purchasing new clothes, attending dances, and in general enjoying the fruits of Ed's success.[49]

Well aware that his business ventures were not paying off, Lemmon turned some of his land parcels over to Perkins County to cover his taxes. In an attempt to regain control over his dwindling finances and capitalize on high wartime prices, in 1915 he and his son James entered the sheep business. For a renowned cattleman like Ed, investing in sheep demonstrated the direness of his situation. While he had never been particularly antagonistic towards sheepmen, he probably shared the sentiment held by most other cattle ranchers—sheepmen were an inferior lot. Ed noted that "many and various were the differences between sheep[men] and cattlemen . . . and many were the obstacles placed by cowmen and cowboys in the nomadic movement of the woolly blatters."[50]

Now, less than a decade after selling out of the cattle business, Ed began tending some of those "woolly blatters" himself. Twenty years later, he recalled the experience: "After the open-range was in a manner a thing of the past and sheep somewhat took the place of cattle, we found the old broken-down cowboy invariably made a good sheep-herder, especially if he had been a good beef herder, and the older and more decrepit, if he could set a horse all day, the more competent he was in the new role."[51] An old, broken-down cowboy himself, Ed was more than competent, but tending sheep must have been a blow to his pride. That October, he and James purchased twenty-five hundred head and moved them to a tract in North Dakota. At times, their sheep also grazed on school sections—the two sections of land in each township leased to farmers and ranchers, the proceeds from which supported the local school. In order to look after the flock, Ed moved out of his house and stayed in sheep camp. After seven years of sleeping indoors, he may have welcomed the opportunity to spend nights under the stars once again.[52]

The following year, Ed and James expanded their livestock operation by purchasing four hundred head of cattle from Minnesota, running them on land they owned in Corson County, South Dakota, on the Standing Rock reservation. James had done well since arriving in Lemmon in 1909. After a successful stint at First State Bank, he started in 1915 as secretary-treasurer of the Western Livestock and Investment Company. Within two years, he became the principle shareholder in a similar venture known as the Dakota

Livestock and Investment Company. He kept an office in the Palace Hotel on Main Street (until the building burned down on 10 November 1917) and probably used his position to help Ed reenter the livestock business. They bought three hundred more cattle in 1918 and an additional forty-two hundred in 1919, with Ed traveling to Arizona to procure them. He spent almost a month near Prescott, attending a roundup and reveling in the action. For a brief period, he returned to his life of twenty years earlier, traveling the country by train in search of high-quality, low-cost cattle; swapping stories with cowboys on the range; and conducting business as an important man of the world. Back in Lemmon, though, Ed still could not get a handle on his finances. In 1917 and 1918, his name appeared on the rolls of those owing back taxes in Perkins County. He completed his final term as commissioner during the latter year, but the embarrassment of his tax delinquency must have been acute. Lemmon experienced an additional setback in 1920, when he suffered a complete loss on the forty-two hundred head of Arizona cattle.[53]

North-central South Dakota experienced a slight drought during 1919, and the dry conditions limited the forage available for Lemmon's cattle on his Standing Rock ranch. Had the 1919–1920 winter been mild, the majority of his underweight beeves might have reached spring alive. Unfortunately, heavy snow fell in mid-October, followed by freezing rain and low temperatures. Unused to a frigid northern winter and inexperienced at finding grass beneath the snow, his thin Arizona cattle fared poorly. By March, few remained alive. Later that month, a warm spell appeared to signal the approach of spring. While his cowhands rode to Morristown to attend a dance, Ed remained at the ranch. That evening, a blizzard rolled in, burying his cabin in snow and trapping the men in town. When the weather finally cleared a week later, they returned and noticed a lone steer bellowing near the cabin. The cowboys entered and found Ed, still very much alive, sitting near the fire. Dejected and no doubt unnerved by the noise outside, he supposedly said, "Take that rifle and shoot that son-of-a-bitch, cause he's the last one."[54] This failure must have hit Ed particularly hard, because he had never before lost money on a cattle herd.

As President Warren G. Harding prepared to take the oath of office in March 1921, Ed's land enterprises and business ventures in town had become a near-total loss. With his other sources of income foundering, the sixty-three-year-old, who had already lived to see fifteen different presidents take office, continued with the enterprise he knew best—raising livestock. That year, Rosella moved out to her husband's cow camp near McLaughlin, where she cooked and kept up the small "Indian shack" he and his Sioux cowhands shared. For two years, Lemmon ran perhaps fifteen hundred head on his land near Spring Creek on the Standing Rock Indian Reservation. Having spent two decades heading a large cattle outfit and dismissing groups of less than one hundred head as insignificant, Ed probably resented the size of his herd and longed for the days of the open range. As he wrote years later, "There will always be enough farmers to hinder stocking cattle in big numbers, and the range will have to be handled with that in mind. But the West-river country is *cow country* and that's the way it always should've been."[55] Dissatisfied with an operation that could not meet his expectations, Ed finally closed out his cattle business for good in June 1923. He was sixty-six years old.[56]

Beginning with the founding of Lemmon, Ed had thrown himself into the role of town builder, working tirelessly and spending no small portion of his personal fortune trying to establish communities in North Dakota and South Dakota. He provided leadership and financial support to several area towns, much as the wealthy Billings family had done with their Montana namesake city during the late nineteenth century. Like Frederick Billings, Ed Lemmon demonstrated what historian Carroll Van West has described as "a tradition of civic capitalism."[57] When Ed retired from business in 1923, Mobridge had 3,500 residents, Lemmon more than 1,100, Hettinger over 800, and Reeder 250. Almost 8,000 people lived in Perkins County, South Dakota, while 5,500 resided in Adams County, North Dakota. The expansion of the railroad, the opening of homestead lands on the Standing Rock and Cheyenne River reservations, and the efforts of men like Ed had played a crucial role in the region's development.

Yet as the city of Lemmon grew, its namesake regressed. In many ways, Ed had sacrificed his own prosperity for the good of the town, but he was not a martyr. Just as portions of the Northern Great Plains experienced boom and bust—Perkins County may have had eight thousand residents in 1920, but eleven thousand people had called it home a decade earlier—so, too, did Ed Lemmon. Even though he could not manage to keep his wealth, the results of his efforts—railroads, towns, and families—remain evident even in the twenty-first century. It might be tempting to dismiss Lemmon's endeavors as quixotic, given the region's relatively sparse population and geographic isolation, both then and now. One may also consider his actions insignificant, because he failed in so many of his town-building efforts. Such judgments, however, lack perspective. Lemmon, South Dakota, may not have been Chicago, but it served as the most important economic and social hub of a region covering hundreds of square miles. That it did not become Chicago should surprise no one, given the tremendous environmental and geographical differences in the regions surrounding the two communities. For those homesteaders who came to the area Ed Lemmon helped to develop, his small rural community served their needs in much the same way the Windy City did the entire Midwest.[58]

Despite the setbacks (and perhaps because of them), Ed could not simply drift into a quiet retirement; it was not in his nature. While his son James took the helm as the family businessman and continued to guide the growth and development of the Lemmon area, Ed sought to tell his story—and the story of an industry and a region—through a series of articles, reminiscences, and other writings. During the next two decades, he would spend the majority of his time crafting a legacy.

8 LEGACY

Few people can work at a vocation for more than half a century without having difficulty letting go. Ed Lemmon was no different. When Lemmon sold the last of his cattle in 1923, his retirement marked the end of a fifty-three-year career as a cowboy, reservation trespasser, roundup boss, cattleman, and town builder. Having lost much of the fortune he had earned in the cattle industry to land speculation, failed businesses, and his wife's excessive spending, Ed began looking for a way to maintain the notability he had earned as one of the best-known cattlemen on the Northern Great Plains. The short, bald, sixty-six-year-old had always thrived on activity, but after numerous broken bones and a lifetime spent outdoors, his aging body could not muster the unfailing energy of his youth. Despite an expanding waistline and a crippled leg, he still longed for the action of roping and herding cattle on horseback.

Because he could no longer experience the "blood and thunder" of the range in person, Lemmon took to reading extensively about the West. He consumed western novels by Zane Grey and other authors with vigor, reliving his own adventures with cowboys, Indians, and outlaws through their pages. He also took to writing his own stories, compiling largely factual accounts of his life. He had loved listening to stories since childhood, when his father vividly described harrowing incidents in Oregon, California, and other places. Ed continued this tradition in cow camp, entertaining cowboys with sometimes embellished accounts of his own adventures and those of his family. In retirement, he acquired a typewriter and made the transition from punching cows to punching keys. When newspapers started publishing his reminiscences, he realized, as had Montana pioneer Granville Stuart, that "his personal story had become his greatest asset."[1] Ed wrote as a way to remember and relive the "good old days," though he also sought financial gain from the endeavor. Above all, he produced hundreds of pages of stories,

"Ed" Lemmon
at the
McLaughlin S.D.
Fair + Rodeo
Fiske Foto

Ed Lemmon at the McLaughlin Fair and Rodeo.
State Historical Society of North Dakota, 1952-04274

recollections, insights, and opinions as a means to secure his place as a founding figure in the West. He was building a legacy.[2]

Ed's interest in publishing stories about his life emerged in 1925, when he sought out an editor to compile his recollections into a book. On 16 August 1925, the *Anaconda* (Montana) *Standard* published a long article about Lemmon and his efforts to get Mrs. E. C. Kurtz to help complete a "history of his life and experiences in the West."[3] The Kurtz family had once lived in Lemmon, and Ed traveled to Montana to seek their assistance. He had not yet taken to writing and instead planned to tell his reminiscences to Mrs. Kurtz so that she could edit and organize them into a volume for publication. That Ed's initial foray into history appeared in the *Standard* is significant, given that Anaconda, Montana, was only twenty-five miles from Deer Lodge, the town that prospector, rancher, vigilante, and foreign diplomat Granville Stuart had advocated as Montana's state capital years earlier. As one of Montana's most important men, Stuart had received widespread recognition in the state's newspapers, including the *Standard*. In 1925, the same year Lemmon began dictating his personal history, Stuart's memoirs, titled *Forty Years on the Frontier*, appeared in print. Stuart's experiences in cattle ranching and town building overlapped with Lemmon's, and the Anaconda newspaper editor likely recognized their similarities and sought to attract readers by featuring several of Lemmon's stories.[4]

Mrs. Kurtz's efforts to compile Ed's reminiscences resulted in a few being printed as newspaper articles, but she could not meet the challenge of organizing them into a book. In the winter of 1926, after some of Ed's stories appeared in the *Lemmon Tribune*, James encouraged his father to continue to seek out an editor, promising "to go in on it" if they could be published.[5] Later that year, Ed began working with North Dakota historian Lewis F. Crawford on a book based on his experiences as an open-range cowboy. Rather than dictating the accounts as he had done with Kurtz, Ed typed them and sent the pages to Crawford for editing. Crawford, who served as superintendent of the State Historical Society of North Dakota, had already published several works, including a biography of frontiersman Ben Arnold. His experience made him well qualified to edit Lemmon's stories, but the old cattleman's poorly written and haphazardly organized submissions made the job difficult. As Ed noted in a handwritten letter to his new editor on 7 December 1926, his recent writings were "absolutely the first typing I ever did, So do not criticize my work." He also knew that some of his accounts contained fictitious or unverified information, but he hoped they could rival some of the "Blood-Curdling Stories" then in print. "Bear in mind I have at least 10 more good Indian stories," he wrote on one occasion. "Also bear in mind there is no fiction excepting the Petrified Buffalo story and possibly Tom Tinkham's Denver to Beatrice trip. Also possibly my Great, Great, Great, Grandfather's story of falling from the Log Cabin. . . . I can vouch for all others, as they are truth and not fiction."[6]

Ed typed his stories in a rambling, free-flowing style that often covered decades of time and several different topics in just a few paragraphs. He followed his memories wherever and whenever they took him, with entertainment, education, and self-promotion as the ultimate goals. His writings could best be described as the stories he had told around the campfire put down on paper. While Ed possessed an exceptional memory and had a broad range of experiences on which to draw, organizing his numerous jumbled accounts posed an immense challenge for Crawford and several other would-be editors, including Nellie Snyder Yost. In 1969, twenty-five years after Ed's death, Yost published a volume of his reminiscences titled *Boss Cowman: The Recollections of Ed Lemmon, 1857–1946.* She described the challenges involved in the endeavor: "Lemmon had written his story after the fashion of most elderly people when reminiscing, recounting the events as he recalled them, with no continuity whatever. He often began a story and then was reminded of another, whereupon he promptly took off on a new track, and perhaps even on the third, before that chapter of his life was ready for newsprint. In later episodes he would go back to the unfinished stories. Consequently, it took endless digging and sorting to put the tales together at all, and then into a meaningful sequence."[7] Crawford, who continued to receive regular submissions from Lemmon throughout the 1920s, suffered through the same difficulties Yost experienced.

While Ed immersed himself in writing his reminiscences, Rosella soured over their financial situation. Following their marriage in 1900, Rosella had enjoyed a comfortable lifestyle due to Ed's successful cattle ventures. When his fortune started to run out in the 1910s, she grew increasingly frustrated. Unlike her husband, who valued material things primarily for their functionality, Rosella loved her beautiful home and expensive clothes. Ed enjoyed spending time with common cowboys on the range, but such an environment was loathsome to his wife. She had detested living in the shack on Standing Rock and resented Ed for forcing her to cook and clean for his Indian cowboys. She became irate when she discovered that Ed had cut off her line of credit at several stores because he no longer had the funds to cover her expenses. Rosella reached her breaking point in the mid-1920s when she had to move to the second floor of their once-opulent home so they could rent out the first floor to boarders. In addition to acquiring debts related to his failed livestock endeavors, Ed had again fallen behind on their property taxes. He leased the house's lower floor to generate enough income so they could avoid foreclosure and continue living there. On 19 April 1927, a month before Ed's seventieth birthday, Rosella filed for divorce.[8]

She immediately attempted to discredit her husband in order to win a financial settlement. Rosella alleged that Ed and James were conspiring to conceal more than fifty thousand dollars' worth of property and sheep in order to deprive her of just compensation. She further claimed that Ed deliberately sought to "injure and wrong" her by refusing to pay bills and taxes for no reason other than "to aggravate, annoy, [and] harass" her.[9] Despite the abundant evidence, Rosella could not bring herself to admit that her husband was broke. She asserted through her attorneys that he "has been and now is a man of much more than ordinary business ability and capacity, during all of said time engaged in business activities in rather a large way; possessed of and handling large business and property interests and has received and is accustomed to receive and is able to make and receive a substantial and sufficient income from his business and business activities and ample [income] with which to provide plaintiff's needs in the way of support, food, clothing, medical attention and the necessaries of life."[10]

Despite Rosella's accusations, the court determined that Ed had "no money or property of any kind" except the house and one small parcel of land.[11] Because of his circumstances, he avoided paying alimony but had to cover her court costs and attorneys' fees. He also had to sell Rosella the house and the four lots on which it sat—valued in total between twenty-five hundred and four thousand dollars—for "one dollar and other valuable considerations in hand."[12] The divorce became final on 27 October 1927. Ed, who had moved in with James and Della several months earlier, continued to stay with his son and daughter-in-law while Rosella occupied and rented out part of the house. She would live there until 1933, when she sold the property and moved to Sturgis.[13]

Lemmon had been broke long before the 1929 stock market crash that devastated Wall Street and kicked off the Great Depression, so the nationwide financial distress and accompanying drought did not immediately affect him any more acutely than the rest of the local population. Throughout the 1930s, he spent several months of each year living in the Don Pratt Hotel in Belle Fourche, where he worked as a wool buyer for the National Wool Marketing Corporation based in Boston, Massachusetts. His son James had become heavily involved in the sheep business, and in the familiar turnaround that tends to come with old age, Ed looked to James as his primary benefactor. James owned several large flocks, which he ran in Grant and Sioux counties in North Dakota; helped found and direct the Co-Operative Wool Growers of South Dakota, a wool-marketing consortium; and, among many other business and civic ventures, served as president of the National Wool Marketing Corporation. In this capacity, he no doubt helped his aging, destitute father get a job with the company. James also became actively involved in the local Northwest Production Credit Association (PCA), a New Deal program President Franklin D. Roosevelt established in 1933 as part of the Farm Credit Act. During his twenty-four years as manager of the PCA, James would develop it into South Dakota's largest livestock-loan company.[14]

While James expanded his business interests, Ed spent much of his time typing his reminiscences. On 1 April 1932, the *Belle Fourche Bee* began running a new column by Lemmon, called "Developing the West," with a reminiscence entitled "My First Entrance into the Dakotas" as its first installment.[15] Lemmon's "Developing the West" column would become his regular forum for sharing stories, regional and personal history, open-range cattle-handling tactics, and thoughts on a wide variety of subjects, including the news of the day. Ed typed many of his articles on the back of Don Pratt Hotel stationery and submitted them to the newspaper for editing. In an attempt to draw readers, he gave his stories colorful titles, such as "Settling Quicksand with Bodies of Buffalo on Emigrant Trip Early in 1883"; "The End of Three Toes, the Killer"; "It Was a Long, Long

Trail, with Many Hardships, but the Competent Trail Boss Brought His Animals Through in Good Shape on the Ninety to One Hundred Day Trip"; "Killing of Jack Horn and Criticisms Therefor"; "Strapping Dead Indians between Horses Legs and Sinking in River"; and hundreds of others.[16] Preparing his columns for print must have been a chore, because Ed supplemented his poorly typed stories with handwritten footnotes, strikeovers, rewrites, additions, corrections, and often illegible scrawl. The old cattleman recognized his limitations in this regard, noting, "I know nothing about Paragraphing Or punctuations,,Which will have to be done by Type,Setter."[17]

Lemmon's published articles offered a unique perspective into life in the West. As a longtime resident of the Northern Great Plains, he wrote stories that appealed to readers' natural fascination with local history. Ed remained one of the area's most recognized figures, thanks in part to his *Belle Fourche Bee* pieces. Having written the vast majority of his stories strictly from memory, he made numerous errors, ranging from dates and places to circumstances and participants in particular events. He sought, however, to produce factual accounts of his life, and when he did stray into areas beyond his personal expertise, he usually noted that his comments were based on hearsay.

Lemmon's reminiscences provided a wealth of information about life as a range cowboy, but many of his articles simply attempted to extol the value of his own activities as a cattleman and town builder. Had he not suffered from stage fright, Lemmon could have been one of the region's most popular speakers at banquets, weddings, funerals, and other gatherings. Because he was afraid of public speaking, he used the only other available means of sharing his experiences—the written word. Yet for all his story-worthy exploits, Ed appears occasionally to have suffered from writer's block. He began what would become more than a decade of weekly newspaper articles when he was seventy-five years old, so it is not surprising that he often failed to recall new material for his columns. When he could not summon any personal stories from memory, Ed reflected on current events or shared secondhand tales, with a good measure of added hyperbole. He did not always differentiate between first and secondhand experiences, which caused consternation among his would-be publishers.

During the 1930s, Lemmon made numerous attempts to get his writings published. He had continued sending stories to Crawford, but the historian was busy finishing his three-volume *History of North Dakota*, published in 1931, and made little progress on Lemmon's project. Never known for his patience, Ed looked for other options. In 1933, he began writing to the Nebraska State Historical Society, requesting information and sending copies of his recollections. Addison E. Sheldon, secretary of the historical society, corresponded with him and sent his submissions out for review. The results were not favorable. Reviewer George Hansen detailed the inaccuracies of Lemmon's stories in several letters to Sheldon; in particular, he drew attention to critical errors in Ed's account of Wild Bill Hickok's 1861 killing of David McCanles, James Woods, and James Gordon at the Rock Creek Pony Express station. Hansen recommended that Ed's stories not be published. Famed author and historian Mari Sandoz also reviewed Lemmon's writings, commenting: "They are full of glaring inaccuracies, etc., that even my limited knowledge detects but there is without doubt a personal flavor and if the man could write at all he could make something worth reading, both as history, if he would be willing to do a little checking, etc., and as good narration. But as it stands!"[18] Excerpts from a few of his stories made their way into Nebraska State Historical Society publications, but Lemmon longed for something more substantial.[19]

When Crawford passed away in 1936, his books and papers passed to North Dakota Congressman Usher L. Burdick, who later recalled:

> Among them was the mass of material which Lemmon had forwarded, including cattle history, history of wild men of the west, wild women of the west, cattle trails from Texas, the cow days in the Black Hills, and data of Lemmon's experiences on the range. It is apparent that Crawford never got around to write the story. I also found many photographs which Mr. Lemmon wanted used. I discovered at once that this was a most interesting mass of material and should be published.
>
> I got in touch with Mr. Lemmon in 1936 and agreed to write the story, utilizing any spare time I had aside from the arduous

duties confronting a Congressman. I assembled the material and classified it preparatory to writing the final draft, but I was confronted by the same problem that delayed Mr. Crawford. Mr. Lemmon kept up a brisk submission of articles, some of which I received in manuscript form. A great amount of this data was in slightly different form from what I already had, but there was little difference in the facts. The work of comparing these articles and hunting for new facts has been a long and arduous undertaking.[20]

Burdick's efforts continued throughout the 1930s and 1940s, finally culminating in a manuscript called "History of the Range Cattle Trade of the Dakotas."[21]

During his later years, Lemmon participated in the Work Projects Administration's Federal Writers' Project, submitting a number of accounts for keeping in the Wyoming State Library. Lemmon also served as a source of information for other authors. He corresponded with August H. Schatz as he prepared to write *Longhorns Bring Culture*, a history of southwestern Dakota Territory. Ed and Sam Moses, a former detective for the Western South Dakota Stock Growers Association, shared their recollections with Schatz and read portions of his manuscript prior to its publication. In 1940, amateur historian Raymond S. Griffiths declared Lemmon "one of the best living authorities on range history. His ability to remember details and even the smallest incidents is phenomenal. He has been a source of information for stories and books about the old west as it was and as it has been distorted."[22] With his personal fortune gone and the days of open-range cattle ranching a distant memory, writing represented Ed's greatest opportunity—however remote—for financial success. It also served as a way for him to share his experiences and remain relevant. With few possessions to pass along, Ed worked diligently to develop a legacy that could carry on after his death.[23]

Although Lemmon spent a great deal of time writing during the early 1930s, he remained active in local events, attending fairs, ribbon cuttings, and celebrations. In 1932, he participated in several important observances. In June, the organizers of the new Petrified Wood Park in Lemmon honored Ed during their opening ceremony; in July, he led the processional parade for the "Old Timers Picnic," a large gathering of former open-range cowboys held near Bixby; and in early September, he attended the dedication of a new monument to Lakota Sioux chief Sitting Bull. Throughout the decade, Lemmon became a regular at the old timers' events, rarely missed an area rodeo, and managed to enjoy himself despite the difficulties of the Great Depression. With help from his son James, he eked out a living, "still eating three squares per day and doling out candy to the kids."[24]

In June 1936, Ed and James were in Belle Fourche registering for the annual meeting of the South Dakota Stock Growers Association when they received word that Ed's youngest son, George, had died. George had moved from Colorado to Lemmon in the 1910s, working at Ed's banks and as a brand inspector for the Stock Growers Association. After the United States entered World War I, he enlisted and served at Camp Funston, Kansas, until 1919. Upon being discharged, George joined his father and older brother in their sheep enterprise and later went into business for himself in Montana. He married Mildred Spear, and the couple had two children, James Edward and Harold Marius. On the day he died, George and a few friends were swimming in Isabel Lake, two miles north of Isabel, South Dakota, when he suffered a "violent attack of cramps" about 150 feet from shore and drowned.[25] George's family interred his body in Greenhill Cemetery in south Lemmon.

By the late 1930s, personal loss and the strain and uncertainty of the Great Depression had finally begun to take a toll on Lemmon. Although he was a natural optimist—he expressed hope for the future in his newspaper columns and offered forward-looking advice for conserving moisture and preventing soil erosion—by 1937 his financial situation had taken precedence over preserving his legacy for posterity. "I do not claim to any great part in developing the West," he said, "for my sole aim at times was to add to my exchecker, with very few philanthropic views in my mind, but, oh, how disappointing these last few years of drouth and depression have been."[26]

Lemmon's struggle to earn a living forced him to explore creative solutions. For several years he had worked as a wool buyer for the National Wool Marketing Corporation, but at the age of eighty he was having limited success and could no longer afford to live at the

Ed Lemmon, half kneeling at right, at "Old Timers" event, 1930s.
South Dakota State Historical Society

Don Pratt Hotel in Belle Fourche. With few other options, Ed wrote
to one of South Dakota's congressmen, requesting an investigation
into his military service. He had guided a military contingent following the 1890 Wounded Knee Massacre and hoped to be allowed
to collect federal benefits and live at the state veterans' home in Hot
Springs. Admission to the home required a minimum of thirty days'
military service, however, and since Ed had served for just one day,
he did not qualify. He also attempted to collect reparations from the
federal government for the Indian raid on Liberty Farm, which occurred seven decades earlier in August 1864. He was disappointed,
but not surprised, when the government dismissed his petition for
lack of sufficient evidence.[27]

Despite his financial hardships, Ed's good humor rarely failed.
He traveled widely, visiting scores of friends and neighbors in Perkins County, the Black Hills, and numerous places along the way.
Although he always used a cane—an intricately carved diamond
willow featuring fifty livestock brands—he remained relatively un-
hindered by his crippled right leg. "It isn't a bad stick yet and beats
a wooden one by far," he quipped.[28] Ed also spent much of his time
doting on children. He may have been making up for his lack of en-
gagement as a father to his own sons, but "Dad" Lemmon charmed

scores of kids with candy, stories, and kindness. In *Taming the Plains*, a history of Corson County, South Dakota, Rose Tidball described "Dad" as a "shrewd, persuasive man who didn't drink or smoke and the children loved him. He usually had a bag of candy for them and would often joke or play games with them."[29] Another writer summed up a sentiment held by many who knew Lemmon: "He was one that once known you never could forget."[30]

Ed's notability earned him a unique honor in 1941—a full-page picture in *Life* magazine. That September, photographer Eliot Elisofon and writer Roger Butterfield traveled to South Dakota and produced a photographic essay titled, "South Dakota: Its Boundless Plains Are the Heart of a Continent." They drove more than thirty-one hundred miles within the state, searching for interesting places and people. Elisofon and Butterfield's essay featured small photographs of several interesting personalities, including Governor Harlan Bushfield, State Exterminator A. M. Jackley (who killed ninety thousand rattlesnakes in 1940 alone), and South Dakota State College agriculture professor Nils Hansen. Twelve such portraits filled one page, balanced on the opposite page by a full-page portrait of Lemmon leaning on his carved walking stick. His wide-brimmed hat hinted at his cowboy past, as did his contorted right leg. The authors penned the following summary: "The great South Dakotan and great Westerner on the opposite page, George Edward ('Dad') Lemmon, was born at Bountiful, Utah, in 1857, began punching cows in Wyoming at 13. His right leg was broken eight times in falls but he went on to saddle-handle more cattle than any man who ever lived—up to 900 in a single day. Once he had the largest fenced pasture in the world (865,429½ acres). In 1907 he staged a sale of prairie lots on [the] North Dakota border and founded [the] town of Lemmon, where he lives today."[31]

For Ed, the magazine feature was one of the highlights of his life. As the *Lemmon Leader* reported in a short article titled "'Dad' Lemmon Is Thrilled by Page Picture in Life," Ed was the "happiest man in the state."[32] Beyond the satisfaction gained from the compliments and letters of congratulations he received from a number of area citizens, the *Life* recognition marked the culmination of Lemmon's longtime efforts to see his story in print. Although it was not the same as publishing his own book, he found the experience "very satisfying, to say the least."[33]

The *Life* magazine feature would prove to be the last publicly significant moment in Ed's long and eventful life. He lived in the Palace Hotel in Lemmon during most of World War II, relying on his son James for financial support. In August 1945, just days after the United States dropped atomic bombs on the Japanese cities of Hiroshima and Nagasaki, Ed fell ill. He was taken to the Lemmon hospital, which occupied the second story of the Bank of Lemmon building on Main Street. On Saturday afternoon, 25 August—just two weeks before the Japanese surrendered to end World War II— George Edward Lemmon passed away. He was eighty-eight. Three days later, James placed Ed's body next to that of his son George in Greenhill Cemetery on the south side of the community he had founded. The R. S. Evanson Funeral Home charged $625.90 for the funeral. Because Ed had only $582.80 in assets when he died, James paid the difference.[34]

Following Ed's death, the Lemmon family slowly disappeared from its namesake town. Rosella, who had moved to Sturgis years earlier, passed away in 1964. Four years later Ed's two remaining sons—James and Roy Edward—also died. Roy had spent much of his career in California as a Hollywood stunt man and returned to South Dakota before his death. He and James were both interred in Greenhill Cemetery. James had been one of Lemmon's strongest businessmen and community leaders, working diligently to promote and strengthen the prairie town. His wife Della, who had experienced a series of physical and mental health problems, passed away in 1970. She and James had had no children.

Ed Lemmon outlived most of his peers and business partners, crediting the virtue of vigorous activity with helping to keep him in shape. He claimed that Ben and George Sheidley, Richard Lake, and Thomas Tomb had all died due to "softening of the brain. Too much brain work and not enough manual exercise."[35] Like Theodore Roosevelt, Lemmon lived a "strenuous life" full of action.

Lemmon's role in the development of the Northern Great Plains has been memorialized in countless ways. Many of his contributions to the region's nomenclature began when he was alive, with the town of Lemmon the most notable example. In 1931, Don MeLoy built a small store fifty miles south of Lemmon, which he named "Usta" in honor of Ed's corrupted Indian name. In 1957, the City of Lemmon erected a stone monument honoring Ed in the city park as part of its fiftieth anniversary celebration. The following year, James successfully nominated his father for induction into the National Cowboy Hall of Fame in Oklahoma City. In 1969, Nellie Snyder Yost published her edited version of Ed's reminiscences, *Boss Cowman*, which helped to rekindle regional interest in the pioneer cattleman. Two years later, the City of Lemmon started what has become an annual affair—the Boss Cowman Celebration and Rodeo. Taking its name from Yost's book, the rodeo recognizes a distinguished area rancher or couple each year as "Boss Cowman Honorees," a testament to Ed Lemmon's influence. In 1994, Ed was inducted posthumously into the South Dakota Hall of Fame, and in the second decade of the twenty-first century, efforts are underway to renovate his house in Lemmon into a museum.[36]

Ed Lemmon lived a life full of adventure, excitement, fun, and hard work. He loved jokes and stories, slept in bedrolls belonging to other cowboys, and rode so recklessly that he broke his leg multiple times in horse falls. At twenty years of age, he guided trail drives. By age thirty-four, he had become range manager for one of the largest cattle outfits on the Northern Great Plains, turning a free-spirited bunch of toughs into first-rate cowhands while developing tradecraft and cattle-handling techniques that other cattle outfits throughout the region copied. As one of the most recognized authorities on open-range cattle handling, he exerted an influence that extended far beyond the Flying V and Reverse L7 outfits.

In almost ninety years on the Great Plains, Lemmon played an integral role in its growth and development. His efforts to build a personal financial fortune helped to bring non-Indian settlers into the region, making Lemmon—sometimes unknowingly—one of the key figures guiding its history. As a cowboy and cattleman, he relied on Indian lands—both legally and illegally—to build a cattle empire. When South Dakota became the last vestige of the open range in the United States, Lemmon enjoyed a prominent role as one of its most important actors. He subsequently used his range skills to guide the Chicago, Milwaukee & St. Paul Railroad west across the

"DAD" LEMMON, 84, WALKS
THE STREETS OF A PRAIRIE
TOWN HE FOUNDED IN 1907

George Edward ("Dad") Lemmon as he appeared in *Life*, 6 October 1941.

Missouri River, becoming a town builder and losing a fortune in the process. In his later life, Ed helped to define the history of the region through the published reminiscences that earned him widespread recognition.

As "Dean of the Range," Lemmon symbolized the hearty stock of the West River country. His skill in open-range cattle handling, his knowledge of the people and environment of the Northern Great Plains, and his role in its development were unmatched.[37] A few years before his death, the *Rapid City Daily Journal* summed up his life this way: "The story of 'Dad' Lemmon's life is an epic of the last frontier, the great west which still has thousands of ranches, but in which the scene is constantly changing. No living man is better acquainted with this area or has watched its progress more closely through three-score years and ten."[38] Lemmon could not have asked for a better legacy.

NOTES

Introduction

1. By the time of Lemmon's death in 1945, historians had already attempted to assess and interpret the significance of the region he had called home. In recent years, scholars have engaged in an interesting debate regarding the American West. Specifically, the question has been whether "the West" is a geographical place or part of a process that has helped to define the United States as a nation. The debate originated in 1893 when a young Frederick Jackson Turner delivered an essay titled "The Significance of the Frontier in American History" at the World's Columbian Exposition in Chicago. Turner argued that the process of civilizing a "savage" land and its people had produced a unique American identity. Further, the American frontier had officially closed as of the 1890 census, when the United States reached a population density of at least two people per square mile. Since that moment, numerous historians have struggled to assess the validity of Turner's thesis, which, some assert, overlooked important actors, including women, American Indians, ethnic groups, and the environment. For these varied viewpoints on the history of the West, *see* William Cronon, *Nature's Metropolis: Chicago and the Great West* (New York: W. W. Norton & Co., 1991); Patricia Nelson Limerick, *The Legacy of Conquest: The Unbroken Past of the American West* (New York: Norton, 1987); Frederick Jackson Turner, *The Significance of the Frontier in American History*, ed. Harold P. Simonson (New York: Frederick Ungar Publishing Co., 1963); Walter Prescott Webb, *The Great Plains* (Boston: Ginn & Co., 1931); Elliott West, *The Way to the West: Essays on the Central Plains* (Albuquerque: University of New Mexico Press, 1995); Richard White, *"It's Your Misfortune and None of My Own:" A New History of the American West* (Norman: University of Oklahoma Press, 1991); and Donald Worster, *Rivers of Empire: Water, Aridity, and the Growth of the American West* (New York: Pantheon Books, 1985).

2. Louis S. Warren, *Buffalo Bill's America: William Cody and the Wild West Show* (New York: Alfred A. Knopf, 2005), pp. xi, 540–42.

3. *Belle Fourche Bee* (hereafter *BFB*), 5 Jan. 1934. *See also* "Rosie Kelley with the Buckskin Bellie of Cheyenne," Work Projects Administration collection, Pioneer Cabinet, Wyoming State Archives, Cheyenne.

4. Lemmon actually translated Huste three different ways: Crooked Ass, Crooked Rump, and Crooked Hip, none of which was correct. Cowboy Ike Blasingame noted, "The Indians called him Hoostay, which simply means 'crippled,' and they held him in high regard. Gradually everyone began calling him

Hoostay, a name which stuck with him always" (Blasingame, *Dakota Cowboy: My Life in the Old Days* [Lincoln: University of Nebraska Press, 1964], p. 222). Usta, a location in Perkins County, South Dakota, is a corruption of Lemmon's nickname. He occasionally camped near the site, which is on the Moreau River. *Faith Country Heritage, 1910–1985* (Faith, S.Dak.: Faith Historical Committee, 1985), p. 364; *BFB*, 9 Nov. 1934, 1 Mar. 1935; Eugene Buechel and Paul Manhart, eds., *Lakota Dictionary: New Comprehensive Edition* (Lincoln: University of Nebraska Press, 2002), p. 94.

5. In Lakota, the phrase is "t'aspáŋ zi p'a." "T'aspáŋ" means apple and "zi" means "yellow," thus the Americanized version became *Taspaze*, or "Yellow Apple." Buechel and Manhart, eds., *Lakota Dictionary*, pp. 300, 428.

6. Bert L. Hall, comp., *Roundup Years: Old Muddy to Black Hills* ([Winner, S.Dak.]: Western South Dakota Buck-a-roos, 2000), p. 301. *See also* ibid., pp. 19, 300.

7. Ed Lemmon, *Boss Cowman: The Recollections of Ed Lemmon, 1857–1946*, ed. Nellie Snyder Yost (Lincoln: University of Nebraska Press, 1969). Yost came up with the term "Boss Cowman" on her own. No evidence suggests that Lemmon was ever referred to by this title, and no other source refers to Lemmon as such. The City of Lemmon annually hosts the Boss Cowman Celebration in honor of Ed Lemmon. This event began after Yost published Lemmon's writings and took its name from the book.

1. Youth

1. *Belle Fourche Bee* (hereafter *BFB*), 13 Jan. 1933.

2. Ike Blasingame, *Dakota Cowboy: My Life in the Old Days* (Lincoln: University of Nebraska Press, 1964), p. 222. *See also BFB*, 16 Feb. 1934.

3. *Developing the West*, vol. 13, p. 5, MSS 691, Wyoming State Archives, Cheyenne (hereafter *DW*). This collection is a compilation of stories written by Lemmon and published in the *Belle Fourche Bee* during the 1930s. Comprising fourteen "volumes" or packets, the articles are arranged in no discernible order and carry no reference to the dates of their publication in the *Bee*. Many of them are slightly different from the versions that appeared in the newspaper.

4. According to Lemmon, this recognition took place in the corridor of the Brown Palace Hotel, although it is not noted in any official association documents. Lemmon restated this assertion numerous times in his writings and was apparently never challenged on the point. Ike Blasingame, too, related that "Ed is said to have 'saddle handled' more cattle than any man in like position" (Blasingame, *Dakota Cowboy*, p. 221). *See also* ibid., pp. 221–23; *DW*, vol. 13, p.5; Ed Lemmon, as told to Usher L. Burdick, "History of the Range Cattle Trade of the Dakotas," unpublished manuscript, call no. 01667, American Heritage Center, University of Wyoming, Laramie, p. 192; Mrs. Lloyd I. Sudlow, ed., *Homestead*

Years, 1908–1968 (Bison, S.Dak.: *Bison Courier*, 1968), p. 178; *BFB*, 31 Jan. 1936, 7 Jan. 1938; "South Dakota: Its Boundless Plains Are the Heart of a Continent," *Life*, 6 Oct. 1941, pp. 108–9; and Ed Lemmon, *Boss Cowman: The Recollections of Ed Lemmon, 1857–1946*, ed. Nellie Snyder Yost (Lincoln: University of Nebraska Press, 1969), p. vii. Though Yost's work is based on Lemmon's personal papers, it is so heavily edited that it can be relied on only for general reference.

5. Blasingame, *Dakota Cowboy*, p. 222.

6. *BFB*, 23 July 1937.

7. Obituary of James Hervey Lemmon, Sr., n.d., unknown newspaper, Virginia Grabow collection, Tigard, Ore.; Lemmon, "History of the Range Cattle Trade," p. 13; John Mack Faragher, *Women and Men on the Overland Trail*, 2d ed. (New Haven, Conn.: Yale University Press, 2001).

8. *DW*, vol. 13, p. 1; Robert H. Ruby and John A. Brown, *The Cayuse Indians: Imperial Tribesmen of Old Oregon* (Norman: University of Oklahoma Press, 1972), pp. 109–12, 128–43; Robert H. Ruby, John A. Brown, and Cary C. Collins, *A Guide to the Indian Tribes of the Pacific Northwest*, 3d ed. (Norman: University of Oklahoma Press, 2010), pp. 17–19.

9. *DW*, vol. 13, pp. 1–2.

10. *BFB*, 28 Jan., 17, 24 June, 1 July, 21 Oct. 1938; *DW*, vol. 7, p. 6.

11. *BFB*, 22 Nov. 1937.

12. Ed's bent for storytelling occasionally led him into areas where his expertise was limited. When challenged on his boldest assertions, he defended them with vigor, though in the rare instances in which others presented evidence that refuted his claims, he acknowledged that some of his information came from hearsay. For example, in 1934 Ed claimed that the Sioux Indians annually sacrificed a young maiden to the Great Spirit by dropping her from the falls of the Yellowstone River. *Rapid City Daily Journal* (hereafter *RCDJ*), 5 Dec. 1934. Several individuals challenged his assertion, including Thomas L. Riggs, a missionary to the Sioux for over six decades. *RCDJ*, 5 Feb. 1935. When faced with statements contradicting his assertions, Ed backed off, stating, "I never witnessed such a sacrifice but have heard talk of them" (*RCDJ*, 7 Feb. 1935). Ed defended his assertions in *BFB*, 1 Mar. 1935.

13. *DW*, vol. 8, p. 8, vol. 13, pp. 1–4; *BFB*, 10 June 1938; obituary of James Hervey Lemmon, Sr.

14. Lucy was born 20 September 1826 in Rindge, New Hampshire. David Lemmon, record of James H. Lemmon, Sr., family, and Virginia Grabow, untitled biography of James Hervey Lemmon, Jr., p. 5, both in Grabow collection; Lemmon, "History of the Range Cattle Trade," pp. 13–14, 16; *DW*, vol. 3, pp. 13–14; Lemmon, *Boss Cowman*, pp. 7–9. For background on westward migration, *see* John D. Unruh, Jr., *The Plains Across: The Overland Emigrants and the Trans-Mississippi West, 1840–60* (Chicago: University of Illinois Press, 1979); and Mi-

chael L. Tate, *Indians and Emigrants: Encounters on the Overland Trails* (Norman: University of Oklahoma Press, 2006).

15. Leonard J. Arrington and Davis Bitton, *The Mormon Experience: A History of the Latter-day Saints*, 2d ed. (Urbana: University of Illinois Press, 1992), pp. 8, 50; William Alexander Linn, *The Story of the Mormons: From the Date of Their Origin to the Year 1901* (New York: Russell & Russell, 1963), pp. 31, 92.

16. *BFB*, 21 Sept. 1934.

17. *DW*, vol. 9, p. 7.

18. Ibid., vol. 9, p. 6.

19. Bagley, *Blood of the Prophets: Brigham Young and the Massacre at Mountain Meadows* (Norman: University of Oklahoma Press, 2002), p. 4.

20. *DW*, vol. 6, p. 11. Lucy also bore three other children who did not survive infancy, two boys named David and a girl named Mandana. Lemmon, *Boss Cowman*, p. 11; David Lemmon, record of James H. Lemmon, Sr., family. "The Blue Juniata" begins, "Wild rov'd an Indian girl, bright Alfarata, where sweep the waters of the blue Juniata" (Dale Cockrell, *The Ingalls Wilder Family Songbook*, Music of the United States of America 22 [Middleton, Wisc.: A-R Editions, for the American Musicological Society, 2011], pp. 237–38). *See also* Juanita Brooks, *The Mountain Meadows Massacre* (Norman: University of Oklahoma Press, 1979). For a collection of firsthand accounts of the massacre, *see* Douglas Seefeldt, ed., *"Horrible Massacre of Emigrants!!": The Mountain Meadows Massacre in Public Discourse*, mountainmeadows.unl.edu.

21. *BFB*, 10 Nov. 1933, 28 Dec. 1934; Lemmon, "History of the Range Cattle Trade," p. 266; Lyn Ryder, *Road Ranches along the Oregon Trail, 1858 to 1868: Between Marysville, Kansas and Fort Kearny, Nebraska* (Niwot, Colo.: Prairie Lark Publications, 1995), p. 66; "Lemmon: G. E. 'Dad' Ed," George E. Lemmon file, Lemmon Public Library, Lemmon, S.Dak.

22. *BFB*, 18 Jan. 1935; Lemmon, "History of the Range Cattle Trade," p. 266.

23. The structures comprising Liberty Farm Station have long since been removed and plowed under, but James's and Ed's descriptions of the topography still hold true today. National Park Service, "Pony Express Historic Resources Study, Chapter Four: Division One: Stations between St. Joseph and Fort Kearney (continued)," nps.gov/parkhistory; *DW*, vol. 6, p. 11.

24. James H. Lemmon, "Early Days on the Little Blue," *Proceedings and Collections of the Nebraska State Historical Society* 15 (1907): 128.

25. Ibid.

26. Ibid. *See also* William E. Lass, *From the Missouri to the Great Salt Lake: An Account of Overland Freighting* (Lincoln: Nebraska State Historical Society, 1972). Hundreds of freight wagons from Nebraska had traveled to Utah during the Mormon War to supply the United States Army. James probably sought to capitalize on this trade by selecting a site along their key travel route.

27. *BFB*, 28 Dec. 1934.

28. Fred Reinfeld, *Pony Express* (Lincoln: University of Nebraska Press, 1966); Nancy Pope, "The Story of the Pony Express," Smithsonian National Postal Museum, postalmuseum.si.edu; Merrill Mattes and Paul Henderson, "The Pony Express: Across Nebraska from St. Joseph to Fort Laramie," *Nebraska History* 41 (June 1960): 83–122.

29. *DW*, vol. 5, p. 1.

30. *BFB*, 11 Oct. 1935.

31. Lemmon to Howard Hickok, n.d., reprinted in Ed Lemmon, *The West as I Lived It: Stories by Ed Lemmon*, comp. Phyllis Schmidt (Pierre, S.Dak.: State Publishing Co., 2007), p. 355.

32. Ibid., p. 356. *See also BFB*, 9 June 1933; and Lemmon, "History of the Range Cattle Trade," pp. 135–36. For a detailed analysis of Ed's problematic memories of Hickok, *see* George W. Hansen to Addison E. Sheldon, 8 May 1934, box 1, folder 1, G. E. Lemmon, 1857–1946 Collection, RG2016.AM, Nebraska State Historical Society, Lincoln (hereafter NSHS).

33. James V. Frederick, *Ben Holladay, the Stagecoach King: A Chapter in the Development of Transcontinental Transportation* (Glendale, Calif.: Arthur H. Clark Co., 1940), pp. 60, 63–66.

34. *BFB*, 21 Oct. 1932, 30 Oct. 1936.

35. Frederick, *Ben Holladay*, p. 165; James Lemmon, "Early Days," p. 131.

36. "Lemmon: G. E. 'Dad' Ed."

37. J. Evetts Haley, *Charles Goodnight: Cowman and Plainsman* (Norman: University of Oklahoma Press, 1949), p. 241.

38. *DW*, vol. 7, pp. 9–10, vol. 10, pp. 11–12.

39. Ibid., vol. 6, p. 11.

40. Ibid.; *BFB*, 10 Feb. 1939.

41. *BFB*, 28 Dec. 1934.

42. Ibid., 21 Oct. 1932, 28 Dec. 1934, 19 Nov. 1937; *DW*, vol. 11, pp. 20–21; Ryder, *Road Ranches*, p. 66. Following the end of the Colorado gold rush in the early 1860s, the quartz mining industry became a big business. *See* Hubert Howe Bancroft and Frances Fuller Victor, *History of Nevada, Colorado, and Wyoming, 1540–1888* (San Francisco, Calif.: History Co., 1890); and Elliott West, *The Contested Plains: Indians, Goldseekers, and the Rush to Colorado* (Lawrence: University Press of Kansas, 1998).

43. James Lemmon, "Early Days," p. 128.

44. Kenneth Carley, *The Dakota War of 1862: Minnesota's Other Civil War*, 2d ed. (St. Paul: Minnesota Historical Society Press, 2001), pp. 1–8; Gary Clayton Anderson, *Kinsmen of Another Kind: Dakota-White Relations in the Upper Mississippi Valley, 1650–1862* (Lincoln: University of Nebraska Press, 1984), pp. 261–79; Michael Clodfelter, *The Dakota War: The United States Army versus the*

Sioux, 1862–1865 (Jefferson, N.C.: McFarland & Co., 1998), pp. 66–67, 155–58; George E. Hyde, *Red Cloud's Folk: A History of the Oglala Sioux Indians* (Norman: University of Oklahoma Press, 1937), pp. 101–13; Frederick, *Ben Holladay*, pp. 190–93; Robert W. Larson, *Red Cloud: Warrior-Statesman of the Lakota Sioux* (Norman: University of Oklahoma Press, 1997), pp. 80–82.

45. Frank A. Root and William Elsey Connelley, *The Overland Stage to California: Personal Reminiscences and Authentic History of the Great Overland Stage Line and Pony Express from the Missouri River to the Pacific Ocean* (Topeka, Kans.: Crane & Co., 1901), pp. 353–60; John G. Ellenbecker, *Oak Grove Massacre (Oak, Nebraska): Indian Raids on the Little Blue River in 1864* (Marysville, Kans.: *Marysville Advocate-Democrat*, 1927). According to James, twenty-three people died during the attacks within thirty-five miles of Liberty Farm. Lemmon, "Early Days," p. 128. Ed Lemmon's own secondhand account of the raid on Liberty Farm suffers from several inaccuracies. He was, however, just seven years old and living in Marysville, Kansas at the time. *See DW*, vol. 11, pp. 20–21; and James C. Olson, *Red Cloud and the Sioux Problem* (Lincoln: University of Nebraska Press, 1965), p. 25.

46. [William G. Cutler, ed.], *History of the State of Kansas*, vol. 2 (Chicago: A. T. Andreas, 1883), p. 915.

47. Clodfelter, *Dakota War*, pp. 202–13.

48. *See* ibid.; and Duane P. Schultz, *Month of the Freezing Moon: The Sand Creek Massacre, November 1864* (New York: St. Martin's Press, 1990).

49. Lemmon, "History of the Range Cattle Trade," pp. 338–39; *BFB*, 21 Oct. 1932; Frederick, *Ben Holladay*, pp. 191–92.

50. *BFB*, 28 Dec. 1934, 6 Aug. 1937, 12 Dec. 1939; *DW*, vol. 5, p. 3, vol. 8, pp. 10–14; James Lemmon, "Early Days," pp. 128–31.

51. James Lemmon, "Early Days," pp. 128–31. James and Ed Lemmon's accounts of this incident are slightly different. Unsurprisingly, James's seems more genuine. *See DW*, vol. 11, pp. 6–7. For an analysis of the two interpretations, *see* George W. Hansen to Addison E. Sheldon, 14 Nov. 1933 and 9 May 1934, both in box 1, folder 1, NSHS.

52. Quoted in Hansen to Sheldon, 9 May 1934.

53. Charles Edgar Ames, *Pioneering the Union Pacific: A Reappraisal of the Builders of the Railroad* (New York: Appleton-Century-Crofts, 1969), pp. 98–103, 119, 122; Frederick, *Ben Holladay*, pp. 252–62; *BFB*, 11 May 1939. *See also* Robert G. Athearn, *Union Pacific Country* (Lincoln: Bison Books, 1971), pp. 42–43.

54. *BFB*, 11 May 1939.

55. Ames, *Pioneering the Union Pacific*, p. 118.

56. *DW*, vol. 5, p. 3, vol. 11, pp. 6–7; *BFB*, 6 Aug. 1937, 21 Dec. 1939; Lemmon, "History of the Range Cattle Trade," pp. 263–64. Tie-cutting rates varied, but some individuals could command forty-nine dollars per month, plus a twenty-

nine-cent bonus for every tie cut above fifteen per day. *See* Athearn, *Union Pacific Country*, p. 44; and "Report of Samuel B. Reed, of Surveys and Explorations from Green River to Great Salt Lake City," Survey, Salt Lake Region, 1864 file, box 2, series 1, subgroup 14, unit 1, Union Pacific Railroad (Omaha, Nebr.) Collection, RG3761.AM, Nebraska State Historical Society, Lincoln.

57. *DW*, vol. 11, p. 11.

58. Quoted in Athearn, *Union Pacific Country*, p. 61.

59. Ames, *Pioneering the Union Pacific*, p. 234.

60. *BFB*, 22 July 1938; Lemmon to the State Historical Society of Wyoming, n.d., Work Projects Administration collection, Pioneer Cabinet, Wyoming State Archives, Cheyenne (hereafter Pioneer Cabinet).

61. *Cheyenne Leader*, 14 Feb. 1868. *See also BFB*, 22 July 1938; Lemmon to the State Historical Society of Wyoming, n.d.; Mark Ellis, *Law and Order in Buffalo Bill's Country: Legal Culture and Community on the Great Plains, 1867–1910* (Lincoln: University of Nebraska Press, 2007); and Charles A. Vollan, "Hell on Wheels: Community, Respectability, and Violence in Cheyenne, Wyoming, 1867–1869" (Ph.D. diss., University of Nebraska–Lincoln, 2004), pp. 78–79. The Saturday, 7 March 1868 edition of the *Cheyenne Leader* included "Lemon hervey" in its list of individuals with mail to collect at the post office. James received mail as well, suggesting that Hervey may have begun conducting business under his own name. For reports on the shootings in Cheyenne, *see* the *Cheyenne Leader*, 1868 and 1869.

62. *BFB*, 10 Nov. 1933. *See also* ibid., 11 May 1934; *Cheyenne Leader*, 23 Mar. 1861; and Vollan, "Hell on Wheels," p. 261. This Charles Martin is not to be confused with the man of the same name who served as secretary of the National Live Stock Association.

63. Emanuel H. Saltiel and George H. Barnett, *History and Business Directory of Cheyenne and Guide to the Mining Regions of the Rocky Mountains* (1868; facsimile ed., New Haven, Conn.: Yale University Library, 1975), p. 23.

64. Vollan, "Hell on Wheels," pp. 272–74. *See also* Frederick Allen, *A Decent, Orderly Lynching: The Montana Vigilantes* (Norman: University of Oklahoma Press, 2004).

65. *DW*, vol. 3, pp. 3–4. The company founded by General Isaac Coe and Levi Carter provided a large portion of the ties used for the Union Pacific construction in western Nebraska and Wyoming. *See* Scott Thybony, Robert G. Rosenberg, and Elizabeth Mullett Rosenberg, *The Medicine Bows: Wyoming's Mountain Country* (Caldwell, Idaho: Caxton Printers, 1986), pp. 61–63.

66. *DW*, vol. 3, pp. 3–4; *BFB*, 24 Dec. 1937.

67. "Prairie Dog Arnold of Cheyenne, 1868–1870" and "Rosie Kelley with the Buckskin Bellie of Cheyenne," both in Pioneer Cabinet; *BFB*, 25 May 1934, 14 Aug. 1936, 24 Dec. 1937, 22 July 1938; Lemmon, *The West as I Lived It*, p. 365.

68. The church's horse herd roamed on what is today's Antelope Island State Park. A sandbar on the island's southeast side provided ready access for herders to trail livestock on and off. No records exist to verify this transaction; however, Ed Lemmon mentions the "Church Island horses" numerous times in his writings, and the circumstances regarding Young's use of horses for compensation is consistent with earlier uses of the Antelope Island herd. *BFB*, 8 Dec. 1933, 18 Jan. 1935; Michael W. Homer, "An Immigrant Story: Three Orphaned Italians in Early Utah Territory," *Utah Historical Quarterly* 70 (Summer 2002): 205–6; James H. Beckstead, *Cowboying: A Tough Job in a Hard Land* (Salt Lake City: University of Utah Press, 1991), pp. 11, 13, 53, 55; "After Completion of the Union Pacific Railroad, 1869, and Driving of the Golden Spike at Promontory Point, Utah, in May 1869," Pioneer Cabinet.

69. *New York Times*, 26 Nov. 1875; Haley, *Charles Goodnight*, p. 241; *BFB*, 6 May 1932, 13 Apr., 9 Nov. 1934, 1 Mar. 1935. Iliff (1831–1878) is the namesake of the Iliff School of Theology in Denver, Colorado.

70. While staying at the Chalk Bluffs, Ed may have instructed Minnie Pinneo in horseback riding. Pinneo later earned some renown as a world-class horse racer, winning prizes in several large races in the eastern United States and in Europe. She may have raced some of James's Church Island horses in these contests. The Pinneo family, who also lived in Cheyenne at this time, was well acquainted with the Lemmons, so Minnie and Ed probably rode together. *See BFB*, 18 Jan. 1935.

71. *BFB*, 27 May 1932. *See also* ibid., 6 May 1932; *DW*, vol. 10, p. 9; and "My Lost Opportunity to Kill an Indian," Pioneer Cabinet.

72. *DW*, vol. 10, p. 9.

73. Lemmon to Crawford, 7 Dec. 1926, G. E. Lemmon Papers, MSS 20019, State Historical Society of North Dakota, Bismarck.

2. Cowboying

1. "After Completion of the Union Pacific Railroad, 1869, and Driving of the Golden Spike at Promontory Point, Utah, in May 1869," Work Projects Administration collection, Pioneer Cabinet, Wyoming State Archives, Cheyenne.

2. Ibid.

3. Ibid.; obituary of James Hervey Lemmon, Sr., n.d., unknown newspaper, Virginia Grabow collection, Tigard, Ore.; Lyn Ryder, *Road Ranches along the Oregon Trail, 1858 to 1868: Between Marysville, Kansas and Fort Kearny, Nebraska* (Niwot, Colo.: Prairie Lark Publications, 1995), p. 66. Benjamin Royce received a patent to the 160 acres on 10 February 1873. Ed Lemmon, *Boss Cowman: The Recollections of Ed Lemmon, 1857–1946*, ed. Nellie Snyder Yost (Lincoln: University of Nebraska Press, 1969), p. 68n5; Virginia Grabow, untitled biography of James Hervey Lemmon, Jr., pp. 23–24, Grabow collection.

4. "After Completion of the Union Pacific Railroad."

5. *Belle Fourche Bee* (hereafter *BFB*), 28 Dec. 1934, 29 July 1938; manuscript population schedule, Cheyenne, Laramie County, W.T., in U.S., Department of the Interior, Census Office, *Ninth Census of the United States, 1870*, National Archives Microfilm Publication M593, roll 1748, sheet 413B.

6. *BFB*, 21 May 1937. Cowboys often rode in front of a stampeding herd, "leading" it in a particular direction and trying to stop or slow the stampede. In this case, the cowboys were unable to stop the herd, and the bosses told their men to get out of the way ("quit the leads") before the herds collided.

7. Ibid. Hervey Lemmon married Lew Slover's sister Elizabeth in 1878.

8. W. H. Hamilton, *Dakota: An Autobiography of a Cowman* (Pierre: South Dakota State Historical Society Press, 1998), p. 1.

9. Alfred T. Andreas, *History of the State of Nebraska* (Chicago: The Western Historical Company, 1882), p. 1478.

10. *BFB*, 27 May 1932.

11. Ibid.

12. Ibid.

13. Ibid.

14. Ibid. *See also* ibid., 21 Dec. 1939; and *Developing the West*, vol. 5, pp. 3–4, MSS 691, Wyoming State Archives, Cheyenne (hereafter *DW*).

15. *BFB*, 17 Feb. 1933. *See also* ibid., 27 May 1938. The *Bee* reprinted a similar article with a slightly different title in two separate issues five years apart.

16. *DW*, vol. 12, pp. 4–5.

17. *BFB*, 7 Jan. 1938.

18. Grabow, untitled biography of James Hervey Lemmon, Jr., p. 75.

19. *Lemmon Tribune*, 17 Feb. 1927.

20. *BFB*, 25 Jan. 1935.

21. Ibid., 7 Jan. 1938.

22. Blasingame, *Dakota Cowboy: My Life in the Old Days* (Lincoln: University of Nebraska Press, 1964), p. 87.

23. *DW*, vol. 10, p. 1.

24. Ibid., vol. 13, p. 10. *See also* ibid., vol. 7, pp. 3–4, vol. 10, p. 1, vol. 11, p. 17, vol. 13, p. 10; and *BFB*, 21 Feb. 1936.

25. *DW*, vol. 10, p. 1, vol. 13, p. 10.

26. Ibid., vol. 13, p. 10.

27. *BFB*, 7 Jan. 1938.

28. Ibid., 18 Jan. 1935; Grabow, untitled biography of James Hervey Lemmon, Jr., p. 65.

29. *BFB*, 16 Feb. 1934.

30. Ibid. *See also DW*, vol. 13, p. 5; and Lemmon, "Killing of Jack Horn and Criticisms Therefor," Ed Texley collection, Hettinger, N.Dak.

31. *BFB*, 16 Feb. 1934.

32. Lemmon, "Fifty-three Years of Open-Range Cattle Handling," Texley collection; Russell Tronstad, Jim Sprinkle, and George Ruyle, eds., *Arizona Rancher's Management Guide*, University of Arizona College of Agriculture and Life Sciences Cooperative Extension, ag.arizona.edu.

33. J. Evetts Haley, *Charles Goodnight: Cowman and Plainsman* (Norman: University of Oklahoma Press, 1949), pp. 188, 280; Lemmon, *Boss Cowman*, p. 80; Lemmon, as told to Usher L. Burdick, "History of the Range Cattle Trade of the Dakotas," unpublished manuscript, call no. 01667, American Heritage Center, University of Wyoming, Laramie, pp. 127–28; Watson Parker, *Deadwood: The Golden Years* (Lincoln: University of Nebraska Press, 1981).

34. Herbert S. Schell, *History of South Dakota*, 4th ed., rev. John E. Miller (Pierre: South Dakota State Historical Society Press, 2004), pp. 126–39; Paul L. Hedren, ed., *The Great Sioux War, 1876–77: The Best from* Montana The Magazine of Western History (Helena: Montana Historical Society Press, 1991), pp. 8–21; Jill St. Germain, *Broken Treaties: United States and Canadian Relations with the Lakotas and the Plains Cree, 1868–1885* (Lincoln: University of Nebraska Press, 2009), pp. 257–86.

35. *BFB*, 6 Oct. 1933.

36. Ibid., 5 May 1934, 25 Jan. 1935; Nellie Snyder Yost, *The Call of the Range: The Story of the Nebraska Stock Growers Association* (Denver, Colo.: Sage Books, 1966), pp. 54–56, 67; Howard Smith and Ann Harry, *The Trail of the Sheidley Cattle Company: An Account of Cattle Ranching on the Western Plains in the Era of the Open Range—and Wealth Therefrom* (Tiffin, Ohio: Herald Printing Co., 2002), chaps. 1–6.

37. *BFB*, 19 Feb. 1937.

38. Ibid.

39. Ibid. *See also* Smith and Harry, *Trail of the Sheidley Cattle Company*, p. 24; Yost, *Call of the Range*, pp. 94–95; *DW*, vol. 10, pp. 5–6; and Lemmon, *Boss Cowman*, pp. 86–88.

40. *DW*, vol. 2, p. 1.

41. Cathie Draine, ed., *Cowboy Life: The Letters of George Philip* (Pierre: South Dakota State Historical Society Press, 2007), p. 110. Cattle ranchers tended to dislike shepherds, as historian Richard W. Slatta phrased it, out of "equal parts of prejudice and belief in the destructiveness of grazing sheep." Cattlemen believed that sheep grazed prairie grasses too close to the ground, reducing the range's ability to regrow the following year. Racial prejudice may also have been a factor because many sheepmen were Hispanic or Basque. In addition, some shepherds did not tend their flocks on horseback, and cowboys felt the longstanding superiority that mounted men have felt over men afoot. Slatta, *Cowboys of the Americas* (New Haven, Conn.: Yale University Press, 1990), p.

186. Many cowboys reflected on the hard work for little compensation. *See* Richard W. Slatta, "Long Hours and Low Pay: Cowboy Life on the Northern Plains," *South Dakota History* 32 (Fall 2002): 194–216.

42. Haley, *Charles Goodnight*, p. 249. For a few examples, *see* Sara R. Massey, ed., *Black Cowboys of Texas* (College Station: Texas A&M University Press, 2000), pp. 183–84, 200–202; Philip Durham and Everett L. Jones, *The Negro Cowboys* (New York: Dodd, Mead & Co., 1965), p. 43; Charles L. Sonnichsen, *Cowboys and Cattle Kings: Life on the Range Today* (Norman: University of Oklahoma Press, 1950), p. 88; and James K. Folsom, ed., *The Western: A Collection of Critical Essays* (Englewood Cliffs, N.J.: Prentice Hall, 1979), p. 19.

43. Blasingame, *Dakota Cowboy*, pp. 99–100. Cowboy George Philip also noted this phenomenon, which many would refer to as Saint Elmo's Fire, but some cowboys called "balls of fire" (Draine, ed., *Cowboy Life*, p. 71).

44. *DW*, vol. 3, p. 3.

45. Draine, ed., *Cowboy Life*, p. 19.

46. *BFB*, 6 Apr. 1934; Yost, *Call of the Range*, pp. 86, 136; Smith and Harry, *Trail of the Sheidley Cattle Company*, pp. 6, 30, 32, 34.

47. *BFB*, 21 Sept. 1934.

48. Ibid.

49. Ibid. *See also DW*, vol. 7, p. 3, vol. 11, p. 17, vol. 13, p. 10.

50. *BFB*, 12 Apr. 1935. For numerous other examples of cowboys dealing with poor weather, *see* Hamilton, *Dakota*; and Blasingame, *Dakota Cowboy*.

51. *BFB*, 23 Sept. 1932.

52. Joe Starita, *The Dull Knifes of Pine Ridge: A Lakota Odyssey* (Lincoln: University of Nebraska Press, 2002), pp. 40–55; *BFB*, 19 Aug., 23 Sept. 1932, 2 Dec. 1938.

53. *BFB*, 28 Oct. 1938.

54. Draine, ed., *Cowboy Life*, pp. 45–47, 174–79.

55. Slatta, "Long Hours and Low Pay," p. 200; *BFB*, 23 July 1937, 28 Oct. 1938; Slatta, *Cowboys of the Americas*, pp. 68–74.

56. *BFB*, 28 Oct. 1938.

57. Ibid.

58. Ibid.

3. Trespassers

1. Portions of this chapter appeared in Nathan Sanderson, "'We Were All Trespassers': George Edward Lemmon, Anglo-American Cattle Ranching, and the Great Sioux Reservation," *Agricultural History* 85 (Winter 2011): 50–71.

2. A number of historians have noted the connection between cattle ranchers and Indian reservations on the Northern Great Plains, but few have examined the role of illegal grazing before the General Allotment Act of 1887. In *When Indians Became Cowboys*, Peter Iverson argues that "Obviously, other forces

helped fuel the effort to defeat the Indians and confine them to reservations. However, especially in the northern plains, cattlemen played a major role in this process" (p. 31). Iverson focuses on Indian efforts to start cattle herds of their own and centers his examination in the twentieth century, after the Dawes Act and other legislation had taken a heavy toll on Indian lands. In *The Plains Sioux and U.S. Colonialism from Lewis and Clark to Wounded Knee*, Jeffrey Ostler touches on the impact of illegal grazing, noting that in 1887 Indians on the Rosebud Reservation in Dakota Territory tried to prevent white trespassing because the Indians needed the range to graze their own horses and cattle. However, Ostler's excellent work says little about grazing in the early 1880s. Stuart Banner's book *How the Indians Lost Their Land* has a chapter on the 1887 General Allotment Act that describes how whites justified allotment under the guise of protecting Indians from trespassers. Banner notes that white reformers criticized the reservation system because it "left the Indians too vulnerable to having their land expropriated" by whites, which provided an excuse to "divide the reservations into individually owned parcels" (p. 267). By giving each Indian title to a designated piece of land, reformers felt that they could better protect Indian land rights. Of course, the "excess" land would then be available for settlement by whites. These and other histories have laid the groundwork for a study of illegal grazing on the Great Sioux Reservation in the pre-allotment era and add insight into this complex relationship. Iverson, *When Indians Became Cowboys: Native Peoples and Cattle Ranching in the American West* (Norman: University of Oklahoma Press, 1994); Ostler, *The Plains Sioux and U.S. Colonialism from Lewis and Clark to Wounded Knee* (Cambridge, U.K.: Cambridge University Press, 2004), pp. 140–41; Banner, *How the Indians Lost Their Land: Law and Power on the Frontier* (Cambridge, Mass.: Belknap Press of Harvard University Press, 2005). For cattle grazing in western Dakota, *see* Bob Lee and Dick Williams, *Last Grass Frontier: The South Dakota Stock Grower Heritage* (Sturgis, S.Dak.: Black Hills Publishers, 1964). There are a number of monographs concerning the 1887 General Allotment Act, including Delos S. Otis, *The Dawes Act and the Allotment of Indian Lands* (Norman: University of Oklahoma Press, 1973); Sister Mary Antonio Johnston, *Federal Relations with the Great Sioux Indians of South Dakota, 1887–1933* (Washington, D.C.: Catholic University of America Press, 1948); and Wilcomb E. Washburn, *The Assault on Indian Tribalism: The General Allotment Law (Dawes Act) of 1887* (Philadelphia: Lippincott, 1975). For an excellent look into white efforts to assimilate American Indians, *see* Frederick E. Hoxie, *A Final Promise: The Campaign to Assimilate the Indians, 1880–1920* (Lincoln: University of Nebraska Press, 1984). For a detailed study of Indian land policy, *see* Janet A. McDonnell, *The Dispossession of the American Indian, 1887–1934* (Bloomington: Indiana University Press, 1991).

3. Edward Lazarus, *Black Hills, White Justice: The Sioux Nation versus the United States, 1775 to the Present* (New York: HarperCollins, 1991), p. 451.

4. Lee and Williams, *Last Grass Frontier*, p. 23; *Belle Fourche Bee* (hereafter *BFB*), 3 Mar. 1933; D. L. Turner, "To Lease the Moon: Burton C. ('Cap') Mossman and the Diamond A Cattle Ranch in South Dakota," *South Dakota History* 42 (Spring 2012): 1–27.

5. Howard Smith and Ann Harry, *The Trail of the Sheidley Cattle Company: An Account of Cattle Ranching on the Western Plains in the Era of the Open Range—and Wealth Therefrom* (Tiffin, Ohio: Herald Printing Co., 2002), pp. 1–36; Lee and Williams, *Last Grass Frontier*, pp. 106–8; *BFB*, 5 May 1934.

6. Lee and Williams, *Last Grass Frontier*, pp. 76, 95, 106–8; Smith and Harry, *Trail of the Sheidley Cattle Company*, p. 147.

7. Andrew C. Isenberg, *The Destruction of the Bison: An Environmental History, 1750–1920* (Cambridge, U.K.: Cambridge University Press, 2000), pp. 140–43; Richard White, *"It's Your Misfortune and None of My Own": A New History of the American West* (Norman: University of Oklahoma Press, 1991), pp. 216–20; Pekka Hämäläinen, "The Rise and Fall of Plains Indian Horse Cultures," *Journal of American History* 90 (Dec. 2003): 844–45.

8. *BFB*, 26 May 1933. *See also* James R. Johnson and Gary E. Larson, *Grassland Plants of South Dakota and the Northern Great Plains*, ed. Mary Brashier (Brookings: South Dakota State University, 1999), pp. 10–13.

9. Smith and Harry, *Trail of the Sheidley Cattle Company*, pp. 36–38.

10. *BFB*, 18 Nov. 1932.

11. Ibid.

12. Ibid.; *United States v. Sioux Nation of Indians*, 448 U.S. 371, p. 380.

13. *BFB*, 26 May 1933. Lemmon considered this winter even worse than that of 1886–1887.

14. Ibid., 22 June 1939.

15. Ibid., 26 Aug. 1932.

16. Ibid.

17. Ibid., 13 Jan. 1933.

18. Ibid., 18 Nov. 1932.

19. United States, Department of the Interior, Office of Indian Affairs (hereafter OIA), *Annual Report of the Commissioner of Indian Affairs to the Secretary of the Interior for the Year 1881* (Washington, D.C.: Government Printing Office, 1881), p. 45. *See also* Lee and Williams, *Last Grass Frontier*, p. 75.

20. OIA, *Annual Report of the Commissioner of Indian Affairs to the Secretary of the Interior for the Year 1882* (Washington, D.C.: Government Printing Office, 1882), p. 35.

21. OIA, *Annual Report of the Commissioner of Indian Affairs to the Secretary*

of the Interior for the Year 1883 (Washington, D.C.: Government Printing Office, 1883), p. 35.

22. *BFB*, 22 June 1939.

23. McDonnell, *Dispossession of the American Indian*, p. 1.

24. The strong sense of community among Indians has been demonstrated in numerous works. For Indian agents' views on the "problems" associated with Indian society, *see* the annual reports of the commissioner of Indian affairs, 1881–1889.

25. Quoted in Julia B. McGillycuddy, *McGillycuddy, Agent: A Biography of Dr. Valentine T. McGillycuddy* (Stanford, Calif.: Stanford University Press, 1941), p. 103. *See also* Candy Moulton, *Valentine T. McGillycuddy: Army Surgeon, Agent to the Sioux* (Norman, Okla.: Arthur H. Clark, 2011).

26. Iverson, *When Indians Became Cowboys*, p. 28.

27. Ibid., p. 52. Indians near the Rosebud Agency started to oppose illegal grazing as early as 1887. *See* Ostler, *Plains Sioux and U.S. Colonialism*, p. 140.

28. *BFB*, 11 Nov. 1932.

29. Dennis C. Pope, *Sitting Bull, Prisoner of War* (Pierre: South Dakota State Historical Society Press, 2010), pp. 3–5, 7–13, 23–25, 34, 36–38.

30. Lee and Williams, *Last Grass Frontier*, pp. 128–29.

31. Ibid., pp. 108, 133–41; Smith and Harry, *Trail of the Sheidley Cattle Company*, p. 69.

32. Lee and Williams, *Last Grass Frontier*, p. 141.

33. Ibid.

34. *BFB*, 17 Apr. 1936.

35. Ibid., 26 Aug. 1932.

36. Quoted in Lee and Williams, *Last Grass Frontier*, p. 26.

37. *BFB*, 26 Aug. 1932.

38. On other occasions, cattlemen loosened particular nuts on the scales so that they would record heavier weights. *See* Lee and Williams, *Last Grass Frontier*, p. 25.

39. *BFB*, 26 Aug. 1932.

40. Ibid. In another account, Lemmon suggests that the large steer was returned to the company by an Indian accomplice, who brought him back before every issue. Lemmon, as told to Usher L. Burdick, "History of the Range Cattle Trade of the Dakotas," unpublished manuscript, call no. 01667, American Heritage Center, University of Wyoming, Laramie, pp. 377–78.

41. Ike Blasingame, *Dakota Cowboy: My Life in the Old Days* (Lincoln: University of Nebraska Press, 1964), p. 27. *See also* Lee and Williams, *Last Grass Frontier*, p. 108; Swan Bros. & Frank to William Sheidly [*sic*], 14 Dec. 1883, Betsey Sheidley Fletcher collection, Sheidley Family Papers, Mission Hills, Kans.; Ed Lemmon, *Boss Cowman: The Recollections of Ed Lemmon, 1857–1946*, ed. Nel-

lie Snyder Yost (Lincoln: University of Nebraska Press, 1969), p. 213; and *Faith Country Heritage, 1910–1985* (Faith, S.Dak.: Faith Historical Committee, 1985), pp. 278, 715.

42. Lee and Williams, *Last Grass Frontier*, p. 108.

43. OIA, *Annual Report of the Commissioner of Indian Affairs to the Secretary of the Interior for the Year 1884* (Washington, D.C.: Government Printing Office, 1884), p. 37.

44. Ibid., pp. 37–38.

45. *BFB*, 5 Apr. 1935.

46. Ibid.

47. Ibid.

48. Ibid.

49. Ibid.

50. August H. Schatz, *Longhorns Bring Culture* (Boston: Christopher Publishing House, 1961), p. 39. *See also* Annie D. Tallent, *The Black Hills; or, The Last Hunting Ground of the Dakotahs* (St. Louis, Mo.: Nixon-Jones Printing Co., 1899), pp. 685–86.

51. *BFB*, 23 June 1933; Virginia Grabow, untitled biography of James Hervey Lemmon, Jr., pp. 60–61, Virginia Grabow collection, Tigard, Ore.; "Lemmon: G. E. 'Dad' Ed," George E. Lemmon file, Lemmon Public Library, Lemmon, S.Dak.

52. Hervey was survived by his wife, Elizabeth, whom he had married in 1878, and his only child, a seven-year-old daughter named Edna.

53. *BFB*, 15 Feb. 1935.

54. For examples, *see* Lemmon, "History of the Range Cattle Trade," chap. 12.

55. McDonnell, *Dispossession of the American Indian*, p. 1.

56. Banner, *How the Indians Lost Their Land*, pp. 257–58.

57. Hoxie, *A Final Promise*, p. 46.

58. Ibid., p. 47.

59. Lemmon shipped from various points, including Ogallala, Valentine, and Chadron in Nebraska and Smithwick and Belle Fourche in Dakota Territory. *See* Smith and Harry, *Trail of the Sheidley Cattle Company*, pp. 36–37; and contents of Union Pacific Railroad Freight Department folder, box 28, series 1, subgroup 2, Union Pacific Railroad (Omaha, Nebr.) Collection, RG3761.AM, Nebraska State Historical Society, Lincoln. Shrinkage could have a tremendous effect on the weight and quality of the cattle once they arrived in Chicago. In 1895, Lemmon chose to ship from Forest City, South Dakota, rather than from Belle Fourche, because the train ride for the cattle was thirty-one hours instead of sixty-one. When trailed properly, cattle would gain weight rather than lose it, so it was better to trail them a longer distance to Forest City, on the east side of the Missouri River, rather than trail them the far shorter distance to Belle Fourche

and keep them on the train for thirty additional hours. On average, the cattle shipped from Forest City weighed forty pounds more and earned $0.20 more per hundredweight than cattle shipped from Belle Fourche. *BFB*, 1 Apr. 1938.

60. W. H. Hamilton, *Dakota: An Autobiography of a Cowman* (Pierre: South Dakota State Historical Society Press, 1998), p. 35.

61. Lee and Williams, *Last Grass Frontier*, pp. 154-57; Edmund Morris, *The Rise of Theodore Roosevelt* (New York: Modern Library, 2001), pp. 375-78; Clyde A. Milner II and Carol A. O'Connor, *As Big as the West: The Pioneer Life of Granville Stuart* (Oxford, U.K.: Oxford University Press, 2009), pp. 258-65.

62. Smith and Harry, *Trail of the Sheidley Cattle Company*, pp. 140-41; *BFB*, 13 May 1938.

63. Lee and Williams, *Last Grass Frontier*, pp. 154-61.

64. *BFB*, 5 Aug. 1938.

4. Roundups

1. Webb, *The Great Plains* (Boston: Ginn & Co., 1931), p. vi. Glidden, a native of DeKalb, Illinois, received a patent for barbed wire in 1874. *See* David J. Wishart, ed., *Encyclopedia of the Great Plains* (Lincoln: University of Nebraska Press, 2004), p. 35.

2. Webb, *Great Plains*, p. 238.

3. Ibid., p. 240. *See also* Cynthia M. Kahn, ed., *The Merck Veterinary Manual*, 9th ed. (Whitehouse Station, N.J.: Merck & Co., 2005), pp. 749-64; Center for Food Security and Public Health, Iowa State University, "*Rhipicephalus (Boophilus) annulatus*: Cattle Tick, Cattle Fever Tick, American Cattle Tick," cfsph. iastate.edu; and Andrew R. Graybill, *Policing the Great Plains: Rangers, Mounties, and the North American Frontier, 1875-1910* (Lincoln: University of Nebraska Press, 2007), chap. 4.

4. For a detailed study of the development of western South Dakota after 1900, *see* Paula M. Nelson, *After the West Was Won: Homesteaders and Town-Builders in Western South Dakota, 1900-1917* (Iowa City: University of Iowa Press, 1986).

5. J. Frank Dobie, *The Longhorns* (New York: Grosset & Dunlap, 1941), p. 35.

6. Howard Smith and Ann Harry, *The Trail of the Sheidley Cattle Company: An Account of Cattle Ranching on the Western Plains in the Era of the Open Range—and Wealth Therefrom* (Tiffin, Ohio: Herald Printing Co., 2002), pp. 15-20, 122-24. Charles Goodnight, who ranched on the southern plains, also recognized the value of crossbreeding with Hereford cattle. J. Evetts Haley, *Charles Goodnight: Cowman and Plainsman* (Norman: University of Oklahoma Press, 1949), pp. 318-20.

7. *See* Bill O'Neal, *The Johnson County War* (Austin, Tex.: Eakin Press, 2004).

8. Clay, *My Life on the Range* (Chicago: By the Author, 1924), pp. 338–39. *See also* Hazel Adele Pulling, "History of the Range Cattle Industry of Dakota," *South Dakota Historical Collections* 20 (1940): 508; and Nelson, *After the West Was Won*, pp. 151–53.

9. Bob Lee and Dick Williams, *Last Grass Frontier: The South Dakota Stock Grower Heritage* (Sturgis, S.Dak.: Black Hills Publishers, 1964), p. 160; Smith and Harry, *Trail of the Sheidley Cattle Company*, p. 147.

10. *Developing the West*, vol. 8, p. 6, MSS 691, Wyoming State Archives, Cheyenne (hereafter *DW*); *Belle Fourche Bee* (hereafter *BFB*), 13 Dec. 1935.

11. *DW*, vol. 8, p. 6.

12. *BFB*, 13 Dec. 1935.

13. *DW*, vol. 8, p. 6.

14. Ed had several difficult experiences crossing streams and recounts three challenging river crossings in *BFB*, 20 Jan. 1933. Some less-experienced cowboys waited for swollen rivers to drop rather than tempt fate. Young cowboy Earl Martin waited two days and nights after a series of heavy rains before crossing the Cheyenne River in 1901. Molly Kruckenberg and Richard W. Slatta, eds., "'$30 a month for all summer and dont have to work Sundays': Letters from Cowboy Earl J. Martin," *South Dakota History* 38 (Summer 2008): 132.

15. John O. Baxter, *Cowboy Park: Steer-Roping Contests on the Border* (Lubbock: Texas Tech University Press, 2008), p. 4; Ed Lemmon, *Boss Cowman: The Recollections of Ed Lemmon, 1857–1946*, ed. Nellie Snyder Yost (Lincoln: University of Nebraska Press, 1969), p. 138.

16. Lee and Williams, *Last Grass Frontier*, p. 161; J. Sterling Morton and Albert Watkins, *History of Nebraska: From the Earliest Explorations of the Trans-Mississippi Region* (Lincoln, Nebr.: Western Publishing & Engraving Co., 1918), p. 682; "Railroad Network Expansion in the United States," *Railroads and the Making of Modern America*, railroads.unl.edu.

17. Louise Carroll Wade, *Chicago's Pride: The Stockyards, Packingtown, and Environs in the Nineteenth Century* (Urbana: University of Illinois Press, 1987), p. 48; W. Joseph Grand, *Illustrated History of the Union Stockyards: Sketch-book of Familiar Faces and Places at the Yards* (Chicago: Thomas Knapp Printing & Binding Co., 1896), p. 15.

18. Wade, *Chicago's Pride*, pp. 104–7, 199–201.

19. Lee and Williams, *Last Grass Frontier*, pp. 161–62.

20. Grand, *Illustrated History of the Union Stockyards*, pp. 49–51.

21. Edmund Morris, *Theodore Rex* (New York: Modern Library, 2001), pp. 435–39, 447–48; William Cronon, *Nature's Metropolis: Chicago and the Great West* (New York: W. W. Norton & Co., 1991), pp. 252–53.

22. *BFB*, 29 Apr. 1938.

23. Lemmon, as told to Usher L. Burdick, "History of the Range Cattle Trade of the Dakotas," unpublished manuscript, call no. 01667, American Heritage Center, University of Wyoming, Laramie, pp. 193–235.

24. Ibid., pp. 215–16.

25. Ibid., p. 196.

26. *BFB*, 25 Oct. 1935.

27. Ibid.

28. Lemmon, "History of the Range Cattle Trade," p. 215. Whether Ed personally knew Martha ("Calamity") Jane Canary is unclear. In the 1 March 1935 edition of the *Belle Fourche Bee*, he mentions a conversation he had with Calamity Jane and Valentine T. McGillycuddy while traveling on a train as "invited guests" to Deadwood's annual Days of '76 celebration, but Canary had died twenty years before the celebration began in 1923. Moreover, she was away from the Black Hills from 1878 to 1895, so even if he did know her, a "professional" relationship between them is highly unlikely. *See* James D. McLaird, *Calamity Jane: The Woman and the Legend* (Norman: University of Oklahoma Press, 2005). Poker Alice, while a famous madam of Sturgis, South Dakota, was not herself a working girl. *See* Michael Rutter, *Upstairs Girls: Prostitution in the American West* (Helena, Mont.: Farcountry Press, 2005), pp. 169–74.

29. Lemmon, "History of the Range Cattle Trade," p. 203.

30. Ibid., p. 205.

31. *BFB*, 24 Apr. 1936.

32. Ibid., 6 Oct. 1933, 24 Apr. 1936, 2 Dec. 1938, 30 Nov. 1939.

33. Ibid., 23 June 1933; Ed Lemmon, *The West as I Lived It: Stories by Ed Lemmon*, comp. Phyllis Schmidt (Pierre, S.Dak.: State Publishing Co., 2007), pp. 323–24.

34. *BFB*, 6 Apr. 1939. For interesting descriptions of techniques used in breaking horses to ride, *see* Cathie Draine, ed., *Cowboy Life: The Letters of George Philip* (Pierre: South Dakota State Historical Society Press, 2007), pp. 179–81; and W. H. Hamilton, *Dakota: An Autobiography of a Cowman* (Pierre: South Dakota State Historical Society Press, 1998), pp. 45–46.

35. Ike Blasingame, *Dakota Cowboy: My Life in the Old Days* (Lincoln: University of Nebraska Press, 1964), p. 96.

36. Hamilton, *Dakota*, p. 37.

37. Lemmon, "History of the Range Cattle Trade," pp. 115–16.

38. *BFB*, 6 Apr. 1939.

39. Ibid., 10 Mar. 1933, 6 Apr. 1939; Lemmon, *The West as I Lived It*, pp. 323–24; "Climate Custer – South Dakota," *U.S. Climate Data*, usclimatedata.com; *DW*, vol. 6, pp. 1–6; August H. Schatz, *Longhorns Bring Culture* (Boston: Christopher Publishing House, 1961), pp. 87–95. Charles Goodnight constructed the first "chuck-box" in 1866, and the design remained virtually unaltered until the end

of open-range cattle ranching in the early twentieth century. Haley, *Charles Goodnight*, p. 122.

40. Lemmon, *The West as I Lived It*, pp. 323–24; *BFB*, 24 Aug. 1934, 11 Mar. 1938, 6 Apr. 1939. Because the job was lonely and dangerous, the position of nighthawk was among the least desirable. In 1888, Lemmon hired Frank ("Pickles") Koshirak to be his nighthawk, a job he kept for more than twenty years. Koshirak was a rough character whose odor and sour personality earned him his uncommon nickname. Pickles Creek in present-day Perkins County, South Dakota, is so named because one day when Lemmon's cattle herd was grazing nearby, Pickles used the creek for his annual bath.

41. Blasingame, *Dakota Cowboy*, p. 222.

42. Lemmon, *The West as I Lived It*, pp. 323–24; *BFB*, 6 Apr. 1939.

43. Lemmon, *The West as I Lived It*, p. 323; *BFB*, 16 Feb. 1934.

44. *BFB*, 16 Feb. 1934.

45. *DW*, vol. 8, p. 5.

46. *BFB*, 16 Feb. 1934.

47. Ibid.

48. Ibid.

49. Bert L. Hall, comp., *Roundup Years: Old Muddy to Black Hills* ([Winner, S.Dak.]: Western South Dakota Buck-a-roos, 2000), p. 336.

50. *BFB*, 16 Feb. 1934.

51. Moroni's family placed his body in the Lemmon plot at the Oak Grove cemetery overlooking the Little Blue River, between his brother Hervey and mother Lucy. His epitaph reads, "A good son, a brother dear; a faithful friend lies buried here."

52. Lemmon, *Boss Cowman*, pp. 238–39; *BFB*, 16 Feb. 1934.

53. *BFB*, 16 Feb. 1934.

54. Ibid.

55. Ibid.

56. Ibid.

57. *U.S. Statutes at Large* 25, 50th Cong., 2d sess., pt. 2, chap. 405 (1889); Benjamin Harrison, "Proclamation 295 – Sioux Nation of Indians," 10 Feb. 1890, accessible through *The American Presidency Project*, University of California Santa Barbara, presidency.ucsb.edu; Herbert T. Hoover, "The Sioux Agreement of 1889 and Its Aftermath," *South Dakota History* 19 (Spring 1989): 56–94; Robert M. Utley, *The Lance and the Shield: The Life and Times of Sitting Bull* (New York: Henry Holt & Co., 1993), chap. 22. The act also established the Crow Creek reservation on the east side of the Missouri River across from the Lower Brule reservation, but Crow Creek was not part of the former Great Sioux Reservation.

58. Utley, *Lance and the Shield*, p. 287.

59. Ibid., chaps. 23–24; Robert M. Utley, *The Last Days of the Sioux Nation*

(New Haven, Conn.: Yale University Press, 1963), chaps. 5, 9; Edward A. Milligan, *Dakota Twilight: The Standing Rock Sioux, 1874–1890* (Hicksville, N.Y.: Exposition Press, 1976), pp. 108–9.

60. *BFB*, 18 Nov. 1932, 19 May, 1 Sept. 1933, 7 Feb. 1936, 23 Dec. 1938; Lemmon, "History of the Range Cattle Trade," pp. 389–95; *DW*, vol. 10, pp. 7–9.

61. Utley, *Last Days of the Sioux Nation*, chap. 12. *See also* Jeffrey Ostler, *The Plains Sioux and U.S. Colonialism from Lewis and Clark to Wounded Knee* (Cambridge, U.K.: Cambridge University Press, 2004), chaps. 13–15.

62. *BFB*, 19 May, 1 Sept. 1933, 23 Dec. 1938; Lemmon, "History of the Range Cattle Trade," pp. 389–95; *DW*, vol. 10, pp. 7–9; Peggy Samuels and Harold Samuels, *Frederic Remington: A Biography* (Garden City, N.Y.: Doubleday, 1982), pp. 148–53.

63. *BFB*, 18 Nov. 1932.

64. Ibid., 18 Nov. 1932, 19 May, 1 Sept. 1933, 23 Dec. 1938; Lemmon, "History of the Range Cattle Trade," pp. 389–95; *DW*, vol. 10, pp. 7–9; Samuels and Samuels, *Frederic Remington*, pp. 148–53; Renée Sansom Flood, *Lost Bird of Wounded Knee: Spirit of the Lakota* (New York: Scribner, 1995), pp. 54–56.

65. *BFB*, 18 Nov. 1932.

66. Ibid., 18 Nov. 1932, 19 May, 1 Sept. 1933, 23 Dec. 1938; Lemmon, "History of the Range Cattle Trade," pp. 389–95; *DW*, vol. 10, pp. 7–9, Lee and Williams, *Last Grass Frontier*, p. 178; Samuels and Samuels, *Frederic Remington*, pp. 148–53. One of the massacre's survivors, Zintkala Nuni, the "Lost Bird of Wounded Knee," would begin her career in "Indian" Pete Culbertson's Wild West show in 1907 at Lemmon, South Dakota. Flood, *Lost Bird of Wounded Knee*, pp. 247–50. Interestingly, Remington's painting *In from the Night Herd* adorned the cover of the first published book about Lemmon, *Boss Cowman*, edited by Nellie Snyder Yost.

67. Blasingame, *Dakota Cowboy*, p. 222.

5. Cattlemen

1. Richard W. Slatta, *Cowboys of the Americas* (New Haven, Conn.: Yale University Press, 1990), pp. 97–99; David E. Lopez, "Cowboy Strikes and Unions," *Labor History* 18 (Summer 1977): 325–40. *See also* D. L. Turner, "To Lease the Moon: Burton C. ('Cap') Mossman and the Diamond A Cattle Ranch in South Dakota," *South Dakota History* 42 (Spring 2012): 1–27.

2. Clark left his estate—worth more than two hundred thousand dollars—to his wife, Charlotte Gifford Clark. Bob Lee and Dick Williams, *Last Grass Frontier: The South Dakota Stock Grower Heritage* (Sturgis, S.Dak.: Black Hills Publishers, 1964), pp. 178–80; Howard Smith and Ann Harry, *The Trail of the Sheidley Cattle Company: An Account of Cattle Ranching on the Western Plains in the Era of the Open Range—and Wealth Therefrom* (Tiffin, Ohio: Herald Printing Co.,

2002), pp. 151–54; *Belle Fourche Bee* (hereafter *BFB*), 2 Sept. 1932, 26 May 1933, 5 May 1934.

3. *BFB*, 6 Dec. 1935.

4. Ben Sheidley had died in 1883. Smith and Harry, *Trail of the Sheidley Cattle Company*, p. 71; *Faith Country Heritage, 1910–1985* (Faith, S.Dak.: Faith Historical Committee, 1985), pp. 278–85; *BFB*, 26 May 1933.

5. *BFB*, 29 Nov. 1935.

6. Ibid. *See also* Ike Blasingame, *Dakota Cowboy: My Life in the Old Days* (Lincoln: University of Nebraska Press, 1964), pp. 221–22.

7. *BFB*, 29 Nov. 1935.

8. Ibid., 5 Apr. 1935.

9. *Developing the West*, vol. 6, p. 1, MSS 691, Wyoming State Archives, Cheyenne (hereafter *DW*). Charles Goodnight's system differed from Lemmon's in several ways, including selecting "three steady men" for the drags. J. Evetts Haley, *Charles Goodnight: Cowman and Plainsman* (Norman: University of Oklahoma Press, 1949), pp. 244–59.

10. Haley, *Charles Goodnight*, p. 136.

11. *DW*, vol. 6, p. 4.

12. Haley, *Charles Goodnight*, pp. 250–51; Richard W. Slatta, *The Cowboy Encyclopedia* (Santa Barbara, Calif.: ABC-CLIO, 1994), pp. 97, 372; Philip Ashton Rollins, *The Cowboy: An Unconventional History of Civilization on the Old-Time Cattle Range* (Norman: University of Oklahoma Press, 1997), p. 36; W. H. Hamilton, *Dakota: An Autobiography of a Cowman* (Pierre: South Dakota State Historical Society Press, 1998), pp. 143–44; Walter Prescott Webb, *The Great Plains* (Boston: Ginn & Co., 1931), pp. 205, 265; *BFB*, 21 May 1937; *DW*, vol. 11, p. 10.

13. *BFB*, 15 Oct. 1937.

14. Ibid.

15. Ibid., 20 May 1932.

16. Ibid., 15 Oct. 1937.

17. Haley, *Charles Goodnight*, p. 122.

18. *BFB*, 31 Aug. 1934. Lemmon claimed to have spent an evening with Goodnight at his Texas ranch in 1884, but this story seems to be another fabrication. *BFB*, 14 Feb. 1936.

19. Ibid., 31 Aug. 1934; Ed Lemmon, *Boss Cowman: The Recollections of Ed Lemmon, 1857–1946*, ed. Nellie Snyder Yost (Lincoln: University of Nebraska Press, 1969), p. 246; Haley, *Charles Goodnight*, pp. 244–59.

20. *DW*, vol. 10, p. 3. While in Sidney, Nebraska, in 1877, Lemmon saw a woman he had known years before but failed to speak to her because he was self-conscious about his leg. As he matured, he overcame his shame and developed deep reserves of self-confidence. *DW*, vol. 9, p. 11.

21. *BFB*, 22 Dec. 1933.

22. Ibid., 5 Apr. 1935.

23. Ibid.

24. Blasingame, *Dakota Cowboy*, p. 222.

25. "Ed Lemmon, 82, Spent 57 Years in Cattle Business," unidentified newspaper clipping, 19 July 1939, George E. Lemmon file, Lemmon Public Library, Lemmon, S.Dak. *See also BFB*, 23 July 1937.

26. *BFB*, 23 July 1937.

27. Ibid., 22 Dec. 1933.

28. Bruce Siberts and Walker D. Wyman, *Nothing but Prairie and Sky: Life on the Dakota Range in the Early Days* (Norman: University of Oklahoma Press, 1954), p. 47. *See also BFB*, 1 Jan. 1937.

29. *BFB*, 26 July 1935. *See also DW*, vol. 11, pp. 16–17.

30. Rose Tidball, *Taming the Plains* ([Keldron, S.Dak.]: By the Author, 1976), p. 39.

31. Lee and Williams, *Last Grass Frontier*, p. 175. *See also* Frederick Allen, *A Decent, Orderly Lynching: The Montana Vigilantes* (Norman: University of Oklahoma Press, 2004).

32. Lee and Williams, *Last Grass Frontier*, p. 169. *See also* ibid., pp. 167–70; *BFB*, 7 Apr. 1933; Clyde A. Milner II and Carol A. O'Connor, *As Big as the West: The Pioneer Life of Granville Stuart* (Oxford, U.K.: Oxford University Press, 2009), pp. 217–48.

33. *BFB*, 26 July 1935. *See also* "Visionary Absorption of Small Cattle Holders by So Called Cattle Kings," Work Projects Administration collection, Pioneer Cabinet, Wyoming State Archives, Cheyenne.

34. Bill O'Neal, *The Johnson County War* (Austin, Tex.: Eakin Press, 2004); John W. Davis, *Wyoming Range War: The Infamous Invasion of Johnson County* (Norman: University of Oklahoma Press, 2010). Similar "large versus small" battles were waged in Texas as well. *See* Andrew R. Graybill, *Policing the Great Plains: Rangers, Mounties, and the North American Frontier, 1875–1910* (Lincoln: University of Nebraska Press, 2007), pp. 79–81.

35. *DW*, vol. 2, p. 1.

36. Ibid.; *BFB*, 30 Dec. 1932.

37. *DW*, vol. 11, pp. 17–18.

38. James R. Johnson and Gary E. Larson, *Grassland Plants of South Dakota and the Northern Great Plains*, ed. Mary Brashier (Brookings: South Dakota State University, 1999), pp. 10–13.

39. Lee and Williams, *Last Grass Frontier*, p. 188.

40. Philip helped to save the American Bison from extinction by gathering and breeding bison on his ranch west of Fort Pierre, South Dakota. Bison from his ranch were used to populate herds throughout the United States, including those in South Dakota's Custer State Park. Wayne C. Lee, *Scotty Philip: The Man*

Who Saved the Buffalo (Caldwell, Idaho: Caxton Printers, 1975). While Philip contributed directly to saving the species, he may not have been its most influential proponent. *See* David Nesheim, "How William F. Cody Helped Save the Buffalo without Really Trying," *Great Plains Quarterly* 27 (Summer 2007): 163–75.

41. Lee and Williams, *Last Grass Frontier*, p. 210.

42. Ibid., pp. 188–205, 225; *BFB*, 7 Apr. 1933, 1 Feb. 1935. In 1937, the Western South Dakota Stock Growers Association became the South Dakota Stockgrowers Association. Even in the twenty-first century, the group remains a voice in the South Dakota cattle industry.

43. Haley, *Charles Goodnight*, pp. 318–20; *BFB*, 1 Jan., 4 June, 15 Oct. 1937, 26 Oct. 1939; John Clay, *My Life on the Range* (Chicago: By the Author, 1924), p. 226; *DW*, vol. 5, p. 10; Lemmon, *Boss Cowman*, p. 239. For examples of the nationwide changes attributed to the railroads, *see* [William G. Thomas, ed.], *Railroads and the Making of Modern America*, railroads.unl.edu.

44. U.S., Department of the Interior, Office of Indian Affairs, *Sixtieth Annual Report of the Commissioner of Indian Affairs to the Secretary of the Interior* (Washington, D.C.: Government Printing Office, 1891), pp. 197–98.

45. Quoted in *BFB*, 9 Nov. 1934. *See also* ibid., 9 Nov. 1934, 1 Mar. 1935. This incident may have taken place in 1897 rather than 1892, at another hearing regarding cattle trespassing on the Pine Ridge Reservation. *See* John Simpson, *West River: Stories from the Great Sioux Reservation* (Hamill, S.Dak.: Rattlesnake Butte Press, 2000), pp. 72–78.

46. Herbert S. Schell, *History of South Dakota*, 4th ed., rev. John E. Miller (Pierre: South Dakota State Historical Society Press, 2004), p. 250; David A. Wolff, *Seth Bullock: Black Hills Lawman*, South Dakota Biography Series 3 (Pierre: South Dakota State Historical Society Press, 2009), pp. 120–28.

47. *BFB*, 14 Apr. 1933.

48. Ibid., 3 Jan. 1936.

49. Ibid., 14 Apr. 1933.

50. Ibid.

51. Ibid.

52. Ibid., 1 Apr. 1938.

53. Ibid., 30 Mar. 1939.

54. Lee and Williams, *Last Grass Frontier*, pp. 55, 76–77, 94, 108, 180; Smith and Harry, *Trail of the Sheidley Cattle Company*, pp. 34, 45–46.

55. Smith and Harry, *Trail of the Sheidley Cattle Company*, pp. 163–68; *BFB*, 14 Oct. 1932, 15 Oct. 1937; Lemmon, *Boss Cowman*, p. 239.

56. Smith and Harry, *Trail of the Sheidley Cattle Company*, pp. 163–68; *BFB*, 30 Oct. 1936.

57. *BFB*, 31 Jan. 1936. *See also* Smith and Harry, *Trail of the Sheidley Cattle*

Company, pp. 163–68; *BFB*, 14 Oct. 1932, 30 Oct. 1936, 15 Oct. 1937; and Lemmon, *Boss Cowman*, p. 239.

58. G. E. Lemmon to W. L. Stocking, 6 Nov. 1896, Betsey Sheidley Fletcher collection, Sheidley Family Papers, Mission Hills, Kans.

59. Bryan lost despite traveling more than eighteen thousand miles and delivering 746 speeches in twenty-seven states during the campaign. "William Jennings Bryan's 1896 Campaign," *Railroads and the Making of Modern America*, railroads.unl.edu.

60. Quoted in Mrs. Lloyd I. Sudlow, ed., *Homestead Years, 1908–1968* (Bison, S.Dak.: *Bison Courier*, 1968), p. 178.

61. Quoted in Bert L. Hall, comp. *Roundup Years: Old Muddy to Black Hills* ([Winner, S.Dak.]: Western South Dakota Buck-a-roos, 2000), pp. 515–16.

62. *BFB*, 23 Dec. 1932, 24 Aug. 1934; *DW*, vol. 7, p. 2; Sudlow, ed., *Homestead Years*, pp. 178–79; J. Leonard Jennewein and Jane Boorman, eds., *Dakota Panorama* ([Worthing, S.Dak.]: Brevet Press, 1961), p. 360.

63. Quoted in Sudlow, ed., *Homestead Years*, p. 179. *See also* Louis S. Warren, *Buffalo Bill's America: William Cody and the Wild West Show* (New York: Alfred A. Knopf, 2005), pp. x–xi.

64. Smith and Harry, *Trail of the Sheidley Cattle Company*, pp. 168–70; *BFB*, 3 Mar. 1933; *Faith Country Heritage, 1910–1985*, p. 278.

65. *BFB*, 6 Dec. 1935.

66. *DW*, vol. 11, p. 18.

67. *BFB*, 6 Dec. 1935.

68. Ibid., 12 Oct. 1934; "Lemmon: G. E. 'Dad' Ed," George E. Lemmon file, Lemmon Public Library, Lemmon, S.Dak. The exact year of their divorce is unknown, if they indeed formally divorced. On 11 June 1900, census worker John P. Smith recorded Bertha as having been married for fourteen years. This enumeration was completed three months after Ed married Rosella Boe, so it is possible that Ed and Bertha were still legally married when he wedded Rosella. Manuscript population schedule, Rapid City, Pennington County, S.Dak., in U.S., Department of the Interior, Census Office, *Twelfth Census of the United States, 1900*, National Archives Microfilm Publication T623, roll 1553, sheet 8B. *See also* unidentified newspaper clipping, 14 Feb. 1896, Virginia Grabow collection, Tigard, Ore.; Kristin L. Hoganson, *Fighting for American Manhood: How Gender Politics Provoked the Spanish-American and Philippine-American Wars* (New Haven, Conn.: Yale University Press, 1998), p. 6; and Matthew Basso, Laura McCall, and Dee Garceau, eds., *Across the Great Divide: Cultures of Manhood in the American West* (New York: Routledge, 2001).

69. *BFB*, 11 Aug. 1933. *See also* Charles F. Martin, comp., *Proceedings of the Second Annual Convention of the National Live Stock Association* (Denver, Colo.: Denver Chamber of Commerce, 1899), p. 325; and *BFB*, 6 Nov. 1936.

70. *BFB*, 11 Aug. 1933.

71. Ibid., 15 Jan. 1937.

72. *DW*, vol. 7, pp. 9–10. Ed is off by one year in the title of this story—he married Rosella on 4 March 1900. *Lemmon Leader*, 25 May 1964; *Rosella B. Lemmon v. George E. Lemmon* (1927), Clerk of Courts, Perkins County, Bison, S.Dak.

73. *DW*, vol. 7, pp. 9–10.

74. "Lemmon: G. E. 'Dad' Ed"; "Married," transcription from unidentified newspaper, n.d., Grabow collection; manuscript population schedule, Palisade, Mesa County, Colo., in U.S., Department of Commerce, Bureau of the Census, *Thirteenth Census of the United States, 1910*, National Archives Microfilm Publication T624, roll 122, sheet 6B.

75. Lemmon, as told to Usher L. Burdick, "History of the Range Cattle Trade of the Dakotas," unpublished manuscript, call no. 01667, American Heritage Center, University of Wyoming, Laramie, p. 192; *DW*, vol. 13, p. 5; Hall, comp., *Roundup Years*, p. 19; Blasingame, *Dakota Cowboy*, p. 221.

6. The Largest Fenced Pasture in the World

1. *Developing the West*, vol. 13, p. 5, MSS 691, Wyoming State Archives, Cheyenne (hereafter *DW*). *See also Belle Fourche Bee* (hereafter *BFB*), 31 Jan. 1936; Peter Iverson, *When Indians Became Cowboys: Native Peoples and Cattle Ranching in the American West* (Norman: University of Oklahoma Press, 1994), p. 42; John H. Burkholder, "Poised to Profit: Fort Pierre and the Development of the Open Range in South Dakota," *South Dakota History* 41 (Fall 2011): 323–52; and Roger Butterfield and Eliot Elisofon, "South Dakota: Its Boundless Plains Are the Heart of a Continent," *Life*, 6 Oct. 1941, pp. 108–9.

2. Donovin Arleigh Sprague, *Standing Rock Sioux*, Images of America Series (Charleston, S.C.: Arcadia, 2004), p. 7; Robert W. Larson, *Gall: Lakota War Chief* (Norman: University of Oklahoma Press, 2007), pp. 174–75.

3. Jones to Frank P. Woodbury, 15 Jan. 1902, William A. Jones Papers, 1892–1911, MSS 495, Wisconsin Historical Society Archives, Madison. The majority of the documents from this collection cited in this chapter are found in box 1, folders 1–2; box 2, folders 1–4; and box 5, folders 8–9, which will be cited collectively as "Jones Papers."

4. Ibid.

5. Collection description, Jones Papers; Janet A. McDonnell, *The Dispossession of the American Indian, 1887–1934* (Bloomington: Indiana University Press, 1991), p. 1; Stuart Banner, *How the Indians Lost Their Land: Law and Power on the Frontier* (Cambridge, Mass.: Belknap Press of Harvard University Press, 2005), pp. 257–58; Herbert S. Schell, "Widening Horizons at the Turn of the Century: The Last Dakota Land Boom," *South Dakota History* 12 (Summer 1982): 93–117.

6. Bingenheimer to Jones, 27 May 1901, Jones Papers.

7. Jones to Editor, *The Outlook*, 12 Apr. 1902, Jones Papers. *See also* Burkholder, "Poised to Profit," pp. 330-31; and Iverson, *When Indians Became Cowboys*, pp. 40-41.

8. Jones to Editor, *The Outlook*, 12 Apr. 1902; U.S., Senate, Committee on Indian Affairs, *Leasing of Indian Lands: Hearings before the Committee on Indian Affairs, United States Senate*, S. Doc. 212, 57th Cong., 1st sess., 1902 (hereafter S. Doc. 212), pp. 10-31.

9. Herbert S. Schell, *History of South Dakota*, 4th ed., rev. John E. Miller (Pierre: South Dakota State Historical Society Press, 2004), p. 251; Ike Blasingame, *Dakota Cowboy: My Life in the Old Days* (Lincoln: University of Nebraska Press, 1964), pp. 35-36; Bob Lee and Dick Williams, *Last Grass Frontier: The South Dakota Stock Grower Heritage* (Sturgis, S.Dak.: Black Hills Publishers, 1964), pp. 231-32.

10. Schell, *History of South Dakota*, p. 251; Blasingame, *Dakota Cowboy*, pp. 35-36; Lee and Williams, *Last Grass Frontier*, pp. 218, 231-32.

11. Kennan, "Have Reservation Indians Any Vested Rights?" *The Outlook*, 29 Mar. 1902, p. 759. *See also* Construction, *The Railway Age*, 8 Feb. 1901, p. 108; Stanley W. Johnson, *The Milwaukee Road's Western Extension: The Building of a Transcontinental Railroad* (Coeur d'Alene: Museum of North Idaho, 2007), pp. 27-29; and James Fredric Hamburg, *The Influence of Railroads upon the Processes and Patterns of Settlement in South Dakota* (New York: Arno Press, 1981), pp. 258-63.

12. Iverson, *When Indians Became Cowboys*, pp. 34-35.

13. Quoted in S. Doc. 212, p. 92.

14. Quoted ibid.

15. Bingenheimer to Jones, 27 May 1901; S. Doc. 212, pp. 91-94; Donal F. Lindsey, *Indians at Hampton Institute, 1877-1923* (Urbana: University of Illinois Press, 1995); David Wallace Adams, *Education for Extinction: American Indians and the Boarding School Experience, 1875-1928* (Lawrence: University Press of Kansas, 1995). These types of debates were not limited to the Sioux. *See* Paul C. Rosier, *Rebirth of the Blackfeet Nation, 1912-1954* (Lincoln: University of Nebraska Press, 2001).

16. Quoted in Kennan, "Have Reservation Indians Any Vested Rights?" p. 759.

17. U.S., Senate, Committee on Indian Affairs, *Leasing of the Indian Lands on Standing Rock Reservation*, S. Rep. 1846, 57th Cong., 1st sess., 1902 (hereafter S. Rep. 1846), p. 7.

18. S. Doc. 212, pp. 13-15.

19. Lewis L. Gould, *The Presidency of Theodore Roosevelt* (Lawrence: University Press of Kansas, 1991), pp. 1-18; Kathleen Dalton, *Theodore Roosevelt: A Strenuous Life* (New York: Alfred A. Knopf, 2002), pp. 199-201; Edmund Morris, *Theodore Rex* (New York: Modern Library, 2001), pp. 3-16.

20. Jones to Bingenheimer, 9 Oct. 1901, Jones Papers.

21. Jones to Editor, *The Outlook*, 12 Apr. 1902.

22. Ibid.

23. Ibid.; S. Doc. 212, pp. 10–31.

24. Roche to Jones, 30 Dec. 1901, Jones Papers.

25. S. Doc. 212, p. 27. *See also* ibid., pp. 14, 28.

26. Herbert Welsh, *The Action of the Interior Department in Forcing the Standing Rock Indians to Lease Their Lands to Cattle Syndicates* (Philadelphia: Indian Rights Assn., 1902), p. 4.

27. Ibid., p. 5.

28. S. Doc. 212, p. 90; S. Rep. 1846, p. 21. Louis Primeau had previously served as interpreter for Indian agent James McLaughlin. *See* Robert M. Utley, *The Lance and the Shield: The Life and Times of Sitting Bull* (New York: Henry Holt & Co., 1993), pp. 263, 287–88.

29. Jones to Editor, *The Outlook*, 12 Apr. 1902.

30. S. Doc. 212, pp. 11, 13.

31. Lee and Williams, *Last Grass Frontier*, p. 164. Lake, Tomb, and Lemmon had keen insight in this area, for more than one hundred thousand homesteaders would settle in western South Dakota between 1900 and 1915. Paula M. Nelson, *After the West Was Won: Homesteaders and Town-Builders in Western South Dakota, 1900–1917* (Iowa City: University of Iowa Press, 1986), p. xiv.

32. S. Doc. 212, pp. 17–31, 71–98; S. Rep. 1846, pp. 16–18.

33. S. Doc. 212, p. 23.

34. Ibid., pp. 22–23, 71–72, 81–82, 87; Jones to Editor, *The Outlook*, 12 Apr. 1902; map of Lemmon and Walker leases, Jones Papers; S. Rep. 1846, pp. 18–19, 27; Kennan, "Have Reservation Indians Any Vested Rights?" pp. 759–65.

35. S. Doc. 212, pp. 22–23, 71–72, 81–82, 87; Jones to Editor, *The Outlook*, 12 Apr. 1902; map of Lemmon and Walker leases; S. Rep. 1846, pp. 18–19, 27; Kennan, "Have Reservation Indians Any Vested Rights?" pp. 759–65.

36. S. Doc. 212, p. 25.

37. Larson, *Gall*, pp. 174–96.

38. S. Doc. 212, pp. 97–98.

39. Lemmon, as told to Usher L. Burdick, "History of the Range Cattle Trade of the Dakotas," unpublished manuscript, call no. 01667, American Heritage Center, University of Wyoming, Laramie, p. 192.

40. S. Doc. 212, pp. 20–21, 72–73, 77; S. Rep. 1846, pp. 20–21, 25; "Memorandum Agreement Made May 23, 1902," Jones Papers; *BFB*, 15 Sept. 1933.

41. S. Doc. 212, pp. 45–48; *BFB*, 15 Sept. 1933.

42. S. Doc. 212, pp. 71–98.

43. Ibid., p. 90.

44. Welsh, *Action of the Interior Department*, p. 1.

45. S. Rep. 1846, p. 20.

46. Kennan, "Have Reservation Indians Any Vested Rights?" p. 760.

47. Jones to Rattle, 25, 31 Jan. 1902, both in Jones Papers.

48. Quoted in Nellie Snyder Yost, *The Call of the Range: The Story of the Nebraska Stock Growers Association* (Denver, Colo.: Sage Books, 1966), p. 213.

49. Lee and Williams, *Last Grass Frontier*, p. 222; Howard Smith and Ann Harry, *The Trail of the Sheidley Cattle Company: An Account of Cattle Ranching on the Western Plains in the Era of the Open Range—and Wealth Therefrom* (Tiffin, Ohio: Herald Printing Co., 2002), pp. 174–75; Andrew R. Graybill, *Policing the Great Plains: Rangers, Mounties, and the North American Frontier, 1875–1910* (Lincoln: University of Nebraska Press, 2007), pp. 124–30. *See also* D. L. Turner, "To Lease the Moon: Burton C. ('Cap') Mossman and the Diamond A Cattle Ranch in South Dakota," *South Dakota History* 42 (Spring 2012): 1–27.

50. "Sioux Indians in Council at Bull Head Station, Standing Rock Agency—April 12, 1902," Jones Papers; "Memorandum Agreement Made May 23, 1902"; *BFB*, 7 Oct. 1932, 15 Sept. 1933.

51. *BFB*, 13 Jan. 1933.

52. Ibid.

53. Mark David Spence, *Dispossessing the Wilderness: Indian Removal and the Making of the National Parks* (New York: Oxford University Press, 1999), pp. 76–81; "Memorandum Agreement Made May 23, 1902."

54. S. Rep. 1846, p. 2. *See also* Charles J. Kappler to Jones, 20 May 1902, Jones Papers.

55. Jones to Davis, 14 Oct. 1902, Jones Papers.

56. Grinnell to Roosevelt, 18 July 1902, ibid.

57. Ibid.

58. Jones to Henry Bradley, 29 Aug. 1902, Jones Papers; Spence, *Dispossessing the Wilderness*, pp. 55–70, 83–100; Iverson, *When Indians Became Cowboys*; Lee and Williams, *Last Grass Frontier*, p. 229.

59. "Lemmon: G. E. 'Dad' Ed," George E. Lemmon file, Lemmon Public Library, Lemmon, S.Dak.; *BFB*, 3 Jan. 1936.

60. Lee and Williams, *Last Grass Frontier*, p. 162; Graybill, *Policing the Great Plains*, pp. 123–24; J. Evetts Haley, *The XIT Ranch of Texas and the Early Days of the Llano Estacado* (Norman: University of Oklahoma Press, 1967), pp. 84–88; *BFB*, 3 Mar. 1933.

61. *BFB*, 15 Sept. 1933.

62. Ibid., 7 Oct. 1932, 15 Sept. 1933, 6 Apr. 1939.

63. S. Doc. 212, p. 24.

64. *BFB*, 15 Mar. 1935. Overgrazing is somewhat relative; modern rotational grazing practices are far different from the open-range grazing Lemmon em-

ployed on his huge lease. Some historians have asserted that "wasteful and destructive practices were common among ranchers" on the Great Plains. Warren Elofson, "Grasslands Management in Southern Alberta: The Frontier Legacy," *Agricultural History* 86 (Fall 2012): 145.

65. *BFB*, 1 Jan. 1937. The $96,000 that Lemmon owed in 1902 would be more than $2 million in 2015 dollars.

66. Ibid. *See also* ibid., 8 July 1932, 6 Apr. 1939; and *DW*, vol. 13, p. 5.

67. *BFB*, 13 Apr. 1934, 3 Jan. 1936; *DW*, vol. 12, pp. 12–15; obituary of James Hervey Lemmon, Sr., n.d., unknown newspaper, Virginia Grabow collection, Tigard, Ore.

68. Blasingame, *Dakota Cowboy*, p. 218.

69. *BFB*, 13 Jan. 1933, 31 May 1935; "Lemmon: G. E. 'Dad' Ed."

70. *BFB*, 31 Jan. 1936. *See also* ibid., 2 Sept. 1932, 21 Apr. 1933; Mrs. Lloyd I. Sudlow, *Homestead Years, 1908–1968* (Bison, S.Dak.: *Bison Courier*, 1968), p. 179; and August H. Schatz, *Longhorns Bring Culture* (Boston: Christopher Publishing House, 1961), p. 39.

71. Lemmon, "History of the Range Cattle Trade," p. 192. *See also BFB*, 3 Mar. 1933; *DW*, vol. 13, p. 5; and Blasingame, *Dakota Cowboy*, p. 221.

72. *BFB*, 9 Sept. 1932.

73. Ibid., 17 Dec. 1937; *DW*, vol. 13, p. 5; Lee and Williams, *Last Grass Frontier*, pp. 231–32; "Lemmon: G. E. 'Dad' Ed"; Ed Lemmon, *Boss Cowman: The Recollections of Ed Lemmon, 1857–1946*, ed. Nellie Snyder Yost (Lincoln: University of Nebraska Press, 1969), p. 240.

74. *BFB*, 15 Sept. 1933. *See also* ibid., 21 Dec. 1934.

7. Town Building

1. *Doane Robinson's Encyclopedia of South Dakota* (Pierre, S.Dak.: By the Author, 1925), p. 990; James Fredric Hamburg, *The Influence of Railroads upon the Processes and Patterns of Settlement in South Dakota* (New York: Arno Press, 1981), pp. 304–5; Paula M. Nelson, *After the West Was Won: Homesteaders and Town-Builders in Western South Dakota, 1900–1917* (Iowa City: University of Iowa Press, 1986), p. 21.

2. Nelson, *After the West Was Won*, p. xiv; Elwyn B. Robinson, *History of North Dakota* (Lincoln: University of Nebraska Press, 1966), p. 176.

3. Minutes of the special meeting of the board of directors of the Chicago, Milwaukee & St. Paul Railway Co., 28 Nov. 1905, box 6, series 3, Milwaukee Road Archives, Milwaukee Public Library, Milwaukee, Wisc. (hereafter Milwaukee Road Archives). For additional information on the decision to extend the line, *see New York Times*, 29 Nov., 3 Dec. 1905; and Ed Lemmon, *The West as I Lived It: Stories by Ed Lemmon*, comp. Phyllis Schmidt (Pierre, S.Dak.: State Publish-

ing Co., 2007), p. 371. Calkins became president of the Milwaukee Road in 1918. *See* August Derleth, *The Milwaukee Road: Its First Hundred Years* (Iowa City: University of Iowa Press, 2002), p. 204.

4. Derleth, *The Milwaukee Road*, pp. 158–75, 204; Rick W. Mills, *The Milwaukee Road in Dakota* (Hermosa, S.Dak.: Battle Creek Publishing Co., 1998); William Cronon, *Nature's Metropolis: Chicago and the Great West* (New York: W. W. Norton & Co., 1991). *See also* contents of box 6, series 3, Milwaukee Road Archives.

5. Chicago, Milwaukee & St. Paul Railway Company Valuation Department, "History of the Location and Construction of the Lines West of Mobridge, South Dakota, by Valuation Sections and Subsidiary Companies," rev. Nov. 1925, pp. 1–6, available through *Milwaukee Road Archive*, [comp. Michael Sol], milwaukeeroadarchives.com; Stanley W. Johnson, *The Milwaukee Road's Western Extension: The Building of a Transcontinental Railroad* (Coeur d'Alene: Museum of North Idaho, 2007), pp. 53–55; Julius Skaug, ed., *Mobridge: Its First 50 Years* ([Mobridge, S.Dak.: City of Mobridge, 1956]), p. 21.

6. Quoted in Lemmon, *The West as I Lived It*, p. 371.

7. Ibid.; Lemmon, as told to Usher L. Burdick, "History of the Range Cattle Trade of the Dakotas," unpublished manuscript, call no. 01667, American Heritage Center, University of Wyoming, Laramie, p. 48; *Lemmon: The First 100 Years* (Lemmon, S.Dak.: Print Shop, 2007), p. 1. Lemmon is not consistent about the timing of his meetings with Calkins. Given the Milwaukee Railroad's construction timeline, the meeting must have occurred in the winter of 1905–1906.

8. Lemmon, *The West as I Lived It*, p. 371. *See also* Lemmon, "History of the Range Cattle Trade," p. 48; and Chicago, Milwaukee & St. Paul Railway Co. Valuation Dept., "History of the Location and Construction of the Lines West of Mobridge," pp. 1–2. In 1922 Lieutenant Governor (and future governor) Carl Gunderson claimed that "Harry McLaughlin, a mixed blood Indian on the Standing Rock Reservation" selected the route. Gunderson became involved with the Milwaukee Railroad in 1909, so his version is likely based on second-hand information. Gunderson, "A Historical Reminiscence," *South Dakota Historical Collections* 11 (1922): 17.

9. Mills, *Milwaukee Road in Dakota*, p. 22; Herbert S. Schell, *History of South Dakota*, 4th ed., rev. John E. Miller (Pierre: South Dakota State Historical Society Press, 2004), p. 252; Derleth, *The Milwaukee Road*, pp. 172–73. *See also* contents of box 6, series 3, Milwaukee Road Archives.

10. Lemmon, *The West as I Lived It*, p. 371.

11. Ibid.; *Belle Fourche Bee* (hereafter *BFB*), 21 June 1935; *Lemmon: The First 100 Years*, p. 1; "Grantee Index to Deeds" (1904–1910), Register of Deeds, Adams County, Hettinger, N.Dak.

12. Lemmon, *The West as I Lived It*, p. 371.

13. Ibid.

14. Quoted ibid., p. 372. *See also The Cyclopædia of Temperance and Prohibition* (New York: Funk and Wagnalls, 1891), pp. 102, 126–27; Schell, *History of South Dakota*, p. 238; and Robinson, *History of North Dakota*, pp. 219, 258–59.

15. Lemmon, *The West as I Lived It*, pp. 372–73.

16. *Lemmon: The First 100 Years*, p. 2.

17. W. H. Hamilton, *Dakota: An Autobiography of a Cowman* (Pierre: South Dakota State Historical Society Press, 1998), p. 165.

18. Lemmon, *The West as I Lived It*, p. 372.

19. "Lemmon: G. E. 'Dad' Ed," George E. Lemmon file, Lemmon Public Library, Lemmon, S.Dak.

20. Skaug, ed., *Mobridge*, pp. 21–23; Mills, *Milwaukee Road in Dakota*, pp. 22–23; Derleth, *Milwaukee Road*, pp. 172–73; Johnson, *Milwaukee Road's Western Extension*. *See also* contents of box 6, series 3, Milwaukee Road Archives.

21. *BFB*, 31 Aug. 1939.

22. Lemmon to Edna Bauer, 4 Oct. 1908, Virginia Grabow collection, Tigard, Ore. *See also Lemmon: The First 100 Years*, pp. 3–8; Hamburg, *Influence of Railroads*, p. 416; and Lemmon High School Sociology Class of 1989, comp., *The Face of Change: Lemmon, South Dakota, Main Street Businesses, 1907–1989*, ed. Ken Ashmore (Lemmon, S.Dak.: Lemmon Centennial Committee, 1989).

23. *Rosella B. Lemmon v. George E. Lemmon* (1927), Clerk of Courts, Perkins County, Bison, S.Dak.; *Dakota Herald* (Lemmon, S.Dak.), 16 July 2007.

24. *BFB*, 5 Nov. 1937.

25. Lemmon High School Sociology Class, *Face of Change*, p. 19; "Grantee Index to Deeds" (1904–1910); Land Records, 1908–1945, Register of Deeds, Perkins County, Bison, S.Dak.; *Lemmon: The First 100 Years*, p. 5.

26. Nathan Sanderson, "More Than a Potluck: Shared Meals and Community-Building in Rural Nebraska at the Turn of the Twentieth Century," *Nebraska History* 89 (Fall 2008): 120–31.

27. "Lemmon: G. E. 'Dad' Ed"; *Lemmon: The First 100 Years*, pp. 3–11; Rose Tidball, *Taming the Plains* ([Keldron, S.Dak.]: By the Author, 1976), p. 39.

28. Mrs. Lloyd I. Sudlow, ed., *Homestead Years, 1908–1968* (Bison, S.Dak.: Bison Courier, 1968), pp. 2–6.

29. Minutes of the meeting of the executive committee of the Chicago, Milwaukee & St. Paul Railway Co., 19 May 1909, box 6, series 3, Milwaukee Road Archives.

30. *BFB*, 13 Jan. 1933.

31. Ibid.; Hamburg, *Influence of Railroads*, pp. 325–44; Lemmon, "History of the Range Cattle Trade," pp. 48–49; Robert F. Bruner and Sean D. Carr, *The Panic of 1907: Lessons Learned from the Market's Perfect Storm* (Hoboken, N.J.: John Wiley & Sons, 2007), pp. 4–5, 197.

32. Herbert S. Schell, "Widening Horizons at the Turn of the Century: The Last Dakota Land Boom," *South Dakota History* 12 (Summer 1982): 93–117; Hamburg, *Influence of Railroads*, pp. 325–52; Mills, *Milwaukee Road in Dakota*, p. 23; Schell, *History of South Dakota*, pp. 253–54. A fifteenth town, Faith, formed the terminus of the Faith branch line and is just across the border in Meade County.

33. Schell, *History of South Dakota*, pp. 309–13.

34. Quoted in Mary and Dale Lewis, *LeBeau: A Sputtering Flame* (Wasta, S.Dak.: Lewis Publishing, 2008), p. 96. *See also* Hamburg, *Influence of Railroads*, p. 310.

35. *Lemmon Leader*, 6 Feb. 1968; *Doane Robinson's Encyclopedia*, p. 993; *Lemmon: The First 100 Years*, p. 14; J. Leonard Jennewein and Jane Boorman, eds., *Dakota Panorama* ([Worthing, S.Dak.]: Brevet Press, 1961), p. 234; *Perkins County Signal* (Lemmon, S.Dak.), 26 Apr. 1911.

36. Hamburg, *Influence of Railroads*, p. 366; South Dakota WPA Writers' Project, *South Dakota Place Names* (Vermillion: University of South Dakota, 1941).

37. Nelson, *After the West Was Won*, pp. 86–88; Sudlow, ed., *Homestead Years*, pp. 52, 151–52; *Lemmon: The First 100 Years*, p. 14.

38. *Lemmon: The First 100 Years*, p. 71; "Yellowstone Trail Summary," Petrified Wood Park and Museum, Lemmon, S.Dak.; "History of the Yellowstone Trail," The Yellowstone Trail Association, yellowstonetrail.org; *Perkins County Signal*, 17 Sept., 29 Oct. 1913.

39. *Perkins County Signal*, 16 Aug. 1911; Schell, *History of South Dakota*, p. 253; Donald Worster, *Dust Bowl: The Southern Plains in the 1930s* (New York: Oxford University Press, 1979), pp. 87–89; Timothy Egan, *The Worst Hard Time: The Untold Story of Those Who Survived the Great American Dust Bowl* (Boston: Houghton Mifflin Co., 2006), pp. 56–67; Jonathan Raban, *Bad Land: An American Romance* (New York: Pantheon Books, 1996).

40. *Perkins County Signal*, 12 July 1911.

41. "Grantee Index to Deeds" (1904–1924); Land Records, 1908–1945; *Lemmon v. Lemmon*.

42. *Perkins County Signal*, 14 June 1911. Farmers across the country began to organize during this time. *See* Richard Hofstadter, *The Age of Reform* (New York: Vintage Books, 1955), pp. 109–19.

43. *Perkins County Signal*, 19 July 1911.

44. Schell, *History of South Dakota*, pp. 259–64.

45. *Perkins County Signal*, 15 Jan. 1913.

46. *Developing the West*, vol. 12, p. 5, MSS 691, Wyoming State Archives, Cheyenne (hereafter *DW*).

47. *BFB*, 16 Feb. 1934.

48. *Lemmon v. Lemmon*.

49. Ibid.

50. *BFB*, 17 Apr. 1936. *See also* Richard W. Slatta, *Cowboys of the Americas* (New Haven, Conn.: Yale University Press, 1990), p. 186.

51. *BFB*, 2 Apr. 1937.

52. Ibid.; *Perkins County Signal*, 13 Oct. 1915; *Lemmon Tribune*, 5 Dec. 1918.

53. *Lemmon Herald*, 12 Jan. 1916; *Lemmon Tribune*, 22 Nov. 1917; *Lemmon: The First 100 Years*, p. 180; *BFB*, 29 Apr. 1938; *DW*, vol. 12, pp. 8–9, vol. 13, pp. 6–7; Lemmon, "History of the Range Cattle Trade," pp. 103–4.

54. Quoted in "Summary of 1919 Cattle Loss," Ed Texley collection, Hettinger, N.Dak. For weather data for north-central South Dakota in 1919 and 1920, *see* "Climate at a Glance," National Centers for Environmental Information, National Oceanic and Atmospheric Administration, ncdc.noaa.gov.

55. Ed Lemmon, *Boss Cowman: The Recollections of Ed Lemmon, 1857–1946*, ed. Nellie Snyder Yost (Lincoln: University of Nebraska Press, 1969), p. ix.

56. *Lemmon v. Lemmon*; Sudlow, ed., *Homestead Years*, pp. 184–87; Bert L. Hall, comp., *Roundup Years: Old Muddy to Black Hills* ([Winner, S.Dak.]: Western South Dakota Buck-a-roos, 2000), pp. 77–78.

57. Van West, *Capitalism on the Frontier: Billings and the Yellowstone Valley in the Nineteenth Century* (Lincoln: University of Nebraska Press, 1993), pp. 4, 133–61.

58. U.S., Department of Commerce, Bureau of the Census, *Fourteenth Census of the United States Taken in the Year 1920*, vol. 1, *Population* (Washington, D.C.: Government Printing Office, 1921), p. 128.

8. Legacy

1. Clyde A. Milner II and Carol A. O'Connor, *As Big as the West: The Pioneer Life of Granville Stuart* (Oxford, U.K.: Oxford University Press, 2009), p. xii.

2. *Belle Fourche Bee* (hereafter *BFB*), 20 Jan. 1933.

3. *Anaconda Standard*, 16 Aug. 1925.

4. Ibid. *See also* Milner and O'Connor, *As Big as the West*.

5. George E. Lemmon to Lewis F. Crawford, 7 Dec. 1926, G. E. Lemmon Papers, MSS 20019, State Historical Society of North Dakota, Bismarck.

6. Ibid. *See also* collection description for Lewis F. Crawford Papers, MSS 10058, State Historical Society of North Dakota, history.nd.gov.

7. Yost, "A Note on the Editing," in Ed Lemmon, *Boss Cowman: The Recollections of Ed Lemmon, 1857–1946*, ed. Yost (Lincoln: University of Nebraska Press, 1969), p. 311.

8. *Rosella B. Lemmon v. George E. Lemmon* (1927), Clerk of Courts, Perkins County, Bison, S.Dak.

9. Ibid.

10. Ibid.

11. Ibid.

12. Ibid. *See also* Land Records, book 158, p. 425, Register of Deeds, Perkins County, Bison, S.Dak.

13. *Lemmon Leader,* 28 May 1964.

14. "G. E. 'Dad' Lemmon Summary," George E. Lemmon file, Lemmon Public Library, Lemmon, S.Dak.; David M. Kennedy, *Freedom from Fear: The American People in Depression and War, 1929–1945* (New York: Oxford University Press, 1999); *Lemmon Tribune,* 30 Oct. 1958; *Lemmon Leader,* 8 Feb. 1968; Donald Worster, *Dust Bowl: The Southern Plains in the 1930s* (New York: Oxford University Press, 1979); Timothy Egan, *The Worst Hard Time: The Untold Story of Those Who Survived the Great American Dust Bowl* (Boston: Houghton Mifflin Co., 2006); Paula M. Nelson, *The Prairie Winnows Out Its Own: The West River Country of South Dakota in the Years of Depression and Dust* (Iowa City: University of Iowa Press, 1996). In 1944 James also helped found the South Dakota Association of Cooperatives, serving as its president until 1956.

15. *BFB,* 1 Apr. 1932.

16. *See,* generally, Lemmon, *Developing the West,* MSS 691, Wyoming State Archives, Cheyenne (hereafter *DW*).

17. Lemmon, "Fifty-three Years of Open-Range Cattle Handling," Ed Texley collection, Hettinger, N.Dak.

18. [Sandoz], "G. E. Lemmon Mss," box 1, folder 1, G. E. Lemmon, 1857–1946 Collection, RG2016.AM, Nebraska State Historical Society, Lincoln (hereafter NSHS). There is a remote possibility that Lemmon provided some of the inspiration for one of Sandoz's novels, *The Tom-Walker,* in which the main character, Milton Stone, lost a leg during the Civil War. Sandoz, *The Tom-Walker* (Lincoln: University of Nebraska Press, 1947).

19. Lewis F. Crawford, *History of North Dakota,* 3 vols. (Chicago: American Historical Society, 1931); Hansen to Sheldon, 14 Nov. 1933 and two letters dated 9 May 1934, all in box 1, folder 1, NSHS; Lemmon, "July 12, 1861, Date of Rock Creek Tragedy," *Nebraska History Magazine* 14 (July–Sept. 1933): 198–99; Lemmon, "Interesting Stories of Early Nebraska, 1850–1876," *Nebraska History Magazine* 15 (Apr.–June 1934): 110–13.

20. Lemmon, as told to Usher L. Burdick, "History of the Range Cattle Trade of the Dakotas," unpublished manuscript, call no. 01667, American Heritage Center, University of Wyoming, Laramie, pp. 1–2.

21. Lemmon, *Boss Cowman,* pp. 310–12. In 1931, Hazel Adele Pulling published her dissertation, titled "History of the Range Cattle Industry of Dakota," in *South Dakota Historical Collections* 20 (1940): 467–521. Pulling had interviewed Lemmon during her research and cited him repeatedly in her notes. When Burdick created his compilation of Lemmon's writings, "History of the Range Cattle Trade of the Dakotas," he may have taken his title from Pulling's dissertation.

22. Griffiths, "Half a Century on the Range is Record of West-River Cowman," in *Roundup Years: Old Muddy to Black Hills*, comp. Bert L. Hall ([Winner, S.Dak.]: Western South Dakota Buck-a-roos, 2000), p. 77.

23. *See*, generally, articles by Lemmon in Work Projects Administration collection, Pioneer Cabinet, Wyoming State Archives, Cheyenne; contents of box 2, folder 15, E. P. Lamborn Papers, MS 156, Kansas Historical Society, Topeka; and August H. Schatz, *Longhorns Bring Culture* (Boston: Christopher Publishing House, 1961).

24. *BFB*, 8 July 1932. *See also Lemmon: The First 100 Years* (Lemmon, S.Dak.: Print Shop, 2007), p. 225; Mrs. Lloyd I. Sudlow, ed., *Homestead Years, 1908–1968* (Bison, S.Dak.: *Bison Courier*, 1968), p. 179; and *BFB*, 30 Sept. 1932, 24 Aug., 14 Sept. 1934.

25. *Lemmon Leader and Grand Valley Herald*, 11 June 1936. *See also BFB*, 12 June 1936; *Lemmon Tribune*, 27 June 1918; and *Lemmon v. Lemmon*.

26. Quoted in Sudlow, ed., *Homestead Years*, p. 187. *See also BFB*, 31 Aug. 1934, 5, 26 June 1936.

27. *DW*, vol. 12, p. 10.

28. Lemmon, "History of the Range Cattle Trade," p. 12.

29. Tidball, *Taming the Plains* ([Keldron, S.Dak.]: By the Author, 1976), p. 38.

30. Nat Pierce, unknown article in unknown volume, p. 412, copy in Virginia Grabow collection, Tigard, Ore. *See also* Lemmon, *Boss Cowman*, p. 215. Cowboy Frank Glover carved the cane, which supported Ed during his 1941 *Life* magazine photo shoot. It is on display in the Lemmon Petrified Wood Park Museum.

31. Butterfield and Elisofon, "South Dakota: Its Boundless Plains Are the Heart of a Continent," *Life*, 6 Oct. 1941, p. 108.

32. *Lemmon Leader*, 9 Oct. 1941.

33. *DW*, vol. 13, pp. 5–6.

34. Lemmon High School Sociology Class of 1989, comp., *The Face of Change: Lemmon, South Dakota, Main Street Businesses, 1907–1989*, ed. Ken Ashmore (Lemmon, S.Dak.: Lemmon Centennial Committee, 1989), p. 56; *Lemmon Leader*, 29 Aug. 1945; *In the Matter of the Estate of George Edward Lemmon, Deceased* (1945), Clerk of Courts, Perkins County, Bison, S.Dak.

35. *BFB*, 1 Jan. 1937.

36. *Faith Country Heritage* (Faith, S.Dak.: Faith Historical Committee, 1985), pp. 364–65; South Dakota WPA Writers' Project, *South Dakota Place Names* (Vermillion: University of South Dakota, 1941), pp. 96–97; *Lemmon Tribune*, 13 June 1957; *Lemmon: The First 100 Years*, pp. 219–24; *Dakota Herald* (Lemmon, S.Dak.), 16 July 2007; Neoma E. Rossow, "Town Founder Was Also Top Cattleman," *South Dakota Hall of Fame Magazine*, Fall 1996, pp. 26–27; Roger Holtzmann, "Boss Cowman's Own Words," *South Dakota Magazine*, Mar.–Apr. 2008, pp. 51–56.

37. Cathie Draine, ed., *Cowboy Life: The Letters of George Philip* (Pierre: South Dakota State Historical Society Press, 2007), p. 299.

38. *Rapid City Daily Journal*, 26 May 1941.

BIBLIOGRAPHY

Public Archival Collections

Adams County Courthouse, Hettinger, N.Dak.
    Register of Deeds Office.
American Heritage Center, University of Wyoming, Laramie.
    Ed Lemmon manuscript, ca. 1960–ca. 1969, call no. 01667.
Chester Fritz Library, University of North Dakota, Grand Forks.
    Usher L. Burdick Papers, OGL 21.
Kansas Historical Society, Topeka.
    E. P. Lamborn Papers, MS 156.
Lemmon Petrified Wood Park, Lemmon, S.Dak.
Lemmon Public Library, Lemmon, S.Dak.
    George E. Lemmon file.
Milwaukee Public Library, Milwaukee, Wisc.
    Milwaukee Road Archives.
Nebraska State Historical Society, Lincoln.
    G. E. Lemmon, 1857–1946 Collection, RG2016.AM.
    James Butler ("Wild Bill") Hickok, 1837–1876 Collection, RG2603.AM.
    Union Pacific Railroad (Omaha, Nebr.) Collection, RG3761.AM.
Perkins County Courthouse, Bison, S.Dak.
    Clerk of Courts Office.
    Register of Deeds Office.
State Archives, South Dakota State Historical Society, Pierre.
    Ed Lemmon Biographical File.
State Historical Society of North Dakota, Bismarck.
    George E. Lemmon Papers, MSS 20019.
Wisconsin Historical Society Archives, Madison.
    William A. Jones Papers, MSS 495.
Wyoming State Archives, Cheyenne.
    Developing the West collection, MSS 691.
    Work Projects Administration collection, Pioneer Cabinet.

Private Collections

Grabow, Virginia, Tigard, Ore.
Sheidley Family Papers, Mission Hills, Kans.
    Betsey Sheidley Fletcher collection.
Texley, Ed, Hettinger, N.Dak.

Newspapers

Anaconda (Mont.) *Standard.*

Belle Fourche Bee.

Cheyenne (Wyo.) *Leader.*

Dakota Herald (Lemmon, S.Dak.).

Lemmon Herald.

Lemmon Leader.

Lemmon Leader and Grand Valley Herald.

Lemmon Tribune.

Marysville (Kans.) *Advocate-Democrat.*

National Tribune (Washington, D.C.).

New York Times.

Perkins County Signal (Lemmon, S.Dak.).

Rapid City Daily Journal.

Wyoming Weekly Leader (Cheyenne).

Government Documents

Harrison, Benjamin. "Proclamation 295 – Sioux Nation of Indians," 10 Feb. 1890. *The American Presidency Project.* University of California Santa Barbara. presidency.ucsb.edu.

Mooney, James. *The Ghost-Dance Religion and the Sioux Outbreak of 1890.* In *Fourteenth Annual Report of the Bureau of Ethnology to the Secretary of the Smithsonian Institution.* Ed. John W. Powell. Washington, D.C.: Government Printing Office, 1896.

U.S., Congress. *United States Statutes at Large* 25. 50th Cong., 2d sess., pt. 2, 1889.

U.S., Department of Commerce, Bureau of the Census. *Fourteenth Census of the United States Taken in the Year 1920*, vol. 1, *Population.* Washington, D.C.: Government Printing Office, 1921.

———. *Thirteenth Census of the United States.* 1910. Manuscript population schedules, National Archives Microfilm Publication T624.

U.S., Department of the Interior, Census Office. *Ninth Census of the United States.* 1870. Manuscript population schedules, National Archives Microfilm Publication M593.

———. *Twelfth Census of the United States.* 1900. Manuscript population schedules, National Archives Microfilm Publication T623.

U.S., Department of the Interior, Office of Indian Affairs. *Annual Report of the Commissioner of Indian Affairs to the Secretary of the Interior.* Washington, D.C.: Government Printing Office, 1881–1891.

U.S., Senate, Committee on Indian Affairs. *Leasing of Indian Lands: Hearings before the Committee on Indian Affairs, United States Senate.* S. Doc. 212, 57th Cong., 1st sess., 1902.

————. *Leasing of the Indian Lands on Standing Rock Reservation.* S. Rep. 1846, 57th Cong., 1st sess., 1902.

United States v. Sioux Nation of Indians. 448 U.S. 371, 1980.

Articles

Burkholder, John H. "Poised to Profit: Fort Pierre and the Development of the Open Range in South Dakota." *South Dakota History* 41 (Fall 2011): 323–52.

Butterfield, Roger and Eliot Elisofon. "South Dakota: Its Boundless Plains Are the Heart of a Continent." *Life,* 6 Oct. 1941, pp. 98–109.

Construction. *The Railway Age,* 8 Feb. 1901, p. 108.

Elofson, Warren. "Grasslands Management in Southern Alberta: The Frontier Legacy." *Agricultural History* 86 (Fall 2012): 143–68.

Gunderson, Carl. "A Historical Reminiscence." *South Dakota Historical Collections* 11 (1922): 17–18.

Hämäläinen, Pekka. "The Rise and Fall of Plains Indian Horse Cultures." *Journal of American History* 90 (Dec. 2003): 833–62.

Holtzmann, Roger. "Boss Cowman's Own Words." *South Dakota Magazine,* Mar./Apr. 2008, pp. 51–56.

Homer, Michael W. "An Immigrant Story: Three Orphaned Italians in Early Utah Territory." *Utah Historical Quarterly* 70 (Summer 2002): 196–214.

Hoover, Herbert T. "The Sioux Agreement of 1889 and Its Aftermath." *South Dakota History* 19 (Spring 1989): 56–94.

Kennan, George. "Have Reservation Indians Any Vested Rights?" *The Outlook,* 29 Mar. 1902, pp. 759–65.

Kruckenberg, Molly and Richard W. Slatta, eds. "'$30 a month for all summer and dont have to work Sundays': Letters from Cowboy Earl J. Martin." *South Dakota History* 38 (Summer 2008): 125–47.

Lemmon, George E. "Interesting Stories of Early Nebraska, 1850–1876." *Nebraska History Magazine* 15 (Apr.-June 1934): 110–13.

————. "July 12, 1861, Date of Rock Creek Tragedy." *Nebraska History Magazine* 14 (July-Sept. 1933): 198–99.

Lemmon, James H. "Early Days on the Little Blue." *Proceedings and Collections of the Nebraska State Historical Society* 15 (1907): 127–33.

Lopez, David E. "Cowboy Strikes and Unions." *Labor History* 18 (Summer 1977): 325–40.

Mattes, Merrill and Paul Henderson. "The Pony Express: Across Nebraska from St. Joseph to Fort Laramie." *Nebraska History* 41 (June 1960): 83–122.

Nesheim, David. "How William F. Cody Helped Save the Buffalo without Really Trying." *Great Plains Quarterly* 27 (Summer 2007): 163–75.

Pulling, Hazel Adele. "History of the Range Cattle Industry of Dakota." *South Dakota Historical Collections* 20 (1940): 467–521.

Rossow, Neoma E. "Town Founder Was Also Top Cattleman." *South Dakota Hall of Fame Magazine*, Fall 1994, pp. 26–27.

Sanderson, Nathan. "More Than a Potluck: Shared Meals and Community-Building in Rural Nebraska at the Turn of the Twentieth Century." *Nebraska History* 89 (Fall 2008): 120–31.

————. "'We Were All Trespassers': George Edward Lemmon, Anglo-American Cattle Ranching, and the Great Sioux Reservation." *Agricultural History* 85 (Winter 2011): 50–71.

Schell, Herbert S. "Widening Horizons at the Turn of the Century: The Last Dakota Land Boom." *South Dakota History* 12 (Summer 1982): 93–117.

Slatta, Richard W. "Long Hours and Low Pay: Cowboy Life on the Northern Plains." *South Dakota History* 32 (Fall 2002): 194–216.

Turner, D. L. "To Lease the Moon: Burton C. ('Cap') Mossman and the Diamond A Cattle Ranch in South Dakota." *South Dakota History* 42 (Spring 2012): 1–27.

Books

Adams, David Wallace. *Education for Extinction: American Indians and the Boarding School Experience, 1875–1928*. Lawrence: University Press of Kansas, 1995.

Allen, Frederick. *A Decent, Orderly Lynching: The Montana Vigilantes*. Norman: University of Oklahoma Press, 2004.

Ames, Charles Edgar. *Pioneering the Union Pacific: A Reappraisal of the Builders of the Railroad*. New York: Appleton-Century-Crofts, 1969.

Anderson, Gary Clayton. *Kinsmen of Another Kind: Dakota-White Relations in the Upper Mississippi Valley, 1650–1862*. Lincoln: University of Nebraska Press, 1984.

————— and Alan R. Woolworth, eds. *Through Dakota Eyes: Narrative Accounts of the Minnesota Indian War of 1862*. St. Paul: Minnesota Historical Society Press, 1988.

Andreas, Alfred T. *History of the State of Nebraska*. Chicago: The Western Historical Co., 1882.

Arrington, Leonard J. and Davis Bitton. *The Mormon Experience: A History of the Latter-day Saints*. 2d ed. Urbana: University of Illinois Press, 1992.

Athearn, Robert G. *Union Pacific Country*. Lincoln: Bison Books, 1971.

Bagley, Will. *Blood of the Prophets: Brigham Young and the Massacre at Mountain Meadows*. Norman: University of Oklahoma Press, 2004.

Bancroft, Hubert Howe and Frances Fuller Victor. *History of Nevada, Colorado, and Wyoming, 1540–1888*. San Francisco, Calif.: History Co., 1890.

Banner, Stuart. *How the Indians Lost their Land: Law and Power on the Frontier*. Cambridge, Mass.: Belknap Press of Harvard University Press, 2005.

Barns, Cass G. *The Sod House*. Lincoln: University of Nebraska Press, 1970.

Basso, Matthew, Laura McCall, and Dee Garceau, eds. *Across the Great Divide: Cultures of Manhood in the American West*. New York: Routledge, 2001.

Baxter, John O. *Cowboy Park: Steer-Roping Contests on the Border*. Lubbock: Texas Tech University Press, 2008.

Beckstead, James H. *Cowboying: A Tough Job in a Hard Land*. Salt Lake City: University of Utah Press, 1991.

Blasingame, Ike. *Dakota Cowboy: My Life in the Old Days*. Lincoln: University of Nebraska Press, 1964.

Boyack, Hazel Noble. *A Nobleman in Israel: A Biographical Sketch of Joseph Bates Noble, Pioneer to Utah in 1847*. Cheyenne, Wyo.: Pioneer Printing Co., 1962.

Brooks, Juanita. *The Mountain Meadows Massacre*. Norman: University of Oklahoma Press, 1979.

Brown, Dee. *The Year of the Century: 1876*. New York: Scribner, 1966.

Bruner, Robert F. and Sean D. Carr. *The Panic of 1907: Lessons Learned from the Market's Perfect Storm*. Hoboken, N.J.: John Wiley & Sons, 2007.

Buechel, Eugene and Paul Manhart, eds. *Lakota Dictionary: New Comprehensive Edition*. Lincoln: University of Nebraska Press, 2002.

Carley, Kenneth. *The Dakota War of 1862: Minnesota's Other Civil War*. 2d ed. St. Paul: Minnesota Historical Society Press, 2001.

Clay, John. *My Life on the Range*. Chicago: By the Author, 1924.

Clodfelter, Michael. *The Dakota War: The United States Army versus the Sioux, 1862–1865*. Jefferson, N.C.: McFarland & Co., 1998.

Cockrell, Dale. *The Ingalls Wilder Family Songbook*. Music of the United States of America 22. Middleton, Wisc.: A-R Editions, for the American Musicological Society, 2011.

Crawford, Lewis F. *History of North Dakota*. 3 vols. Chicago: American Historical Society, 1931.

Cronon, William. *Nature's Metropolis: Chicago and the Great West*. New York: W. W. Norton & Co., 1991.

[Cutler, William G.] *History of the State of Kansas*. Chicago: A. T. Andreas, 1883.

The Cyclopædia of Temperance and Prohibition. New York: Funk and Wagnalls, 1891.

Dalton, Kathleen. *Theodore Roosevelt: A Strenuous Life*. New York: Alfred A. Knopf, 2002.

Davis, John W. *Wyoming Range War: The Infamous Invasion of Johnson County*. Norman: University of Oklahoma Press, 2010.

Derleth, August. *The Milwaukee Road: Its First Hundred Years*. Iowa City: University of Iowa Press, 2002.

Dobie, J. Frank. *The Longhorns*. New York: Grosset & Dunlap, 1941.

Draine, Cathie, ed. *Cowboy Life: The Letters of George Philip.* Pierre: South Dakota State Historical Society Press, 2007.

Durham, Philip and Everett L. Jones. *The Negro Cowboys.* New York: Dodd, Mead & Co., 1965.

Egan, Timothy. *The Worst Hard Time: The Untold Story of Those Who Survived the Great American Dust Bowl.* Boston: Houghton Mifflin Co., 2006.

Ellenbecker, John G. *Oak Grove Massacre (Oak, Nebraska): Indian Raids on the Little Blue River in 1864.* Marysville, Kans.: *Marysville Advocate-Democrat,* 1927.

Ellis, Mark R. *Law and Order in Buffalo Bill's Country: Legal Culture and Community on the Great Plains, 1867–1910.* Lincoln: University of Nebraska Press, 2007.

Etcheson, Nichole. *Bleeding Kansas: Contested Liberty in the Civil War Era.* Lawrence: University Press of Kansas, 2004.

Faith Country Heritage, 1910–1985. Faith, S.Dak.: Faith Historical Committee, 1985.

Faragher, John Mack. *Women and Men on the Overland Trail.* 2d ed. New Haven, Conn.: Yale University Press, 2001.

Flood, Renée Sansom. *Lost Bird of Wounded Knee: Spirit of the Lakota.* New York: Scribner, 1995.

Folsom, James K., ed. *The Western: A Collection of Critical Essays.* Englewood Cliffs, N.J.: Prentice Hall, 1979.

Frederick, James V. *Ben Holladay, the Stagecoach King: A Chapter in the Development of Transcontinental Transportation.* Glendale, Calif.: Arthur H. Clark Co., 1940.

Gould, Lewis L. *The Presidency of Theodore Roosevelt.* Lawrence: University Press of Kansas, 1991.

Grand, W. Joseph. *Illustrated History of the Union Stockyards: Sketch-book of Familiar Faces and Places at the Yards.* Chicago: Thomas Knapp Printing & Building Co., 1896.

Graybill, Andrew R. *Policing the Great Plains: Rangers, Mounties, and the North American Frontier, 1875–1910.* Lincoln: University of Nebraska Press, 2007.

Hagan, William T. *Charles Goodnight: Father of the Texas Panhandle.* Norman: University of Oklahoma Press, 2007.

Haley, J. Evetts. *Charles Goodnight: Cowman and Plainsman.* Norman: University of Oklahoma Press, 1949.

———. *The XIT Ranch of Texas and the Early Days of the Llano Estacado.* Norman: University of Oklahoma Press, 1967.

Hall, Bert L., comp. *Roundup Years: Old Muddy to Black Hills.* [Winner, S.Dak.]: Western South Dakota Buck-a-roos, 2000.

Hamburg, James Fredric. *The Influence of Railroads upon the Processes and Patterns of Settlement in South Dakota.* New York: Arno Press, 1981.

Hamilton, W. H. *Dakota: An Autobiography of a Cowman.* Pierre: South Dakota State Historical Society Press, 1998.

Hedren, Paul L., ed. *The Great Sioux War, 1876–1877: The Best from* Montana The Magazine of Western History. Helena: Montana Historical Society Press, 1991.

Hofstadter, Richard. *The Age of Reform.* New York: Vintage Books, 1955.

Hoganson, Kristin L. *Fighting for American Manhood: How Gender Politics Provoked the Spanish-American and Philippine-American Wars.* New Haven, Conn.: Yale University Press, 1998.

Hoxie, Frederick E. *A Final Promise: The Campaign to Assimilate the Indians, 1880–1920.* Lincoln: University of Nebraska Press, 1984.

Hyde, George E. *Red Cloud's Folk: A History of the Oglala Sioux Indians.* Norman: University of Oklahoma Press, 1937.

Isenberg, Andrew. *The Destruction of the Bison: An Environmental History, 1750–1920.* Cambridge, U.K.: Cambridge University Press, 2000.

Iverson, Peter. *When Indians Become Cowboys: Native Peoples and Cattle Ranching in the American West.* Norman: University of Oklahoma Press, 1994.

Jeffrey, Julie Roy. *Converting the West: A Biography of Narcissa Whitman.* Norman: University of Oklahoma Press, 1991.

Jennewein, J. Leonard and Jane Boorman, eds. *Dakota Panorama.* [Worthing, S.Dak.]: Brevet Press, 1961.

Johnson, Elizabeth Meeuwsen. *Black Horse Butte: A Dakota Homestead Community, 1909–1940.* Freeman, S.Dak.: Pine Hill Press, 1995.

Johnson, James R. and Gary E. Larson, *Grassland Plants of South Dakota and the Northern Great Plains.* Ed. Mary Brashier. Brookings: South Dakota State University, 1999.

Johnson, Stanley W. *The Milwaukee Road's Western Extension: The Building of a Transcontinental Railroad.* Coeur d'Alene: Museum of Northern Idaho, 2007.

Johnston, Sister Mary Antonio. *Federal Relations with the Great Sioux Indians of South Dakota, 1887–1933.* Washington, D.C.: Catholic University of America Press, 1948.

Kahn, Cynthia M., ed. *The Merck Veterinary Manual.* 9th ed. Whitehouse Station, N.J.: Merck & Co., 2005.

Kennedy, David M. *Freedom from Fear: The American People in Depression and War, 1929–1945.* New York: Oxford University Press, 1999.

Lake, Stuart N. *Wyatt Earp, Frontier Marshal.* New York: Houghton Mifflin, 1931.

Larson, Robert W. *Gall: Lakota War Chief.* Norman: University of Oklahoma Press, 2007.

———. *Red Cloud: Warrior-Statesman of the Lakota Sioux.* Norman: University of Oklahoma Press, 1997.

Laskin, David. *The Children's Blizzard.* New York: HarperCollins, 2004.

Lass, William E. *From the Missouri to the Great Salt Lake: An Account of Overland Freighting.* Lincoln: Nebraska State Historical Society, 1972.

Lazarus, Edward. *Black Hills, White Justice: The Sioux Nation versus the United States, 1775 to the Present.* New York: HarperCollins, 1991.

Lee, Bob and Dick Williams. *Last Grass Frontier: The South Dakota Stock Grower Heritage.* Sturgis, S.Dak.: Black Hills Publishers, 1964.

Lee, Wayne C. *Scotty Philip, the Man Who Saved the Buffalo.* Caldwell, Idaho: Caxton Printers, 1975.

Lemmon, Ed. *Boss Cowman: The Recollections of Ed Lemmon, 1857–1946.* Ed. Nellie Snyder Yost. Lincoln: University of Nebraska Press, 1969.

———. *The West as I Lived It: Stories by Ed Lemmon.* Comp. Phyllis Schmidt. Pierre, S.Dak.: State Publishing Co., 2007.

Lemmon: The First 100 Years. Lemmon, S.Dak.: Print Shop, 2007.

Lemmon High School Sociology Class of 1989, comp. *The Face of Change: Lemmon, South Dakota, Main Street Businesses, 1907–1989.* Ed. Ken Ashmore. Lemmon, S.Dak.: Lemmon Centennial Committee, 1989.

Lewis, Mary and Dale Lewis. *LeBeau: A Sputtering Flame.* Wasta, S.Dak.: Lewis Publishing, 2008.

Limerick, Patricia Nelson. *The Legacy of Conquest: The Unbroken Past of the American West.* New York: Norton, 1987.

Lindsey, Donal F. *Indians at Hampton Institute, 1877–1923.* Urbana: University of Illinois Press, 1995.

Linn, William Alexander. *The Story of the Mormons: From the Date of Their Origin to the Year 1901.* New York: Russell & Russell, 1963.

McCrady, David G. *Living with Strangers: The Nineteenth-Century Sioux and the Canadian-American Borderlands.* Lincoln: University of Nebraska Press, 2006.

McDonnell, Janet A. *The Dispossession of the American Indian, 1887–1934.* Bloomington: Indiana University Press, 1991.

McGillycuddy, Julia B. *McGillycuddy, Agent: A Biography of Dr. Valentine T. McGillycuddy.* Stanford, Calif.: Stanford University Press, 1941.

McLaird, James D. *Calamity Jane: The Woman and the Legend.* Norman: University of Oklahoma Press, 2005.

Martin, Charles F., comp. *Proceedings of the Second Annual Convention of the National Live Stock Association.* Denver, Colo.: Denver Chamber of Commerce, 1899.

Massey, Sara R., ed. *Black Cowboys of Texas*. College Station: Texas A&M University Press, 2000.

Mattes, Merrill J. *The Great Platte River Road: The Covered Wagon Mainline via Fort Kearney to Fort Laramie*. Lincoln: University of Nebraska Press, 1988.

Milligan, Edward A. *Dakota Twilight: The Standing Rock Sioux, 1874–1890*. Hicksville, N.Y.: Exposition Press, 1976.

Mills, Rick W. *The Milwaukee Road in Dakota*. Hermosa, S.Dak.: Battle Creek Publishing Co., 1998.

Milner, Clyde A. II and Carol A. O'Connor. *As Big as the West: The Pioneer Life of Granville Stuart*. Oxford, U.K.: Oxford University Press, 2009.

Morris, Edmund. *The Rise of Theodore Roosevelt*. New York: Modern Library, 2001.

———. *Theodore Rex*. New York: Modern Library, 2001.

Morton, J. Sterling. *Illustrated History of Nebraska: A History of Nebraska from the Earliest Explorations of the Trans-Mississippi Region*. Ed. Albert Watkins and George L. Miller. 3d. ed. Vol. 1. Lincoln, Nebr.: Western Publishing & Engraving Co., 1911.

——— and Albert Watkins. *History of Nebraska: From the Earliest Explorations of the Trans-Mississippi Region*. Lincoln, Nebr.: Western Publishing & Engraving Co., 1918.

Moulton, Candy. *Valentine T. McGillycuddy: Army Surgeon, Agent to the Sioux*. Norman, Okla.: Arthur H. Clark, 2011.

Nelson, Paula M. *After the West Was Won: Homesteaders and Town-Builders in Western South Dakota, 1900–1917*. Iowa City: University of Iowa Press, 1986.

———. *The Prairie Winnows Out Its Own: The West River Country of South Dakota in the Years of Depression and Dust*. Iowa City: University of Iowa Press, 1996.

Olson, James C. *Red Cloud and the Sioux Problem*. Lincoln: University of Nebraska Press, 1965.

O'Neal, Bill. *Encyclopedia of Western Gunfighters*. Norman: University of Oklahoma Press, 1979.

———. *The Johnson County War*. Austin, Tex.: Eakin Press, 2004.

Ostler, Jeffrey. *The Plains Sioux and U.S. Colonialism from Lewis and Clark to Wounded Knee*. Cambridge, U.K.: Cambridge University Press, 2004.

Otis, Delos S. *The Dawes Act and the Allotment of Indian Lands*. Norman: University of Oklahoma Press, 1973.

Parker, Watson. *Deadwood: The Golden Years*. Lincoln: University of Nebraska Press, 1981.

Petersen, Paul R. *Quantrill of Missouri: The Man, the Myth, the Soldier*. Nashville, Tenn.: Cumberland House, 2003.

Pope, Dennis C. *Sitting Bull, Prisoner of War*. Pierre: South Dakota State Historical Society Press, 2010.

Raban, Jonathan. *Bad Land: An American Romance*. New York: Pantheon Books, 1996.

Reinfeld, Fred. *Pony Express*. Lincoln: University of Nebraska Press, 1966.

Robinson, Doane. *Doane Robinson's Encyclopedia of South Dakota*. Pierre, S.Dak.: By the Author, 1925.

Robinson, Elwyn B. *History of North Dakota*. Lincoln: University of Nebraska Press, 1966.

Rollins, Philip Ashton. *The Cowboy: An Unconventional History of Civilization on the Old-Time Cattle Range*. Norman: University of Oklahoma Press, 1997.

Root, Frank A. and William Elsey Connelley. *The Overland Stage to California: Personal Reminiscences and Authentic History of the Great Overland Stage Line and Pony Express from the Missouri River to the Pacific Ocean*. Topeka, Kans.: Crane & Co., 1901.

Rosa, Joseph G. *Wild Bill Hickok: The Man and His Myth*. Lawrence: University Press of Kansas, 1996.

Rosier, Paul C. *Rebirth of the Blackfeet Nation, 1912–1954*. Lincoln: University of Nebraska Press, 2001.

Ruby, Robert H. and John A. Brown. *The Cayuse Indians: Imperial Tribesmen of Old Oregon*. Norman: University of Oklahoma Press, 1972.

Ruby, Robert H., John A. Brown, and Cary C. Collins. *A Guide to the Indian Tribes of the Pacific Northwest*. 3d ed. Norman: University of Oklahoma Press, 2010.

Rutter, Michael. *Upstairs Girls: Prostitution in the American West*. Helena, Mont.: Farcountry Press, 2005.

Ryder, Lyn. *Road Ranches along the Oregon Trail, 1858 to 1868: Between Marysville, Kansas and Fort Kearny, Nebraska*. Niwot, Colo.: Prairie Lark Publications, 1995.

Saltiel, Emanuel H. and George H. Barnett. *History and Business Directory of Cheyenne and Guide to the Mining Regions of the Rocky Mountains*. 1868. Facsimile ed., New Haven, Conn.: Yale University Library, 1975.

Samuels, Peggy and Harold Samuels. *Frederic Remington: A Biography*. Garden City, N.Y.: Doubleday, 1982.

Sanders, Alvin Howard. *Shorthorn Cattle: A Series of Historical Sketches, Memoirs and Records of the Breed and Its Development in the United States and Canada*. Chicago: Sanders Publishing Co., 1918.

Sandoz, Mari. *The Tom-Walker*. Lincoln: University of Nebraska Press, 1947.

Schatz, August H. *Longhorns Bring Culture*. Boston: Christopher Publishing House, 1961.

Schell, Herbert S. *History of South Dakota*. 4th ed. Rev. John E. Miller. Pierre: South Dakota State Historical Society Press, 2004.

Schultz, Duane P. *Month of the Freezing Moon: The Sand Creek Massacre, November 1864*. New York: St. Martin's Press, 1990.

Siberts, Bruce and Walker D. Wyman. *Nothing but Prairie and Sky: Life on the Dakota Range in the Early Days*. Norman: University of Oklahoma Press, 1954.

Simpson, John. *West River: Stories from the Great Sioux Reservation*. Hamill, S.Dak.: Rattlesnake Butte Press, 2000.

Skaug, Julius, ed. *Mobridge: Its First 50 Years*. [Mobridge, S.Dak.: City of Mobridge, 1956].

Slatta, Richard W. *The Cowboy Encyclopedia*. Santa Barbara, Calif.: ABC-CLIO, 1994.

———. *Cowboys of the Americas*. New Haven, Conn.: Yale University Press, 1990.

Smith, Howard and Ann Harry. *The Trail of the Sheidley Cattle Company: An Account of Cattle Ranching on the Western Plains in the Era of the Open Range—and Wealth Therefrom*. Tiffin, Ohio: Herald Printing Co., 2002.

Sonnichsen, Charles L. *Cowboys and Cattle Kings: Life on the Range Today*. Norman: University of Oklahoma Press, 1950.

South Dakota WPA Writers' Project. *South Dakota Place Names*. Vermillion: University of South Dakota, 1941.

Spence, Mark David. *Dispossessing the Wilderness: Indian Removal and the Making of the National Parks*. New York: Oxford University Press, 1999.

Sprague, Donovin Arleigh. *Standing Rock Sioux*. Images of America Series. Charleston, S.C.: Arcadia, 2004.

Standing Bear, Luther. *My People, the Sioux*. Lincoln: University of Nebraska Press, 1975.

Starita, Joe. *The Dull Knifes of Pine Ridge: A Lakota Odyssey*. Lincoln: University of Nebraska Press, 2002.

St. Germain, Jill. *Broken Treaties: United States and Canadian Relations with the Lakotas and the Plains Cree, 1868–1885*. Lincoln: University of Nebraska Press, 2009.

———. *Indian Treaty-Making Policy in the United States and Canada, 1867–1877*. Lincoln: University of Nebraska Press, 2001.

Stiles, T. J. *The First Tycoon: The Epic Life of Cornelius Vanderbilt*. New York: Alfred A. Knopf, 2009.

Sudlow, Mrs. Lloyd. I. *Homestead Years, 1908–1968*. Bison, S.Dak.: *Bison Courier*, 1968.

Swanberg, W. A. *Jim Fisk: The Career of an Improbable Rascal*. New York: Scribner, 1959.

Tallent, Annie D. *The Black Hills; or, The Last Hunting Ground of the Dakotahs.* St. Louis, Mo.: Nixon-Jones Printing Co., 1899.

Tate, Michael L. *Indians and Emigrants: Encounters on the Overland Trails.* Norman: University of Oklahoma Press, 2006.

Thybony, Scott, Robert G. Rosenberg, and Elizabeth Mullett Rosenberg. *The Medicine Bows: Wyoming's Mountain Country.* Caldwell, Idaho: Caxton Printers, 1986.

Tidball, Rose. *Taming the Plains.* [Keldron, S.Dak.]: By the Author, 1976.

Turner, Frederick Jackson. *The Significance of the Frontier in American History.* Ed. Harold P. Simonson. New York: Frederick Ungar Publishing Co., 1963.

Unruh, John D., Jr. *The Plains Across: The Overland Emigrants and the Trans-Mississippi West, 1840–60.* Chicago: University of Illinois Press, 1979.

Utley, Robert M. *The Lance and the Shield: The Life and Times of Sitting Bull.* New York: Henry Holt & Co., 1993.

———. *The Last Days of the Sioux Nation.* New Haven, Conn.: Yale University Press, 1963.

Van West, Carroll. *Capitalism on the Frontier: Billings and the Yellowstone Valley in the Nineteenth Century.* Lincoln: University of Nebraska Press, 1993.

Wade, Louise Carroll. *Chicago's Pride: The Stockyards, Packingtown, and Environs in the Nineteenth Century.* Chicago: University of Illinois Press, 1987.

Warren, Louis S. *Buffalo Bill's America: William Cody and the Wild West Show.* New York: Alfred A. Knopf, 2005.

Washburn, Wilcomb E. *The Assault on Indian Tribalism: The General Allotment Law (Dawes Act) of 1887.* Philadelphia: Lippincott, 1975.

Webb, Walter Prescott. *The Great Plains.* Boston: Ginn & Co., 1931.

Welsh, Herbert. *The Action of the Interior Department in Forcing the Standing Rock Indians to Lease Their Lands to Cattle Syndicates.* Philadelphia: Indian Rights Assn., 1902.

West, Elliott. *The Contested Plains: Indians, Goldseekers, and the Rush to Colorado.* Lawrence: University Press of Kansas, 1998.

———. *The Way to the West: Essays on the Central Plains.* Albuquerque: University of New Mexico Press, 1995.

White, Richard. *"It's Your Misfortune and None of My Own": A New History of the American West.* Norman: University of Oklahoma Press, 1991.

Wishart, David J., ed. *The Encyclopedia of the Great Plains.* Lincoln: University of Nebraska Press, 2004.

Wolff, David A. *Seth Bullock: Black Hills Lawman.* South Dakota Biography Series 3. Pierre: South Dakota State Historical Society Press, 2009.

Worster, Donald. *Dust Bowl: The Southern Plains in the 1930s*. New York: Oxford University Press, 1979.

———. *Rivers of Empire: Water, Aridity, and the Growth of the American West*. New York: Pantheon Books, 1985.

Yost, Nellie Snyder. *The Call of the Range: The Story of the Nebraska Stock Growers Association*. Denver, Colo.: Sage Books, 1966.

Theses and Dissertations

Vollan, Charles A. "Hell on Wheels: Community, Respectability, and Violence in Cheyenne, Wyoming, 1867–1869." Ph.D. diss., University of Nebraska–Lincoln, 2004.

Electronic Resources

Center for Food Security and Public Health, Iowa State University. "*Rhipicephalus (Boophilus) annulatus*: Cattle Tick, Cattle Fever Tick, American Cattle Tick." cfsph.iastate.edu.

"Climate Custer – South Dakota." *U.S. Climate Data*. usclimatedata.com.

National Centers for Environmental Information, National Oceanic and Atmospheric Administration. "Climate at a Glance." ncdc.noaa.gov.

National Park Service. "Pony Express Historic Resources Study, Chapter Four: Division One: Stations between St. Joseph and Fort Kearney (continued)." nps.gov/parkhistory.

Pope, Nancy. "The Story of the Pony Express." Smithsonian National Postal Museum. postalmuseum.si.edu.

Seefeldt, Douglas, ed. *"Horrible Massacre of Emigrants!!": The Mountain Meadows Massacre in Public Discourse*. mountainmeadows.unl.edu.

[Sol, Michael, comp.] *Milwaukee Road Archive*. milwaukeeroadarchives.com.

South Dakota Hall of Fame. sdhalloffame.com.

[Thomas, William G., ed.] *Railroads and the Making of Modern America*. railroads.unl.edu.

Tronstad, Russell, Jim Sprinkle, and George Ruyle, eds. *Arizona Rancher's Management Guide*. University of Arizona College of Agriculture and Life Sciences Cooperative Extension. ag.arizona.edu.

Yellowstone Trail Association. "History of the Yellowstone Trail." yellowstonetrail.org.

INDEX

Aberdeen, S.Dak., 151

Adair, Hugh, 60

Adams County, N.Dak., 157, 161, 169, 173

African Americans, 106

Agrarian movement, 168–69

Alcohol and tobacco, 6, 9, 11, 14, 101, 156, 169, 186

American bison, xii, 14, 29, 106, 118, 212n40

American Indians: assimilation of, 53, 64; attacking homesteaders, 27–28; Cayuse War, 4; exploitation by whites, 56–58; flight from Indian Terr., 42–43; and Ghost Dance, 90; and Great Sioux War, 35–36; and intermarriage, 118, 123–24, 128–29, 220n8; and land allotments, 64–65; and Lemmon, 23, 46, 51–53, 108; raiding by, 13–16, 185; and reservation system, xi–xii; and Sand Creek Massacre, 14–15; and U.S.-Dakota War, 13–15. *See also* Great Sioux Reservation

Ames, Charles Edgar, 17

Anaconda (Mont.) *Standard*, 176–77

Anderson, John, 115–16

Antelope Island State Park, 198n68

Arapaho Indians, 13–14

Arizona, 108, 172

Arndt, Othe, 99

Arnold, Ben, 177

Austin, Stephen F., xii

Bagley, Will, 7

Baldwin, Frank D., 92

Barbed wire, 68–71, 136, 139, 145, 206n1

Beatrice, Nebr., 13, 16

Belle Fourche, S.Dak., 101, 150; and cattle shipping, 109–12, 205n59; grazing ranges near, 66, 132–33; Lemmon lives in, 180, 184–85

Belle Fourche Bee, xiv–xv, 78, 180–81, 192n3, 208n28

Belle Fourche River, 46

Bickford, O. G., 160

Big Foot (Miniconjou chief), 90

Billings, Frederick, 173

Bingenheimer, George H., 123, 126, 131, 144

Bismarck, N.Dak., 150

Bison, S.Dak., 161–62, 166

Bixby, S.Dak., 184

Black Hills, 35–36, 46–48, 89, 151

Black Hills Live Stock Assn., 103

Black Hills Stock Growers Assn., 103

Black Kettle (Cheyenne chief), 15

Blasingame, Ike, 31, 38, 58, 84, 101, 147, 191n4, 192n4

Blizzards. *See* Weather

Boe, Rosella B. *See* Lemmon, Rosella Boe

Boggs, Bill, 101–2

Boss Cowman: The Recollections of Ed Lemmon, 1857–1946, xiii, xv, 177–78, 188, 192n7, 193n4

Boss Cowman Celebration and Rodeo, 188, 192n7

Boston Indians Committee, 143

Bountiful, Utah, 5–7, 21, 186

Brands and branding: inspection and registration, 103–4, 107, 113, 115, 184; and Lemmon's cane, 185, 225n30; and repping, 43–45; and roundups, 31, 34, 73, 80–81, 84, 147; and stray steers, 74, 85. *See also* Cattle outfits and ranches

Brooke, John R., 91–92

Brothels. *See* Prostitutes and prostitution

Bryan, William Jennings, 114, 214n59

Buchanan, James, 7

Buffalo. *See* American bison

Buffalo Gap, S.Dak., 62, 75–76; 100–101, 117

Bullock, Seth, 109

Burdick, Usher L., xv, 78, 182–83, 224n21

Burke, John, 157

Bushfield, Harlan, 186

Butte County, S.Dak., 150, 157

Butterfield, Roger, 186

"Calamity Jane." *See* Canary, Martha Jane

California Gold Rush (1849), 5

Calkins, R. M., 151–52, 154, 220n3, 220n7

Campbell, Bill, 57

Canary, Martha Jane ("Calamity Jane"), 30, 78, 208n28

Cannonball River, 46, 121, 133

Carlisle Indian Industrial School, 126

Carter, Levi, 197n65

Casey, Edward W., 92

Cattle associations, 103–7, 113, 115, 184. *See also* specific associations

Cattle drives and trailing: to Indian agencies, 54, 56–58, 65, 108; Lemmon's first drive, 36–37; Lemmon's system for, 97–100;

and night guard, 3, 43; outfitting of, 81–83, 98–99, 101, 208n39; and river crossings, 71–73, 207n14; and shrinkage, 39–40, 56–58, 65, 75–76, 111–12; and stampedes, 27, 96–99, 164, 199n6; and stray steers, 74. *See also* Roundups

Cattle grazing: and crop damage, 27; and development of Great Plains, 68–69; on Indian lands, 1, 46, 49–56, 65–66, 121; and line riders, 37; overgrazing, 218n64; and range laws, xi–xii, 37. *See also* Standing Rock Indian Reservation grazing leases

Cattle outfits and ranches, 103; Bosler Brothers, 44; BXB, 48; D. H. Clark & Co., 48–51; Diamond A, 48; Diamond M, 48; Elkhorn ranch, 135; Goodnight (JA brand), 99–100; Grimes & Thornton Co., 58; Hashknife, 29; J. W. Iliff (Bar F brand), 21, 25, 100; Keith and Barton, 44; Lake & Tomb (Reverse L7 brand), 114; Lawhorn and Hardigan, 27; Maltese Cross ranch, 135; Matador, 48, 139; NUN ranch, 101, 113–14, 148; 100 Cattle Co., 40–45; Paxton and Ware, 44; Pine Ridge Agency (FOF brand), 53; Spade Ranch, 139; Turkey Track, 48; VVV, 48; Walworth Brothers, 44; XIT, 145. *See also* Brands and branding; Sheidley Cattle Co.

Cattle ranching: and breeding, 70, 100, 107, 113, 206n6; and fencing, 68–71, 139, 206n1; financing and profitability of, 94, 111, 146; Lemmon's reputation for, 1–3; responsibilities of general manager, 95–96; and shipping, marketing, and slaughtering livestock, 75–77, 108–12; on Standing Rock Indian Reservation, 134–36, 139, 147–49; on world's largest fenced pasture, 2, 121, 145, 148, 186

Cattle rustling, 102–3, 106

Cayuse Indians, 4

Central Pacific Railroad, 21

Chadron, Nebr., 60, 65, 74–75, 101

Chalk Bluffs, 22

Chamberlain, S.Dak., 151

Cheyenne, Wyo., 18–22, 25, 104–5

Cheyenne Indians, 13–15, 18, 36, 42, 46

Cheyenne Leader, 18, 197n61

Cheyenne River, 46–51, 68–69, 72–73, 85

Cheyenne River Indian Reservation, 90, 108, 162–63

Chicago, Ill.: Lemmon attends meetings in, 102, 117, 131, 147, 155; shipping cattle to, 39–40, 65, 108–12, 148, 205n59

Chicago & North Western Railroad, 74–75, 109, 111

Chicago, Milwaukee & St. Paul Railroad, xi, 124–27, 130–34, 137–38, 142–44, 151–58, 162–65, 169

Children's blizzard (1888), 68

Chivington, John M., 14–15

Church of Jesus Christ of Latter-day Saints. *See* Mormons

Clark, Charlotte Gifford, 210n2

Clark, David H.: chooses ranges, 51–52, 66, 69; and cowboys, 102; death, 83, 210n2; and D. H. Clark & Co., 48–55; holds political offices, 49, 71, 94–95; as manager of Sheidley Cattle Co., 36, 58–60, 81, 94–96, 112–13; marriage, 210n2; as

president of cattle association, 55, 94–95, 103

Cleveland, Grover, 66

Cody, William F. ("Buffalo Bill"), xii, xiv, 213n40

Coe, Isaac, 197n65

Colorado, 13–15, 21–22, 25, 119, 164, 195n42

Comstock, William, 139

Connors, Milton C., 71

Co-Operative Wool Growers of South Dakota, 180

Corson County, S.Dak., 163

Cowboys and cowboying: and boredom, 38, 209n40; Lemmon begins career as, 25; Lemmon as manager of, 60–61; Lemmon publishes stories of, 175–78; Lemmon's reputation as, 1–3; nighthawks, 43, 209n40; as sheep herders, 171; and trail drives, 97–98; and trips to town, 101; equipment of, 45, 72. *See also* Cattle drives and trailing; Cattle outfits and ranches; Roundups

Crawford, Lewis F., 23, 177–78, 182

Crow Creek Indian Reservation, 209n57

Culbertson, ("Indian") Pete, 210n66

Custer, George Armstrong, 35–36

Custer County, S.Dak., 80

Czolgosz, Leon, 127

Dakota Livestock & Investment Co., 171–72

Davis, J. W., 143

Daviston, S.Dak., 166

Dawes, Henry L., 64

Dawes Act (1887), 64–66, 68, 123, 201n2

Days of '76 (celebration), 208n28

Deadwood, S.Dak., 35, 103, 208n28
Denver, Colo., 2, 148, 198n69
Denver Pacific Railroad, 19–20
"Developing the West" (*Belle Fourche
    Bee* column), xiv, 180–81, 192n3
Devier, Addie, 78
Deweese, Nebr., 6
Dewey County, S.Dak., 163
DeWitt, Nebr., 17
D. H. Clark & Co. *See* Sheidley
    Cattle Co.
*The Dispossession of the American
    Indian*, 53
Dobie, J. Frank, 70
Donovan, Della. *See* Lemmon,
    Della Donovan
Don Pratt Hotel, 180, 185
Drought. *See* Weather
Dull Knife (Cheyenne chief), 42
Dupree, S.Dak., 165

Eagle Butte, S.Dak., 165
Earling, Albert J., 162
Elgin, N.Dak., 165
Elisofon, Eliot, 186
Enlarged Homestead Act (1909), 167
Evarts, S.Dak., 101, 124–25, 132–33, 138,
    147–48, 151–54

Faith, S.Dak., 163, 165, 222n32
Fall River County, S.Dak., 80, 160
Fall River County Stock Growers
    Protective Assn., 103
Fargo, N.Dak., 151
Farm Credit Act (1933), 180
Farmers Equity Union, 168–69
Federal Writer's Project, 183
A Final Promise, 64
Finch, F. A., 166
First State Bank of Lemmon, 160,
    166–67

Flying V brand. *See* Sheidley
    Cattle Co.
Forest City, S.Dak., 111–12, 138, 151,
    205n59
Forsyth, James W., 91–92
Fort Pierre, S.Dak., 212n40
Fort Yates, N.Dak., 121, 144, 160
Forty Years on the Frontier, 177
Fremont, Elkhorn & Missouri Valley
    Railroad, 65, 74–75, 111

Gamble, Robert J., 134
General Allotment Act (1887), 64–66,
    68, 123, 201n2
Gettysburg, S.Dak., 111
Ghost Dance, 90
Glenham State Journal, 164
Glidden, Joseph F., 68, 206n1
Glover, "Coon," 147
Glover, Frank, 225n30
Gold and gold rushes, 5, 13–14, 35, 89
Goodnight, Charles, xvi, 34, 38, 97–
    100, 206n5, 208n39, 211n18
Gordon, James, 182
Grand, W. Joseph, 76–77
Grand River, 122, 133, 137, 142, 144, 147,
    154
Grant County, N.Dak., 157, 180
Great Depression, 180, 183–84
Great Die-Up (1886–1887), 65–66, 69,
    74
The Great Plains, 69
Great Sioux Reservation: and beef
    rations, 56–58; and Black Hills,
    35–36, 46–48; dismantling and
    opening of, xi–xii, 46–48, 54, 64–65,
    68, 89–90; and grazing rights,
    55–56, 70–71; trespassing on, xii–
    xiii, 46–54, 121. *See also* American
    Indians; specific reservations
Great Sioux War, 36, 46

Green, George, 40–42, 87
Grey, Zane, 23
Griffiths, Raymond S., 183
Grinnell, George Bird, 141, 143
Guide Rock, Nebr., 27
Gunderson, Carl, 220n8

Hamilton, W. H., 27, 157
Hampton Normal and Agricultural
    Institute, 126
Hansen, George, 182
Hansen, Nils, 186
Hardigan (Texas cattleman), 27
Harding, Warren G., 172
Harding County, S.Dak., 150
Harper's Weekly, 92
Hashknife (cattle outfit), 29
Havelock, N.Dak., 165
Hebron, Nebr., 16
Hettinger, N.Dak., 157, 173
Hettinger County, N.Dak., 157
Hickok, James Butler ("Wild Bill"),
    9–10, 35, 182
History of North Dakota, 182
"History of the Range Cattle Industry
    of Dakota," 224n21
"History of the Range Cattle Trade of
    the Dakotas," xv, 72, 182–83, 224n21
Hitchcock, Ethan Allen, 128
Hoffman, Connie, 78
Holladay, Ben, 10–11, 15–16
Homestead Act (1862), 14, 167
Homesteading: and cattle damage
    to crops, 27; and claim jumping,
    25–26; and encroachment on
    Indian lands, xi–xii, 46–48, 54, 139;
    and end of the frontier, 107, 150,
    190–91n1; and Indian attacks, 28–
    29; and land speculation, 167–68;
    and opening of reservation lands,
    70–71, 163–64

Horses: from Church Island, 21–22,
    25, 30–31, 198n68, 198n70; for
    racing, 32–33, 198n70; for roping
    and cutting, 31–32, 41; rounding up
    and rebreaking of, 80–81; roweling
    of, 32; S. I. Bay, 72, 85; stolen, 42–
    43; swimming flooded rivers, 72
Hoxie, Frederick, 64
Hudgins, Jim, 95
Hunkpapa Lakota Indians, xiii, 90–91,
    121–22, 136, 141, 149
Hunter (railroad agent), 126–27

Iliff, John Wesley, 11, 21–22, 25, 31, 63,
    100
Iliff, Wyo., 22
Indian Rights Assn., 133, 137–38
In from the Night Herd, 210n66
Ipswich, S.Dak., 166
Isabel, S.Dak., 162–63, 165, 184
Iverson, Peter, 54, 126
Ivy, John, 147

Jackley, A. M., 186
Jackson, George, 115
Jawbone Railroad, 154
Johnson County War, 70, 102
Jones, James K., 133–35
Jones, William A., 121–24, 127–38,
    142–44
Jordan, Mont., 114
Julesburg, Colo., 15, 21
The Jungle, 77

Kearney, Nebr., 16–17
Kennan, George, 125, 137–38
Kilpatrick, Samuel, 13
Kinney, J. C., 167
Kiowa, Nebr., 27
Kittredge, Alfred B., 135
Kurtz, Mrs. E. C., 176–77

Lake, Richard C., 112–14, 131, 151, 159, 187

Lake, Tomb & Co., 114

Lake, Tomb & Lemmon Co., 116–17, 120, 131–32, 135, 144–49, 156–60

Land allotments, 64–65

Land speculation, 167–68

Lantry, S.Dak., 165

La Plant, S.Dak., 165

Last Grass Frontier, 56

Lawhorn (Texas cattleman), 27

Laws and law enforcement: and code of the open range, xi–xii, 37, 107; and cowboys, 61–62; and leasing of Indian lands, 127–39; and livestock damage to crops, 164; by vigilantes, 18–19

Lee, Bob, 56, 104

Lee, Joe, 6

Leith, N.Dak., 165

Lemmon, Alpharetta Elizabeth, 7, 20, 86, 146

Lemmon, Bertha Reno, 62–63, 77–78, 102, 117–19, 164, 214n68

Lemmon, David, 194n20

Lemmon, Della Donovan, 166, 179–80, 187

Lemmon, Edna, 205n52

Lemmon, Elizabeth Slover, 199n7, 205n52

Lemmon, George Edward, ii, x–xviii, 95, 176, 189; attends school, 13, 20, 27; birth, 6, 186; builds legacy, xiv–xv, 23–24, 174–78, 188–90; as county commissioner, 61–62, 157–58, 160–61, 166, 172; death, 187; description and reputation of, 1–3, 34, 41, 62, 116, 119–20, 147–48, 183, 185–86; divorces of, 63, 102, 117–18, 179–80, 214n68; financial difficulties of, 169–74,

178–80, 184–85; and injuries, 32–34, 84–87, 170; leaves cattle business, 148–50, 173–75; in *Life*, 186–87, 189; marriage to Bertha, 62–63, 77–78, 87, 164; marriage to Rosella, 118–19, 214n68, 215n72; military service of, 185; monument to, 188; near-death experiences of, 88–89, 147; nicknames of, xiii, 191–92n4, 192n5; and women, 63, 78–80, 118

Lemmon, George Edward, stories and articles by, xiv, 16, 60, 84, 182–83, 193n12; "The Bitter with the Sweet," 33; "Developing the West" column, xiv, 180–81, 192n3; "My Lost Opportunity to Kill an Indian," 23, 28–29; reliability of, xvi, 29–30, 177–78, 181–82, 193n12, 211n18

Lemmon, George Reno, 78, 117, 169, 184

Lemmon, Harold Marius, 184

Lemmon, James Edward, 184

Lemmon, James Hervey, Sr. (Lemmon's father): birth and early years, 3–4; and Church Island horses, 21–22, 25, 30–32, 198n68, 198n70; death, 146–47; in Oregon and California, 4–5; and freighting and railroad contracts, 15–21; and Liberty Farm, 7–15, 25–26, 147, 196n45; marriage and children of, 5–7; in Thayer County, Nebr., 26, 30, 36, 40, 45, 86, 146–47

Lemmon, James Hervey, Jr. (Lemmon's brother), 5–6, 10, 12–13, 17–18, 20–21, 24–27, 31, 34, 62–63, 146, 199n7

Lemmon, James Hervey (Lemmon's son), 78, 102, 114, 164–66, 171–74, 177, 180, 187

Lemmon, Lucy Elizabeth Whittmore, 5–8, 14, 16, 20, 25–26, 30, 62, 118, 146, 193n14, 194n20

Lemmon, Mandana, 194n20

Lemmon, Mildred Spear, 184

Lemmon, Moroni Stowell ("Rone"), 6, 10, 13, 20, 34–36, 86, 89, 146, 209n51

Lemmon, Rosella Boe, 118–19, 144, 147, 160, 169–70, 173, 178–80, 187, 214n68

Lemmon, Roy Edward, 78, 117, 187

Lemmon, S.Dak., 159; Boss Cowman Celebration and Rodeo, 188, 192n7; as county seat, 157, 161–62, 166; economic importance of, 173–74; fiftieth anniversary of, 188; First State Bank, 160, 166–67, 171; Fourth of July celebration in, 161, 169; Greenhill Cemetery, 184, 187; growth and development of, 165; Lemmon monument, 188; Lemmon's business and civic activities in, 159–61; Palace Hotel, 172, 187; Petrified Wood Park, 183, 225n30; and railroad, 158; townsite of, 156

Lemmon Brick & Tile Co., 166, 169

Lemmon Leader, 186

Lemmon Tribune, 177

Liberty Creek, 8

Liberty Farm, 7–18, 25–27, 33, 147, 185, 194n23, 196n45

Life, 186–87, 189

Lisco, Nebr., 40

Little Blue River, 8, 11, 13, 15–17, 25, 30, 62, 88–89, 146–47

Little Wolf (Cheyenne chief), 42

Longhorn cattle, 70

Longhorns Bring Culture, 183

"The Lost Bird of Wounded Knee," 210n66

Love, Leonard, 55

Lower Brule Indian Reservation, 90, 108, 121, 209n57

Mabry, Seth ("Major"), 36, 57

McCall, Jack, 35

McCanles, David, 182

McChesney, Charles, 66

McCumpsey, Tom, 30, 32–33, 36

McDonnell, Janet, 53

McGillycuddy, Valentine T., 52–54, 59–60, 208n28

McIntosh brothers (railroad contractors), 165

MacKenzie, Murdo, 94, 139

McKinley, William, 114, 123, 127

McLaughlin, James H., 53–54, 90, 134, 141, 145, 165

McLaughlin, S.Dak., 163, 165

Mahto, S.Dak., 165

Majors, Alexander, 9, 10

Maple Leaf, S.Dak., 165

Marengo, Ill., 5

Martin, Charles (accused murderer), 19, 197n62

Martin, Charles (livestock association secretary), 2, 148

Martin, Earl, 207n14

Marysville, Kans., 13–15, 196n45

Meade County, S.Dak., 222n32

Meadow, S.Dak., 161, 166, 170

MeLoy, Don, 188

Merritt, Ves, 101

Metcalf, Ute, 19–20, 25

Miles City, Mont., 150, 158

Miller, Isaac, 91–92

Milwaukee Road. *See* Chicago, Milwaukee, St. Paul & Pacific Railroad

Minnesota, 13–15, 171

Missouri River: divides S.Dak., 164; homesteading and settlement beyond, 150–51, 167; and railroads, xi–xiii, 151–54, 158, 188–90; swum by cattle, 111–12, 124–25

Mitchell, S.Dak., 151

Mobridge, S.Dak., 154–55, 158, 162, 173

Montana Stock Growers Assn., 103

Moore, Jim, 9–10

Moore, M. E., 160

Moreau Junction, S.Dak., 162–63

Moreau River, 58–59, 66, 68, 72, 80, 108–9, 114, 119, 144, 162, 194n4

Mormons, 6–8, 20–21, 30–31, 103, 198n68. *See also* Young, Brigham

Mormon War, 7, 21, 194n26

Moroni (Mormon angel), 6–7

Moses, Sam, 107, 183

Mossman, Burton C. ("Cap"), 94

Mott, N.Dak., 165

Mountain Meadows Massacre, 7

Murdo, S.Dak., 139

National Cowboy & Western Heritage Museum Hall of Fame, xi, xii, 188

National Live Stock Assn., 2, 118, 147–48

National Wool Marketing Corp., 180, 184

Nebraska State Historical Society, 182

New England, N.Dak., 163, 165

New Leipzig, N.Dak., 165

Northern Wyoming Farmers and Stock Growers' Assn., 105

North Platte, Nebr., 17–18

North Platte River, 5, 36

Oak, Nebr., 27

Ogallala, Nebr., 36, 60, 65, 103

Oglala Lakota County, S.Dak., 91

Oglala Lakota Indians, xii–xiii, 52, 60, 142, 149

"Old-Timers Picnic" (Bixby, S.Dak.), 184–85

"The Opening of the Fighting at Wounded Knee," 92

Oregon Terr., 4–5

Oregon Trail, 5, 8–17

OSO Brand. *See* Sheidley Cattle Co.

The Outlook, 125, 137

Overland Mail Co., 9

Pacific Railway Co., 151–52

Paiute Indians, 7

Palisade, Colo., 119

Panic of 1907, 162

Pawnee National Grassland, 22

Peno Flats roundup (1897), 115–16

Perkins County, S.Dak., 150, 161, 166–67, 172–74

Petrified Wood Park (Lemmon, S.Dak.), 183, 225n30

Pettigrew, Richard F., 55

Pew, Bob, 91–92

Philip, James ("Scotty"), 106, 118, 123, 212n40

Philips, W. P., 96

Pierre, S.Dak., 95, 103, 150–51, 158

Pike's Peak Gold Rush (1858), 13

Pine Ridge Indian Reservation, 23, 52–53, 56, 59–60, 90–92, 103, 108, 121, 142, 144–45, 149

Pinneo, Minnie, 198n70

Pioneering the Union Pacific, 17

Pitt, Joseph, 119

"Poker Alice." *See* Tubbs, Alice Ivers

Polygamy, 6

Pony Express, 9–10, 16, 21, 26, 30, 182

Populist movement, 168–69

Prescott, Ariz., 172

Primeau, Louis P., 130, 137, 217n28

Production Credit Assn., 180
Promontory Summit, Utah, 21
Prostitutes and prostitution, 6, 18,
    78–79
Pulling, Hazel Adele, 224n21

Quammen, Ole S., 166

Race and racism, 200n41
Railroads: and cattle shipping, 39–40,
    65, 74–77, 100, 108–13; crossing
    Missouri River, 151–54, 158,
    188–90; and Panic of 1807, 162; and
    shipping rates, 168–69; and tie-
    cutting contracts, 19–21, 195n56,
    197n65; and transcontinental
    lines, 16–18, 21, 158; western
    expansion of, 55, 109. *See also*
    specific railroads
Ramsland, T. O., 166
Ranches. *See* Cattle outfits and
    ranches
Rapid City, S.Dak., 49, 71, 75, 94, 101,
    117, 119
Rapid City Daily Journal, 190
Rattle, Thomas S., 138
Red Cloud (Lakota chief), xiii, 23, 52,
    54, 91, 108, 145
Red Cloud, Nebr., 27
Red Cloud Agency, 57
"Red River Red" (cowboy), 40–41
Reed, A. S., 139
Reeder, N.Dak., 154, 157, 173
Regent, N.Dak., 165
Remington, Frederic, 92, 210n66
Remington, Jane, 79
Returned Students' Assn., 126–27,
    139, 163
Reverse L7 brand. *See* Sheidley
    Cattle Co.
Richards, Bartlett, 139

Rideout (Mormon missionary), 21
Riggs, Thomas L., 193n12
Roosevelt, Franklin D., 180
Roosevelt, Theodore, 1, 66, 127, 135,
    139, 141, 143, 169
Rose, Bird, 114, 144, 146, 149
Rosebud Indian Reservation, 90, 103,
    108, 121, 163, 201n2, 204n27
Roundups: branding and castrating,
    34, 43, 73, 147; circling, 84–85;
    cutting, 31–32, 43, 96, 147–48;
    Lemmon as roundup boss, 1–3, 36,
    68, 71–74; outfit hierarchy and pay
    scale, 83–84; Peno Flats roundup
    of 1897, 115–16; preparation and
    outfitting of, 80–83; Prescott, Ariz.
    roundup of 1919, 172; repping,
    43–45. *See also* Cattle drives and
    trailing
Royce, Benjamin, 25–26
Russell, William, 9, 10

Sand Creek Massacre (1864), 14–15
Sandoz, Mari, xv, 182, 224n18
Schatz, August H., 183
Schmidt, Phyllis, xiv
Schools and education, 13, 20, 27, 90,
    126, 137, 171
Selfridge, N.Dak., 165
Seventh United States Cavalry
    Regiment, 91
Sewall, E. D., 156
Sheep and sheep business, 21, 36,
    75, 167; and cattlemen, 37, 171,
    200n41; and Lemmon, 171, 179–80,
    184; grazing on Indian lands, 56,
    125
Sheffield, Sam, 114
Sheidley, Ben, 36, 112, 187, 211n4
Sheidley, George, 36, 95, 112–14, 187
Sheidley, Sarah, 114, 116

Sheidley, William, 36, 95, 112–14, 116–17
Sheidley Cattle Co., 119; annual meetings of, 116–17; and Big Dry range, 114; Clark as general manager of, 36, 58–60, 81, 94, 112–13; and D. H. Clark & Co., 48–51; expansion into D.T., 48, 58–59; and Flying V brand, 48–49, 52–53, 60–61, 63, 66, 68, 79–80, 86–87, 100, 105–9, 112–14, 117–21, 164, 188; Lake and Tomb as advisers of, 112–14; and leasing Indian lands, 55–56, 64–65, 70–71; Lemmon as cowboy for, 45–46, 77–78; Lemmon as general manager of, 95–97, 100–102; Lemmon as roundup boss for, 61, 68, 115–16; and Moreau River range, 58–60, 68, 72, 80, 105, 108; and OSO brand, 48; and Reverse L7 brand, 114, 116, 125, 147, 188. *See also* Cattle outfits and ranches
Sheldon, Addison E., 182
Sheridan, Wyo., 150
Shields, N.Dak., 165
Shoemaker, Mandy, 79
S. I. Bay (horse), 72, 85
Sidney, Wyo., 22
Sihasapa Lakota Indians, xiii, 121–22, 136, 141, 149
Sinclair, Upton, 77
Sioux County, N.Dak., 157, 180
Sioux Falls, S.Dak., 151
Sitting Bull (Hunkpapa chief), 54, 90, 184
Slatta, Richard W., 200n41
Slover, Elizabeth. *See* Lemmon, Elizabeth Slover
Slover, Lew, 27, 199n7
Smithwick Station, S.Dak., 85–86, 101, 205n59

South Dakota Hall of Fame, 188
"South Dakota: Its Boundless Plains Are the Heart of a Continent," 186
South Dakota Stockgrowers Assn., 213n42
Spanish-American War, 117, 128
Spear, Mildred. *See* Lemmon, Mildred Spear
Spearfish, S.Dak., 71, 119, 144, 159
Springer, William M., 137
Standing Rock Indian Reservation, 154; bands living on, 121–22; and beef contracts, 108; and Ghost Dance, 90; and illegal grazing, 53–54; opening of, 163, 173; and railroads, 124–25, 152–56, 220n8. *See also* American Indians; Great Sioux Reservation
Standing Rock Indian Reservation grazing leases: bidding process for, 131–33; and controversy, 133–41; fencing of, 129–30, 133, 136–37, 139–47, 165; Lemmon lease as world's largest fenced pasture, 2, 121, 145, 148, 186; Lemmon lives and works on, 141, 147–49, 160, 171–73, 178–79; negotiations for, 122–30; and tribal approval, 130–31
Stanford, Leland, 21
State Historical Society of North Dakota, 177
Steele, Alta, 79
St. Elmo's Fire, 38, 201n43
Stewart, Frank, 106–7
Stuart, Granville, 103, 175, 177
Sturgis, S.Dak., 180, 187
Swift, Gustavus, 75

Taming the Plains, 186
Taylor, Ruben ("Rube"), 21–22
Texas Fever, 68–69

Texley, Ed, xv
Thayer County, Nebr., 26, 36, 40, 45, 86, 146–47
Thunder Hawk (Standing Rock chief), 133
Tidball, Rose, 186
Tiffin, Ohio, 36, 40, 113
Timber Lake, S.Dak., 165
Tinkham, Tom, 177
Tobacco. *See* Alcohol and tobacco
Tomb, Thomas B., 112–14, 131, 151, 159, 187
The Tom-Walker, 224n18
Trail City, S.Dak., 162–63, 165
Trail drives. *See* Cattle drives and trailing
Treaty of Fort Laramie (1868), 35, 48, 89
Trotter, Bill, 9–10
Truesdell, J. A., 137–38
Tubbs, Alice Ivers ("Poker Alice"), 78–79
Turner, Frederick Jackson, 107, 150, 191n1

Union Pacific Railroad, 16–21, 25, 65
Union Stockyards, 75–77
University of North Dakota, xiv–xv
University of Wyoming, xv
U.S. Army, 7, 13–15, 35–37, 194n26
U.S. Department of the Interior, 121, 128, 135, 143
U.S. Federal Reserve System, 162
Usta, S.Dak., 188, 192n4
Utah War (1857), 7, 21, 194n26
Utley, Robert M., 90

Valentine, Nebr., 60, 65, 74–75, 101
Van West, Carroll, 173
Vessey, Robert S., 164
Vigilante law enforcement, 19, 103, 177

Waddell, William, 9, 10
Wade, William, 127–28, 132, 134–35, 142–43
Wakpala, S.Dak., 165
Walker, W. I., 132–37, 139–43, 165
Walking Shooter (Standing Rock chief), 133
Wall, S.Dak., 115
Watauga, S.Dak., 165
Weasel Bear (Standing Rock chief), 133
Weather: drought of 1919, 172; Lemmon and blizzards, 42, 147, 172; lightning and "balls of fire," 38; and Spring roundups, 81; winter of 1880–1881, 51–52; winter of 1886–1887 (the "Great Die-Up"), 65–66, 69, 74; winter of 1887–1888, 68; winter of 1902–1903, 146; winter of 1919–1920, 172
Webb, Walter Prescott, 68–69
Wells, Almond B., 91–92
Wells, Fargo & Co., 16
The West as I Lived It: Stories by Ed Lemmon, xiv
Western Dakota Stock Assn., 103
Western Livestock & Investment Co., 171
Western South Dakota Stock Growers Assn., 106–7, 213n42
West River: and cattle associations, 103–4; and homesteading, 70–71, 163–64; land speculation in, 167–68; land use in, 167, 173
White Butte, S.Dak., 168–69
Whittmore, Benjamin, 5–6
Whittmore, Lucy Elizabeth. *See* Lemmon, Lucy Elizabeth Whittmore
Whittmore, Nathaniel, 5–6
Williams, Dick, 56, 104

Women, 63, 78–80, 118. *See also* Prostitutes and prostitution

Woods, J. M., 106

Woods, James, 182

Work Projects Administration, 183

World's Columbian Exposition (1893), 107, 191n1

World War I, 169, 184

World War II, 187

Wounded Knee Massacre, xvi, 90–92, 185, 210n66

Wovoka (Paiute medicine man), 90

Wyoming, 18, 20, 22, 25, 48, 70, 102–6, 186

Wyoming State Historical Society, xv

Wyoming State Library, 183

Wyoming Stock Growers Assn., 49, 53, 103–6, 113

Yellowstone Trail Assn., 166

Yost, Nellie Snyder, xiii, xv, 178, 188, 192n7

Young, Brigham, 6–7, 21, 198n68. *See also* Mormons

Young Man Afraid of His Horses (Oglala chief), 23, 52, 145

Ziebach County, S.Dak., 163

Zintkala Nuni, 210n66